H. G. Wells's Perennial Time Machine

EDITED BY

GEORGE SLUSSER

PATRICK PARRINDER

DANIÈLE CHATELAIN

H. G. Wells's Perennial

TIME MACHINE

Selected Essays from the

Centenary Conference

"*The Time Machine:*

Past, Present, and Future"

Imperial College, London

July 26–29, 1995

THE UNIVERSITY OF GEORGIA PRESS

ATHENS

Paperback edition, 2016

© 2001 by the University of Georgia Press

Athens, Georgia 30602

www.ugapress.org

Designed by Erin Kirk New

Set in 10.5 on 13 Bulmer

Most University of Georgia Press titles are
available from popular e-book vendors.

Printed digitally

The Library of Congress has cataloged the
hardcover edition of this book as follows:

H. G. Wells's perennial Time machine / edited by George Slusser,
Patrick Parrinder, Danièle Chatelain.

xvi, 216 p. ; 24 cm.

Includes bibliographical references and index.

ISBN 0-8203-2290-3 (alk. paper)

1. Wells, H. G. (Herbert George), 1866–1946. Time machine—
Congresses. 2. Literature and science—Great Britain—History—
20th century—Congresses. Science fiction, English—History
and criticism—Congresses. 4. Time travel in literature—Congresses.
I. Slusser, George Edgar. II. Parrinder, Patrick. III. Chatelain Danièle.

PR5774.T53 H4 2001

823'.912—dc21   2001-023531

Paperback ISBN 978-0-8203-5062-2

Contents

Note on the Text

The edition of *The Time Machine* that has been adopted as standard for the purposes of the present volume is as follows: H. G. Wells, *The Time Machine and the Island of Doctor Moreau*, ed. Patrick Parrinder, World's Classics edition (New York: Oxford University Press, 1996). Quotations from this edition, which offers a modified version of Wells's 1924 Atlantic edition text incorporating later corrections, are identified by chapter and page number in the text of the essays that follow. Quotations from the epilogue are specified as "E." It should be noted that in the Atlantic edition Wells reduced the number of chapters and deleted the chapter titles from the first English edition (London: Heinemann, 1895). The relationship between the old and new chapter divisions is as follows:

Heinemann	*Atlantic/World's Classics*
Chapter/section 1 and 2	1
3	2
4	3
5 and 6	4
7 and 8	5
9	6
10	7
11	8
12	9
13	10
14	11
15 and 16	12
Epilogue	Epilogue

Acknowledgments

The editors wish to thank the contributors and all those who participated in the *Time Machine* centenary symposium at Imperial College, London. Above all, we would like to thank the members of the symposium working party, Sylvia Hardy, Mary Mayer, and Bernard Loing. Special thanks are also due to other members of the H. G. Wells Society for their contributions to the occasion, including John Green, David C. Smith, and Michael Sherborne.

The role of the Eaton Program at the University of California, Riverside, in the *Time Machine* centenary conference was to complement that of the H. G. Wells Society in soliciting speakers who would approach Wells's masterpiece from the point of view of the science fiction tradition on which it has had such a seminal influence. Of those who helped in this regard, we would like specifically to thank Eric Rabkin, Gregory Benford, Paul Alkon, Joseph D. Miller, and the late Frank McConnell. Though only one of the above was able to attend the conference, all were invaluable in their suggestions.

The long-standing commitment of Peter Briscoe, Head of Collection Development, and Sheryl Davis, Acting Head of Special Collections, to the Eaton Collection is much appreciated. Thanks goes also to Emory Elliott, director of the Center for Ideas and Society, for his support, and to Professors David Danow, Lisa Raphals, Stephanie Hammer, and Ye Yang, all of the Comparative Literature Department, for keeping the faith. George Slusser would also like to thank colleague Robert Heath of the Biology Department for his unyielding support of the Eaton enterprise, often in the face of administrative indifference.

Finally, the editors wish to thank Dr. Roscoe Anderson, who has been a most generous benefactor to the Eaton Collection over the years. It is thanks to a gift on his part that *H. G. Wells's Perennial Time Machine* has seen the light of day in its present form. This book is dedicated to Dr. Anderson.

Introduction: *The Time Machine*'s Centennial Audience

GEORGE SLUSSER AND DANIÈLE CHATELAIN

Heureux qui comme Ulysse a fait un beau voyage
—du Bellay, *Regrets*

Wells's Time Traveller surely does not, in the confident Renaissance manner of du Bellay's Ulysses, make a "beau voyage." And though he comes back to the place from which he began, he has no happy homecoming. The voyage is fraught with terrors, and the voyager witness to humanity's end, to the death of Earth and Sun. But the return is worse yet, for he finds no adequate audience to hear his story. The dinner guests, a representative group of professionals from the author's time, do not accept it, and their lack of understanding drives the Traveller to the brink of self-denial—were it not for the physical presence of his machine: "I'm damned if it isn't all going [. . .] Did I ever make a Time Machine, or a model of a Time Machine? Or is it all only a dream? They say life is a dream, [. . .] but I can't stand another that won't fit. It's madness. And where did the dream come from? . . . I must look at that machine. If there *is* one!" (12, 88). The sight of the object that physically took him to the future and back makes him believe again: "It's all right now. The story I told you was true."

But the audience still does not believe, and thus will not understand. Only one among them, the unnamed primary narrator, attempts to make the journey from disbelief to understanding. It is he who tells of the evening when the model is demonstrated: "I think that at that time none of us quite believed in the Time Machine" (2, 12). His narrative frames the Traveller's telling of his voyage, which causes him to ponder: "For my own part, I was unable to come to a conclusion" (12, 89). His revelation seems to come at the end, as he looks upon the Traveller's empty laboratory. Hearing the man-servant's account that there was no physical way out, he must opt for Time: "At that I understood" (12, 90). But does he understand? He remains a man of his time, an apostle of the Advancement of Mankind, hoping the Traveller, if he were to go to the future again, would choose to go to "one of the nearer ages, in which men are still men" (E, 91). His "epilogue" soothes his audience with homilies ("it remains for us to live as though it were not so"), uttering, against all the evidence of the Traveller's story, platitudes about our future race enduring in "gratitude and a mutual tenderness." Apparently satisfied with such weak fare, this narrator's audience is inadequate as well.

Who then was Wells's audience in *The Time Machine*? Commonly, in the travel narrative form Wells adapted, the author's audience identifies with the narrator's audience. The latter is as ignorant of the strange "world" visited as the former. In its need of information, the narrator's audience acts as a conduit whereby the author's imagined or hypothetical audience—the reader—learns about, and comes to understand, the nature of the unknown world. Wells, however, breaking with tradition, did not want his imagined audience to identify with either narrator's inadequate audiences. He was writing, it seems, for a virtual audience, for the audience that would exist in the twentieth century and beyond, an audience that would grapple with such "wonders" as the fourth dimension, temporal displacement, time machines. All disciplines, scientific or literary, that were represented among the Traveller's audience of professionals remained closed to the message of the future. For Wells's virtual audience, however—the readers we have become—these same disciplines have become dialogue partners, wrestling with the multiple complexities of the author's visionary work.

Such was the audience assembled at the four-day centenary conference on *The Time Machine* that took place in July 1995 at Imperial College, London, and was the source of the essays in this volume. This conference, attended by one hundred humanists, scientists, and writers from throughout the world, was jointly sponsored by the H. G. Wells Society, the international body of Wells scholars, and the J. Lloyd Eaton Collection of the University of California, Riverside, the world's largest cataloged collection of science fiction.

The Time Machine has been, and will continue to be, a focal point for strong cross-disciplinary readings. In light of the "two cultures" debate, Wells's novel not only brings together the various and conflicting intellectual currents of his time, scientific and humanistic, but hands them down as intellectual legacy to our world. Here, cultural myths of social progress vie with thermodynamics and entropy; utopian control of the future with random and purposeless "natural selection." Initially relegated by the James-Wells debate to the status of "literature of ideas," *The Time Machine* has gradually been revisioned as a masterpiece of narrative art. As a text for discussion, it continuously reveals surprises when seen through the varied lenses of commentators and critics: surprises about Wells the romancer, the storyteller, the thinker, the scientist. The first section of this volume, "Eternal Readability," offers five strong revisionist readings of the novel: readings that demonstrate the appeal of this text more than a hundred years after its publication.

The second section, "Currents of Its Time," presents five essays that explore our perennial fascination with the intellectual currents that gave rise to *The Time Machine*. Wells's novel, in a sense, is itself a time machine, for it brings to its reader today, in a manner as fresh as in the time it was written, a feel for the contexts—once again literary and scientific—in which it was created. Nourished by the ancient literary forms of imaginary voyage and utopia, it confronts these with contemporary utopian movements as diverse as Morris's medievalism and Fabian socialism. To depict the Traveller's future, it draws equally on Gothic horror stories and journalists' accounts of Edwardian London's underground. As narrative, it blends personal concerns of its author—concerns about class structure, nationalism, and imperialism—with well-informed speculations on history, biology, time.

The final section of this volume, "The Rewriting," contains six essays that reveal the breadth and depth of the novel's influence on modern narrative. *The Time Machine* has inspired numerous rewrites since its publication. Indeed, one might argue that in most literal fashion, it is science fiction's seminal text, having been recrafted in hundreds of known novels and stories. Part of the fun of SF scholarship is discovering new rewrites in unlikely places, in authors as disparate as Robert A. Heinlein and Michael Bishop. *The Time Machine* reappears time after time in film reincarnations, as does its author and his machine. It has become the object of sophisticated theoretical rewrites on a "metanarrative" plane. Finally, such well-known writers as Brian W. Aldiss rewrite Wells's work in the form of personal meditations on its text.

The essays in the first section ask why a reader in our time should read *The Time Machine*. J. R. Hammond, in "*The Time Machine* as a First Novel: Myth and Allegory in Wells's Romance," finds narrative elements as diverse as the Everyman allegory, the quest legend of the Holy Grail, and the fairy tale. It is because of these roots in myth and allegory, he argues, that the book remains as strong a read today as the day it was published. Robert Crossley, in "Taking It as a Story: The Beautiful Lie of *The Time Machine*," locates another reason for the book's continued appeal to readers: the Traveller's art as storyteller. The Traveller, as "miniature model for the author," assumes the role of "Victorian Sindbad." Paul Alkon, in "Was the Time Machine Necessary?," presents the machine as having a concrete narrative function: that of real protagonist. Wells, by making a machine the literal *means* of moving people through time, blends narrative with scientific discourse, and thus makes the term "scientific romance" a reality. Frank Scafella, in "The Rebirth of a Scientific Intelligence: Or, From 'Traveller' to 'Travailer' in *The Time Machine*," considers the work's attraction today in the light of its being "a full-blown allegory of the making of the scientific intelligence, perhaps the first full realization in dramatic form of that vision." Finally, on this same question of the scientific originality of Wells's narrative, W. M. S. Russell's "Time Before and After *The Time Machine*" presents the book's treatment of time as a fourth dimension as "an exciting new chapter in the history of ideas." On the level of ideas alone, Russell argues, this novel has had, and continues to have, a strong impact on physicists and metaphysicians alike.

The second group of essays discusses *The Time Machine* as focal point, and perhaps summum, of the intellectual and literary currents of its time. Kirby Farrell, in "Wells and Neoteny," characterizes the early Wells, in his portrait of Eloi and Morlocks, as blind to neoteny. The reason, Farrell argues, is Wells's education in late-Victorian Darwinism, "whose anxieties valorized lethal competition and adult 'strength,'" characteristics that in neotenic terms are nonadaptive. Sylvia Hardy, in "*The Time Machine* and Victorian Mythology," discusses the role of Victorian anthropology and linguistics, notably the "solar mythology" of Max Müller. Hardy sees the solar myth as giving Wells's narrative a "sub-text," and with it an alternate, cyclical vision of time, as opposed to the time arrow of thermodynamics. John Huntington, in "*The Time Machine* and Wells's Social Trajectory," examines social class as covert context. The author's social strategy in this novel, Huntington argues, is to transform the class differences of his time into species differences. This allows him to discuss in veiled fashion personally painful class matters such as "falling back." Patrick Parrinder, in "From Rome to Richmond: Wells, Universal History, and Prophetic Time," also seeks hidden contexts, and his contribution reveals that concealed in *The Time Machine*'s numerology are two timescales—biological evolution, and a historical timescale on which Wells rewrites Edward Gibbon's *Decline and Fall*, transferring the "universal history" of humankind from Rome to the Traveller's Richmond. Finally, Carlo Pagetti, in "Change in the City: The Time Traveller's London and the 'Baseless Fabric' of His Vision," glosses Wells's description of the Morlocks' subterranean landscape with accounts by contemporary journalists of the London underworld at the heart of "civilized" imperial Britain.

Essays in the third section focus on the diverse ways *The Time Machine* has been rewritten in different forms and media in this century. In what amounts to a theoretical rewriting of Wells's text, Larry W. Caldwell, in "Time at the End of

INTRODUCTION XV

Its Tether: H. G. Wells and the Subversion of Master Narrative," argues that the author, in his first novel, subverts the master narratives of his time in a manner akin to today's postmodernists. If as a historian Wells used the "imposed [. . .] structurations of geology, biology and sociology," as a student of narrative he "remorselessly interrogated epocal logic." The next essay deals with a rewriting of Wells's text that is both filmic and cultural. In his "The Legacy of H. G. Wells's *The Time Machine*: Destabilization and Observation," Joshua Stein considers George Pal's "popular American" film version. Unlike the "subversive" projection of Wells's Traveller—which aims at the "destabilization" of the authority of late-Victorian cultural authority—Pal's Traveller projects a very different future, one that reflects "the American ideology of manifest destiny," coupled with Cold War visions of postapocalypse survival.

If we admit that Wells "invented" time travel, then the myriad stories in this genre written from the 1930s to the 1990s are rewritings of *The Time Machine*. Danièle Chatelain and George Slusser, in "Wells and the Sequency-Simultaneity Paradox: Heinlein's Rewriting of *The Time Machine* in 'By His Bootstraps,'" find Wells's influence at the level of the creative process itself. The paradox Heinlein develops is sequency-simultaneity, and Slusser and Chatelain locate its literary source in the "Mrs Watchett episode." David Leon Higdon, in "A Revision and a Gloss: Michael Bishop's Postmodern Interrogation of H. G. Wells's *The Time Machine*," examines a more recent SF rewriting—Michael Bishop's *No Enemy but Time* (1983). Where Heinlein re-engineered *The Time Machine* into a work that bears resemblance to the modernist geometrical narrative, Bishop, Higdon argues, creates a Borgesian "counter-book." Finally, Brian W. Aldiss, in his essay "Doomed Formicary versus the Technological Sublime," portrays Wells's paradoxical vision in *The Time Machine* as still unresolved a century later, thus a challenge to serious visionary fiction now and in the future. If in *The Time Machine* biology and physics show the future as a "doomed formicary," the machine and story keep alive the "technological sublime." Aldiss sees Wells's response to this paradox as Pascalian: "The more gigantic the works of mankind become, the more he was dwarfed; the more he was dwarfed, the greater his power was seen to be."

Finally, Patrick Parrinder, in his "Afterword: In the Company of the Immortals," offers comments on the history of scholarly and critical readings of *The Time Machine*. Looking forward to the next centenary audience in 2095, Parrinder sees many new ways of reading Wells's seminal text. Essentially, however, two groups will continue to debate it with renewed passion: Wellsian scholars, perennially intrigued by the relation of this first novel to the author's subsequent controversial works; and scientists, philosophers, and SF readers pursuing the elusive ways of time travel and the mystery of human time. Wells's work is, more than a "novel" or a "text," a great "invention." The time machine *was* necessary then. It has engaged the minds and imaginations of that virtual audience Wells was seeking in his new century. As we stand at the start of not just another century but a millennium, that audience will grow vaster in ways we cannot yet imagine.

PART 1

Eternal Readability

A Work for All Time

The Time Machine as a First Novel

Myth and Allegory in Wells's Romance

J. R. HAMMOND

At first sight *The Time Machine* is a decidedly unusual first novel. It is deeply pessimistic in tone, holding out little, if any, hope for mankind—not at all the kind of book one would expect from a young man in his twenties. Unlike most first novels, it does not have the appearance of a disguised autobiography but is concerned, ostensibly at least, with the distant future rather than the here and now. Closer reading, as I hope to show, does not support these first impressions. It is indeed a pessimistic book, but it is also in a very real sense a heroic book, rich in mythological undertones. And while it is not autobiographical, it is deeply rooted in Wells's psychology.

The book first appeared in volume form in the summer of 1895, having first been serialized in the *National Observer* and *New Review*. Let us remind ourselves of the circumstances in which the story was written. Throughout 1894 Wells was living hand-to-mouth as a journalist, writing humorous articles and topical essays published for the most part in the *Pall Mall Gazette*. He and Amy Catherine Robbins were lodging on Mornington Road (now Terrace), Camden Town, but as both were in poor health, and as the summer heat of London was becoming oppressive, they decided to spend the month of August at Sevenoaks in Kent. The move was not a success. They were accompanied by Mrs. Robbins, who strongly disapproved of her daughter's liaison with Wells and lost no opportunity to tell them so. She was herself unwell and inclined to moods in which she would shut herself in her room. Both Wells and Amy were worried by his impending divorce from his wife, Isabel. Moreover, his journalistic career, which had started so promisingly, began to flounder. The *National Observer* was sold over the head of its editor, W. E. Henley; the new editor disliked the time-travelling papers and suspended publication. The literary editor of the *Pall Mall Gazette*, heretofore Wells's staple source of income, went away on holiday, and his temporary assistant declined to accept Wells's contributions. The *Pall Mall Budget*, a weekly offshoot of the *Gazette* that had published a number of his short stories, announced it would shortly close. On top of all these worries, Wells's and Amy's landlady at Sevenoaks discovered their unmarried state and made life unpleasant for them with petty humiliations.

Despite these distractions, a considerable amount of literary work was done during those weeks in lodgings, for Wells had an ambitious project up his sleeve. Henley had told him that he was starting a new monthly journal, the *New Review*, to be launched in January 1895, and he wanted "The Time Traveller" as a serial. If Wells could rewrite the story as a continuous narrative instead of loosely connected installments, Henley would pay him one hundred pounds for the serial rights. Moreover, William Heinemann would undertake to publish the story in book form and would pay an advance of fifty pounds on a printing of ten thousand copies. To Wells, a young writer at the beginning of his career, this seemed untold wealth (one would have to multiply these figures by at least fifty to arrive at present-day values), and he set to work to rewrite *The Time Machine* from beginning to end. Tusculum Villa, 23 Eardley Road, Sevenoaks, has some claim to a place in literary history as the house in which *The Time Machine* was born.

Wells's problem was how to transform the *National Observer* articles into a continuous story in which the Time Traveller would not merely have brief, tantalizing glimpses of the future but would also convey a detailed account of his adventures and a description of the future of civilization. In this task he was greatly encouraged by Henley, who was convinced that Wells possessed the ability to exploit the idea of time travel far beyond the glimpses contained in the *National Observer* papers. Wells set to work with feverish energy, beginning with pasteups of the *National Observer* articles and proceeding through handwritten drafts and revisions of typed versions. He frequently worked far into the night on the warm summer evenings (much to the disgust of the landlady, who thought he was using an excessive amount of lamp oil), and when not writing he and Amy would go for long walks amidst the handsome beech woods of Knole Park. He wrote as one who was inspired, and when he came to write his autobiography forty years later he still recalled the experience vividly.

It is a salutary experience to reread *The Time Machine* in the first edition and try to imagine the impact it must have made on the late-nineteenth-century reader. When the story is read in one sitting rather than in installments, its full literary and imaginative power are apparent. One of the reasons the story exercises such a powerful hold on the imagination is that it contains strong mythological elements. The basic plot of a lone visitant struggling against the forces of darkness conforms to the classic theme of the quest in Arthurian romance. Thus, the Palace of Green Porcelain, which so intrigues the Traveller when seen from a distance, resembles the enchanted castle in a medieval tale of chivalry. Weena, whom the Traveller rescues from drowning and seeks to protect from the Morlocks, corresponds to the rescued princess of legend. The thickets through which the Traveller and Weena struggle in their flight symbolize the forces of darkness and danger they must traverse if they are to be free. (Note the Arthurian echoes of the Traveller's use of the word *mace* to describe the metal lever he uses as a weapon, made even more explicit when the Traveller goes forth "mace in one hand and Weena in the other" [8, 68].) The perilous journey across an unknown landscape is common to many mythologies from time immemorial, as is the Traveller's passing through a series of trials and obstacles. In this sense the story can be seen as a modern version of an ancient story. Rex Weldon Finn, in *The English Heritage,* has pointed out that the tradition of a "race of dark undersized hairy beings who were hardly human and rarely seen" is an ancient one and has its origin in "the small half-subdued primitive peoples, driven to take refuge in caves and hills and forests" in the time of the Celts.[1] The Traveller's descent into the well recalls the voyage to the abyss of the underworld in the legend of Psyche and Cupid, while his fight with the Morlocks is an echo of comparable struggles in the myths of many cultures.

The fact that the Traveller is not named adds to the symbolic quality of the story. In all the 1894–95 versions he has no name; he is simply referred to as the Philosophical Inventor, the Inventor, or the Time Traveller. Like Christian in *The Pilgrim's Progress,* he is Everyman, a sample human being with the normal complement of anger, fear, hunger, and despair. Because he is fallible and subject to moods of disgust and self-doubt, the reader identifies with him in his plight, sharing in his adventures and his attempts to understand the world around him. It is this timeless element that gives the story the quality of a parable, a myth of universal relevance.

The story can be read as an allegory of the human condition with its central situation of a solitary protagonist pitting his intelligence against forces of darkness and danger until finally reaching his goal. The myth of a lone survivor seeking to triumph over obstacles placed in his path by adversaries whose language and motivations he does not understand holds a seminal place in literature and forms the central theme of *Robinson Crusoe* and *Gulliver's Travels.* The Time Traveller has to solve the riddle of life for himself for, as he remarks, "I had no convenient cicerone in the pattern of the Utopian books" (5, 50).

One reading of *The Time Machine,* then, is as a parable. Man must use all his resources of rationality and guile to overcome forces of darkness and unreason. Even when the odds against him seem insurmountable, he must still live "as though it were not so" (E, 91), doing his utmost within the limits of his powers to change his environment. Viewed in this light, the novel is a characteristic Wellsian text. In portraying man's predicament through the fable of the Time Traveller and emphasizing the crucial importance of human intelligence, Wells dramatizes the contrast between determination and choice and places the central emphasis on *individual* responsibility.

Is the story a warning or a prophecy? At the conclusion of his narrative, the Traveller raises either possibility when he declares, "Take it as a lie—or a prophecy. Say I dreamed it in the workshop. Consider I have been speculating upon the destinies of our race until I have hatched this fiction" (12, 87). Whether warning or prophecy, the implication is that the future pattern of civilization *can* be affected by human initiative; that man is not simply a passive observer (as the Traveller's audience is), but an active participant. The human story is the Time Traveller's story writ large.

In common with many narratives depicting a journey—for example, Defoe's *Robinson Crusoe*, Stevenson's *An Inland Voyage,* and Conrad's *Heart of Darkness*—the journey is both literal and metaphorical. That Wells intended an allegorical interpretation to exist beneath the surface narrative is apparent from the extensive use of mythological and dream imagery. At the conclusion of his story, the Time Traveller asks whether it is all a dream and continues, "They say life is a dream, a precious poor dream at times—" (12, 88). Wells's deployment of conventional symbols for a *threshold*—the broken window caused by the departure of the machine from the laboratory, the clap of thunder that greets his arrival in 802,701, the doors beneath the Sphinx that must be opened before he can regain his machine—represents the transition from conscious to unconscious, from the world of everyday reality to the world of the mind. *The Time Machine* is a voyage not only into the future but also into the unconscious. By dramatizing fundamental aspirations and fears in the form of an allegorical fable, Wells created a myth of continuing relevance to our times.

There are numerous parallels between *The Time Machine* and the quest legends of the Holy Grail. In an illuminating study of Alain-Fournier's *Le Grand Meaulnes* (a novel that has some affinity with *The Time Machine*), Robert Gibson has highlighted the conventions of the fairy tale: "the monsters the hero regularly encounters on his travels," "the dark forest which so frequently needs to be traversed," the fairy castle.[2] The classic fairy tale frequently employs the number three: three blind mice, three brothers, three wishes. The same pattern is repeated in *The Time Machine*—the fruit the Traveller eats has a three-sided husk, he wakes to find "three stooping white creatures" (6, 54), there are three fruit trees in the open court of the Palace of Green Porcelain and three Morlocks at his feet in the fight in the forest, and finally he vanishes "three years ago" (12, 90). This repetition of motifs based on a threefold pattern reinforces some of the novel's underlying themes. The number three traditionally represents birth, life, and death (or creation, preservation, and extinction). The Traveller's arrival in 802,701 is comparable to a new birth—"I felt naked in a strange world" (3, 22)—while his adventures parallel the human journey toward enlightenment and death.

The landscape of the story frequently resembles that of a fairy tale. The narrator writes of "the tall pinnacles of the Palace of Green Porcelain and the polished gleam of its walls" (7, 59); he refers to lush valleys, sleeping houses, and "a little open court within the palace" (8, 70). As if to underline the analogy with *The Sleeping Beauty*, he emphasizes Weena's unconsciousness: "She seemed scarcely to breathe. [. . .] I tried what I could to revive her, but she lay like one dead. I could not even satisfy myself whether or not she breathed" (9, 73–74). Fairy tales are often symbolic dramatizations of the painful journey from adolescence to maturity. From this point of view, *The Time Machine* is unusually interesting in both autobiographical and metaphorical terms. Psychologically, it can be seen as a dramatization of Wells's personal struggle to free himself from his past and from all the forces holding him back (the underground rooms at Bromley and Uppark, the claustrophobic world of the draper's shop, his humble origins). In this sense it is very much a young man's book; he was twenty-eight when he wrote it, and looking back on it later he commented that "It seems a very undergraduate performance to its now mature writer."[3] It has much in common with other novels of adolescence including *Le Grand Meaulnes* and John Fowles's *The Magus*— the heuristic mill the protagonist has to undergo, the yearning for enlightenment, the enigmatic Anima figure. All three novels possess a childlike quality in which the central figure struggles to make sense of a world he does not understand. The death of Weena can be said to represent the end of childhood dreams and the beginning of maturity. The Traveller has passed a crisis in his life and from this point onward has to rely on his own resources. He has severed his romantic longings and can contemplate his destiny with stoical detachment.

In the context of Wells's struggle to free himself from the forces holding him back, it is interesting to note the frequency with which images of being pulled back recur in *The Time Machine*: "I disengaged myself from the clutches of the Morlocks" (6, 56), "I felt as if I was in a monstrous spider's web" (9, 74), "The clinging hands slipped from me" (10, 80). In Wells's short story "The Apple"

(1896), the narrator has to pass through "dry branches that stuck like thorns" and "grass like knife blades" before finding the Apple of the Tree of Knowledge, while in "Mr Skelmersdale in Fairyland" (1901), thorns, briars, and twisted roots separate the narrator from the Anima figure of his dreams. Thickets, briars, and other impedimenta frequently recur in dreams and mythology. Metaphorically, *The Time Machine* symbolizes man's perilous journey through the evolutionary cycle: his beginnings as a neophyte, his struggle against the forces of darkness and ignorance, and, finally, his extinction. The poetic quality of the vision of the earth in the distant future is intense in its power. Like Crusoe's sight of the footprint in the sand or the first glimpse of Treasure Island, it is one of those images that haunts the imagination:

> So I travelled, stopping ever and again, in great strides of a thousand years or more, drawn on by the mystery of the earth's fate, watching with a strange fascination the sun grow larger and duller in the westward sky, and the life of the old earth ebb away. At last, more than thirty million years hence, the huge red-hot dome of the sun had come to obscure nearly a tenth part of the darkling heavens. Then I stopped once more, for the crawling multitude of crabs had disappeared, and the red beach, save for its livid green liverworts and lichens, seemed lifeless. And now it was flecked with white. A bitter cold assailed me. Rare white flakes ever and again came eddying down. [...] There were fringes of ice along the sea margin, with drifting masses further out; but the main expanse of that salt ocean, all bloody under the eternal sunset, was still unfrozen. (11, 83–84)

The Traveller's return to his own time is a mirror image of his departure, but in a larger sense his journey is a reversal of the Darwinian concept of evolution: in journeying to the distant future he sees a mirror image of man's own ancestry. In the end all that remains are crabs, marine life, and "green slime" (11, 84) on the rocks; the evolutionary process has unwound to where it began. In his celebrated lecture *Evolution and Ethics* (1893), T. H. Huxley wrote, "If, for millions of years, our globe has taken the upward road, yet, sometime, the summit will be reached and the downward route will be commenced." This was a salutary observation, but it was not widely held at the time. The popular interpretation of Darwin's ideas was that natural selection would lead to ever *higher* forms of life, that evolution was a steady progression. Wells implicitly challenges this assumption; the notion of man as heir to all the ages gives way to a much less satisfying idea that man is simply one of many species and is subject to the same immutable laws governing all forms of life.

Today *The Time Machine* is part of literary history, and it exists against a background of criticism and analysis. It has taken its place within a well-established dystopian tradition. One has to make a conscious effort to imagine the impact the book must have had on readers of 1895, living as they did in a world in which the extinction of man seemed an utterly remote possibility.

The ambivalence of the epilogue is characteristic of all Wells's fiction; indeed, there are very few of his novels that end on a note of resolution. Neither the reader nor the narrator knows whether the Time Traveller has journeyed to the future or the past, or indeed whether he is still alive. We simply do not know: "One cannot choose but wonder" (E, 91). Wells deliberately ends his narrative on this note in order to leave the reader in a state of uncertainty. It was a convention of the Victorian novel that all loose ends be neatly tied up in the concluding pages. By implicitly rejecting this device, Wells signaled that his first novel marked a departure from the established parameters. It represented a new beginning.

The Time Machine is a characteristic Wellsian text in that the protagonist is a man of science who is drawn by emotional and romantic drives. Although the Time Traveller is at pains to record as accurately as possible his impressions of the world about him, his response is frequently expressed in aesthetic terms. He states that "everywhere were fruits and sweet and delightful flowers; brilliant butterflies flew hither and thither" (4, 32). He refers to "beautiful pagoda-like plants" (4, 29), a prospect that was "as sweet and fair a view as I have ever seen" (4, 30). In describing the sunset on his first day he observes, "The sun had already gone below the horizon and the west was flaming gold, touched with some horizontal bars of purple and crimson" (4, 30). He is beckoned by the "tall pinnacles" (7, 59) of the Palace of Green Porcelain and comforted by the beauty of the starlit sky. He is powerfully attracted to Weena. Again and again he refers to the beauty of flowers and blossoms, the effects of light and shadow on landscape and buildings, the wonder of moon and stars. These are not the reactions one would associate with a rational man of science, but they are characteristic of Wells in his novels and short stories. (In an article written in this same year, "The Degeneration of the Ravensbourne," Wells wrote touchingly of the despoliation of the countryside around Bromley, a countryside he had come to know and love as a child.)[4] *The Time Machine* is the work of a man who is determined to establish his scientific credentials and yet is simultaneously drawn to visions of beauty and desire.

The dichotomy is symbolized at numerous points in the narrative, most strikingly when the Traveller passes a statue of a faun and some acacias in his journey toward the Palace of Green Porcelain. In art and mythology the faun is a symbol of eroticism; the fact that the statue is missing its head suggests Wells's disapproval of the languorous decay of the Eloi. Acacias have long been considered a sacred plant, and in Romanesque art they symbolize the soul and immortality. The Palace, with its extensive collection of scientific treasures, represents man's achievements in the field of science and invention; before arriving at its portals, the Traveller passes symbols of profane and sacred love. As a rational being he is drawn toward the museum and the products of man's intelligence. As an emotional being he is aware of drives pulling him in the opposite direction.

To what extent was *The Time Machine* characteristic of its time and to what extent was it a new departure? In one sense it is very much a period piece. The Time Traveller wears "dingy nineteenth-century garments" (4, 26); he wears a tail-coat; there is a reference to Lord Rosebery (Prime Minister from March 1894 to July 1895); a crab's antennae are likened to "carters' whips" (11, 82); the time machine itself has a *saddle*, which suggests a bicycle, a mode of transport then at the height of its popularity. In depicting the indolent Eloi and the brutish Morlocks, the book dramatizes phenomena much in the news in the 1890s—the languorous, decadent aesthetic movement of Oscar Wilde and Aubrey Beardsley and the manual workers who spent much of their lives underground or in darkness. Like Samuel Butler's *Erewhon* and Edward Bellamy's *Looking Backward,* it looks at the future as a way of commenting on the present. On the other hand, a novel that was simply a period piece would hardly have retained its popularity for a century after its publication. Clearly, *The Time Machine* possesses intrinsic qualities that have ensured its survival through changes in taste and literary fashion over a period of more than one hundred years. These qualities further ensure its enduring relevance as an allegory of the human condition and its haunting power as a vision of the future of man.

Why did Wells take such pains over the writing of the story? It is not unusual for a first novel to be very carefully written, but *The Time Machine* is remarkable in being written with such elaborate care over a long period, a process Bernard Bergonzi has described as suggesting that "the young Wells had an artistic scrupulosity almost rivalling that of James himself."[5] Wells clearly felt a deep intellectual and emotional attachment to the story—he referred to it as "my trump card" and "my peculiar treasure"—and sensed it was an idea that would either make or break his career. Beyond this, the meticulous care with which he worked on a succession of drafts over a period of eight years indicates the seriousness of his literary ambitions and his desire to create work of enduring merit. There is a telling moment in the Palace of Green Porcelain when the Traveller, seeing the decayed remnants of books, reflects on the mortality of literary attainment: "Had I been a literary man I might, perhaps, have moralised upon the futility of all ambition. But as it was, the thing that struck me with keenest force was the enormous waste of labour to which this sombre wilderness of rotting paper testified" (8, 68). It is not difficult to see in this passage the young author speculating on his own future and wondering whether all his efforts would be in vain. He could not have known then that the novel would itself become a kind of time machine carrying his name into futurity.

The Time Machine is not only the story of the Traveller and his journey into the future. It is the story of a little-known writer launching his first novel on to the world. *The Time Machine* is a heroic book and a brave book. It is a myth of universal relevance and—at the same time—a personal testament characteristic of Wells.

Notes

1. Rex Weldon Finn, *The English Heritage* (London: Macdonald, 1948), p. 46.

2. Robert Gibson, *Le Grand Meaulnes* (London: Grant and Cutler, 1986), pp. 103–4.

3. H. G. Wells, preface to *The Time Machine* (New York: Random House, 1931), p. ix.

4. H. G. Wells, "The Degeneration of the Ravensbourne," *Pall Mall Gazette*, 12 July 1894.

5. Bernard Bergonzi, "The Publication of *The Time Machine* 1894–95," *Review of English Studies*, n.s. 11 (February 1960), p. 51.

Taking It as a Story

The Beautiful Lie of *The Time Machine*

ROBERT CROSSLEY

"Story!" cried the Editor. "Story be damned!" said the Time Traveller.
—Wells, *The Time Machine*

This exclamatory exchange in the Richmond dining room between guest and host makes storytelling into an issue that governs the entire narration of *The Time Machine*. In one sense, H. G. Wells's Editor, characterized by the narrator as "the new kind of journalist" (2, 15), is a forerunner of the obnoxious reporter we have all come to know in the past hundred years, earlier in print and now inescapably on television. He confronts a man in distress, haggard and hungry, and insists on the public's immediate right to claim his experience as a narrative commodity. For his part, the Time Traveller insists that the story must wait until he is ready to tell it and that it does not, in any case, belong at the dinner table. But once the host and guests have retired to the smoking room, the Traveller makes clear that he will not play the Editor's game; he does not accept the new journalistic notion of "story" as sensation, as controversy, as interrogation, as group participation. There will not be an interview. The Editor will hear a story, but he will do so on the Traveller's terms. And those terms involve the ancient storyteller's privilege of telling events in a sequence of his choosing, without having to attend to quibbles, misgivings, or heckling from his audience:

> I can't argue to-night. I don't mind telling you the story, but I can't argue. I will [...] tell you the story of what has happened to me, if you like, but you must refrain from interruptions. I want to tell it. Badly. Most of it will sound like lying. So be it! It's true—every word of it, all the same. (2, 17)

This Victorian Sindbad offers as after-dinner entertainment not a romance, he says, but a confession, not an imaginary voyage, but a chapter of autobiography. His experience, he knows, will sound like fiction; the truth will seem like a lie. A contract must be negotiated:

> "I shan't sleep till I've told this thing over to you. Then I shall go to bed. But no interruptions! Is it agreed?"
>
> "Agreed," said the Editor, and the rest of us echoed "Agreed." (2, 17)

This agreement marks a significant difference between the Heinemann edition of 1895, which with minor variants we all now read, and the 1894 serialized version of *The Time Machine* that appeared in the *National Observer*. Wells made a great many changes and additions in that crucial year when *The Time Machine* suddenly matured in his imagination after a seven-year gestation. But this embargo on interruptions is a change that was central to the form of the book. In 1894 *The Time Machine* was essentially a freewheeling, multivoiced discussion that meandered through the Traveller's account of his journey. The *National Observer*'s Time Traveller (or the Philosophical Inventor, as he was then called) was interrupted and questioned so often by his guests in the course of his description of the future that he complained at one point, "I am a traveller, and I tell you a traveller's tale. I am not an annotated edition of myself."[1] The Heinemann's Traveller acts on this principle from the start, and in having him do so, Wells took the significant step of turning a Platonic dialogue into a framed narrative. A discourse on time travel became a story by and about a time traveller.

Throughout his long evening's tale, the Time Traveller, under the terms of his agreement, takes no questions from his audience. The only momentary pause in the narrative occurs when he reaches into his pocket and lays on the table the two withered flowers he has brought back from the year 802,701. Without comment, he then resumes his tale. But when the entire story has been told, this Traveller, unlike Sindbad, is not showered with gold and praises by his audience. The faces of the Time Traveller's auditors register their doubts, their unasked questions, their suspicions, their embarrassment. Except for the narrator, none of those present appears to have the slightest faith in the authenticity of the tale. As the Traveller scans the perplexed faces looking at him—or trying not to look at him— he concludes the narrative of his adventures:

> No. I cannot expect you to believe it. Take it as a lie—or a prophecy. Say I dreamed it in the workshop. Consider I have been speculating upon the destinies of our race until I have hatched this fiction. Treat my assertion of its truth as a mere stroke of art to enhance its interest. And taking it as a story, what do you think of it? (12, 87)

To this appeal, the Traveller gets no satisfactory reply. The Journalist and Psychologist, eager to make their escape, talk only of the clock and the best place to get a late cab. The Medical Man asks their host where he *really* got those strange flowers. The pushy Editor who issued the call for a story now rejects it all as a "gaudy lie" (12, 89). But the Traveller's question is worth asking and worth answering. After more than a hundred years, what *do* we think of *The Time Machine* as a story?

To read the scholarly commentary on *The Time Machine* is to form the impression that a great many of Wells's critics have said, in effect, "Story be damned!" Much has been made of theories of time in *The Time Machine*. Of Huxleyan devolution. Of the mediation of opposites. Of the mood of the fin-de-siècle. Of future history. Of utopian or dystopian tradition. Take your pick. What have I left out? *The Time Machine* as anthropological field trip, as Oedipal riddle, as antipastoral, as Cassandran prediction, as autobiographical projection, as truncated epic, as socialist parable, as son of *Frankenstein*. It is testimony to the extraordinary richness of Wells's first great book that all these roads lead to wisdom. But how seriously and how often has it been taken as a story, as a beautiful lie, as a product of the dream workshop of a fiction maker?

Wells the critic had little patience with overtly didactic narratives in which doctrine masqueraded as story. He scorned Sarah Grand's [Frances Elizabeth McFall's] *The Heavenly Twins* as "merely an episode intercalated in a hysterical diatribe against the tyranny exercised by man over woman." In a review of Grant Allen's *The British Barbarians*, he wrote, "Let him call his sermon a sermon and be content."[2] Although later commentators frequently accused Wells of falling into the trap of sermonizing, in 1895 the reviewer in the *Saturday Review*, whose pages often featured Wells's own unsigned book reviews, was equally impressed by *The Time Machine*'s narrative as by its ideas. "A story of remarkable ability," said the critic. "As a mere narrative it is excellently told, and the plot is distressingly interesting."[3] On the other hand, if we trust the mature judgment of the author—and I'm not at all sure we *should*—the story, as opposed to the ideas, of *The Time Machine* dated quickly and amounted to "a very undergraduate performance." So Wells himself pronounced in a special preface to a limited edition of *The Time Machine* in 1931.[4] But, of course, this was almost always Wells's line when describing his own work: to play it up as a literature of ideas and to play it down as narrative art.

In his extended comments on the novel in *Experiment in Autobiography*, Wells made it plain that he knew perfectly well both the value and the persistence of "story," despite his campaign to denigrate his own talents as storyteller. "In my hands the Novel proved like a blanket too small for the bed," he wrote about his professed inability to offer a decent narrative cover for all the ideas in his fiction.[5] But a few pages later in the *Autobiography,* he also predicted that while the novel in its early-twentieth-century mode may cease to be written in the future, "stories, parables, parodies of fact will still be told."[6] And, in truth, it is the durability of *The Time Machine* as story that most fully explains its hold on readers after more than a century.

The Time Machine is a fable, in the old Miltonic sense of that literary term: a fabrication, a fiction invented to deceive, a falsehood, a lying story in the mode of a traveller's tall tales, of which Ulysses, that notorious old deceiver, is the prototypical teller. As J. R. Hammond has urged in his study of Wells and the modern novel, we should consider the importance of the subtitle that Wells gave to the Heinemann edition of *The Time Machine*: "An Invention."[7] Surely that subtitle refers not only to the mechanism of crystal and metal fashioned by the man from Richmond in his laboratory, but to the fiction created by the man from Bromley in the laboratory of his imagination. Author and protagonist, fiction maker and machine maker, are both ingenious fabricators. The narrative is told—indeed, performed—by an inventor notorious for indulging what his friends regard as "more than a touch of whim" (2, 12), a habit that casts his narrative into a shadow land between vision and mirage. At the conclusion of the narrative, the auditors in the Richmond smoking room debate whether the teller is memoirist or mountebank, and even the most sympathetic of his listeners—the unnamed person who records the narration for us—asks in his final exchange with the Time Traveller: "But is it not some hoax? [. . .] Do you really travel through time?" (12, 89). The difficulty in separating the man of science, who invents a time machine, from the merry prankster, who enjoys guying his guests, accentuates the problem of the credibility of his narration. "Story be damned," the Time Traveller may say, but making things and making things up are his twin businesses.

Wells has deliberately set up the tale so that the truths exposed in *The Time Machine*—truths about progress, about class, about mortality—come packaged in what the Editor dismisses as a gaudy lie, but what I prefer to celebrate as a beautiful one. The Medical Man, examining the miniature model of the time machine displayed in chapter 1, exclaims, "It's beautifully made" (1, 9). So too is the machinery of Wells's fiction. In fact, in the *National Observer* serialization, the Traveller's auditors, just as incredulous but not as grumpy as those in the Heinemann edition, keep the Traveller talking all night for the sheer pleasure of his narration and on the chance that "there still might be a sufficiently worthy lie wasting in his brain."[8]

It was C. S. Lewis—a great proponent of the fundamental value of story in the literary experience—who pointed out forty years ago that in romance "belief is at best irrelevant."[9] Lewis proposed the test of rereading rather than the test of credibility for romantic fiction. After the "sheer narrative lust" of a first reading has been appeased, Lewis suggested, the reader is in a position to savor the fiction *as story*, re-experiencing the once-surprising turns of plot but now more fully relishing the sense of "surprisingness," the cunning design and beautiful deployment of artifice that becomes more evident on each successive rereading. "It is the quality of unexpectedness, not the *fact* that delights us. It is even better the second time," Lewis insisted.[10]

How well does the story of *The Time Machine* measure up to Lewis's test of rereadability? We might begin with the narrator through whom we receive the Traveller's tale—the man at the dinner party who has transformed the telling into a text, something heard into something read. Nearly the whole of *The Time Machine* is narrated in quotation marks so that as readers, we are constantly aware of the fiction as purported transcript.[11] We are also inevitably aware of the transcript as fiction from the moment when the narrator warns us of "the inadequacy of pen and ink" and his "own inadequacy" at capturing the reality of the night spent listening to the Traveller's story (2, 17). The narrator's skills aside, we read the quotation marks as part of the "machinery" of the fiction whose authenticity is as uncertain for us as the time machine's is for the people gathered in the Richmond smoking room. This is a narrative, after all, *remembered* three years after the event, not transcribed at the telling. Inevitably, the original oral performance has been reinvented on paper. In the epilogue, the narrator tells us how he has been haunted by the Time Traveller's recital, replaying it in his imagination as he also invents sequels to it, both in prehistory and in future history. The inexhaustible mystery of the tale fascinates that narrator and for three years leaves him remembering and wondering. "To me," he writes, "the future is still black and blank—is a vast ignorance, lit at a few casual places by the memory of his story" (E, 91). It has taken the narrator a very long time to set down what he recalls of the Traveller's account of his adventure. In that time, the Traveller has already become a "story" in the journalistic sense of a sensation, as we are told at the close of the final chapter: "The Time Traveller vanished three years ago. And, *as everybody knows now*, he has never returned" (12, 90; emphasis added). In writing down the "invention" known as *The Time Machine*, the narrator ensures that his friend will not simply *be* a story but will be allowed to *tell* his story—at least as reinvented by the narrator.

But it is possible to get a little too literary at this point—or in that fine old

British demurrer, to be "too clever by half" over Wells's narrator. This narrator is so slender an invention himself that he will not bear very close analysis. It is Wells who arranges the story in *The Time Machine*. Over the course of his career, Wells experimented variously and sometimes brilliantly with narrators, but this is not the case in *The Time Machine*.[12] Here the narrator is a convenient cat's-paw for the author—or, to use the appropriate image for this book, this narrator is the miniature model for the full-scale author who stands in the next room and who actually takes us for a ride. To gauge the distinctive qualities and beauties of that storytelling Wells, the artful liar, I want to undertake rereadings of three distinctive moments from *The Time Machine*, which I will call "In the Saddle," "Down the Well," and "On the Beach."

In the Saddle

The first true episode in *The Time Machine*, once we move in from the frame of the dinner party, is concerned with the experience of time travelling itself. It is a glittering example of Wells's narrative art. ("Could anything be more finely imagined or more admirably expressed?" asked the critic at the *Saturday Review*.[13]) In part, this episode works as story because of Wells's remarkable instinct, often commented on, for circumstantial detail in the foreground and a sketchy background. We hear the Traveller tell us how he gave a final tap to the machine he had just assembled, tightened all its screws, oiled it, before seating himself in the saddle. We don't really know what the thing as a whole looks like, but we have the illusion that we've seen it, and we participate in the tension and exhilaration of the moment.

Throughout the thousand-word description of time travelling, we are intensely aware of the Traveller's feelings from the first instant when his monosyllabic verbs and nouns telegraph sensation: "I drew a breath, set my teeth, gripped the starting lever with both hands, and went off with a thud" (3, 18). Wells's early romances often anticipate the special effects of cinema and stop-motion photography, but here the effect is even more startling; the reader is given a taste of the "virtual reality" of a rough and scary ride through time: hands manipulating the joystick, a blinking light painful to the eye, disorienting sound effects, nausea induced by the swaying of the machine, the persistent fear of falling and the expectation of a crash, the hysteria and loss of nerve that finally and irrationally cause the Traveller to jam on the brakes and be catapulted out of the saddle into the year 802,701.

The narration of this scene depends on a striking combination of the verisimilar

with the rhetorical device Ernst Robert Curtius identified as the "inexpressibility topos"—the claim that an experience cannot adequately be captured in
words.[14] "I want to tell" this story, the Traveller cautions his listeners. "[But m]ost
of it will sound like lying" (2, 17). Our narrator adds another layer of inexpressibility to the Traveller's account by insisting that we readers lose a dimension of
the experience that had been available to those who witnessed and heard the
account first-hand:

> You read, I will suppose, attentively enough; but you cannot see the speaker's white,
> sincere face in the bright circle of the little lamp, nor hear the intonation of his voice.
> You cannot know how his expression followed the turns of his story! (2, 17)

But the emphasis on the inexpressible and incommunicable is counterpoised by
a reliance on vivid metaphors designed to create the impression of verisimilitude.
"I am afraid I cannot convey the peculiar sensations of time travelling" (3, 18),
the Traveller warns us. Then he launches into a catalog of approximations of the
impossible to the familiar: Mrs Watchett seems to shoot across the room like a
rocket; night arrives, in a nice reversal, like the turning out of a lamp; the headlong motion of the machine feels like the queasy plunge down a switchback; night
and day alternate like a flapping black wing; the sun appears as a brilliant arch in
the sky and the moon as a dimmer band of light; trees change color like puffs of
vapor; buildings rise and evaporate like dreams; the solid ground under the machine seems to liquefy and flow. The whole of this account is punctuated by like-
nesses and a "series of impressions" (3, 20), all designed to make the inexpressible appear tangible. The entire passage is full of *seeming*s and *suppose*s,
*so-to-speak*s and *kind of*s, "new sensations" filtered through "the veil of my confusion" (3, 20).

The entire account of time travelling is a breathless accumulation of alternately
precise and approximate, vivid and dim impressions. Everything is fluctuating
and flickering, reeling and falling, going hazy and faint, but then twinkling and
flashing. Even the Traveller himself seems to metamorphose during the experience; at high speeds he becomes almost gaseous, "slipping like a vapour through
the interstices of intervening substances" (3, 20), and fears coming to a stop when
the return to solidity, "the jamming of myself, molecule by molecule, into whatever lay in my way," might cause "a profound chemical reaction—possibly a far-
reaching explosion" (3, 20). The combination of observation and evocation
achieved by the Traveller as he bucks and sways in the saddle of the time machine before being finally flung headlong into the year 802,701 is more dazzling,
I think, than the account of sunrise on the moon that caused T. S. Eliot to sus-

pend disbelief in *The First Men in the Moon*.[15] If we take it as a story, the description of the first of all human journeys through time belongs among the grand episodes of make-believe in literature. That we disbelieve in travelling into the future *is* irrelevant. This is a story that lies like the truth. What matters is that *if* time travelling were possible, we are convinced that this is what it might feel like. The "In the Saddle" episode turns fantastic hypothesis into fictional experience. It is a ride that we can look forward to on repeated readings. And that, as Lewis reminds us, is what story is *for*.

Down the Well

Consider how Wells paces his story and generates expectancy. Just after arriving in 802,701, the Traveller casually observes "a pretty little structure, like a well under a cupola" and, with an authorial pun to which Patrick Parrinder calls our notice, remarks blandly on "the oddness of wells still existing" (4, 30).[16] For nearly one-third the length of *The Time Machine*, hints accumulate about this architectural phenomenon. From a hilltop the Traveller notices how "certain circular wells" are a "peculiar feature" of the Thames Valley of the future, and, curious, he peers down several of them and observes how deep they all are, how waterless, how noisy. He gives us a sound effect and a simile: "thud—thud—thud, like the beating of some big engine." He tosses a slip of paper down a well and, when it is "sucked swiftly out of sight," guesses that the wells are ventilators for underground sewers (5, 40–41).

He then seems to put the wells out of mind, but a reader's curiosity has been awakened by the unresolved problem of those recurrently observed artifacts in the landscape. Later, the Traveller sees his first Morlock and follows it to, as he says, "one of those round well-like openings of which I have told you" (5, 47). When the creature disappears, on a hunch the Traveller looks into the well and sees a feature he had missed before: metal handholds attached to the wall of the shaft, down which the Morlock is retreating. The Traveller starts thinking and revising. Perhaps this isn't the entrance to a sewer at all; he asks himself, "[W]hat was hidden down there, at the foot of the shaft?" (5, 47). Discovering that he can get no answer from the useless Eloi, who shrink at the very idea of the wells, he is left to guess that they are entrances to an artificial habitat beneath the surface. Here, he supposes, the other humanoid species of the far future must live and work, but ("though it may seem odd to you," he admits) he makes no immediate effort to test his hypothesis. The suspense builds for another two days. The Traveller knows it is "inevitable" that he will take this route to search for his missing time machine, but he fears the dark descent (6, 50–51). Finally, the Traveller can no longer put off the duty of adventure, and at last Wells appeases the reader's narrative lust for a glimpse of the Underworld.

The actual venture down into the realm of the Morlocks is one into the "mouth" of the well and down its "throat" (6, 53). A reader may be reminded of the medieval hell mouth and of the dark underworlds of Hieronymus Bosch with their entryways through the mouths and gullets of grotesque animals. The receding image of a single star framed in a small circle of sky as the Traveller moves downward may suggest the descent into Dante's starless Inferno, while the "rayless obscurity" and "utter darkness" (6, 54) of the caves may recall the "darkness visible" of Milton's Hell. As he ventures deeper, the Traveller gets intimations of the vast labyrinth of tunnels and galleries carved under the earth, but he never reaches the bottom of the well, and neither he nor the reader has anything like a map of the Underworld. *The Time Machine* has nothing comparable to the pictorial depth and detail of the subterranean world in *The First Men in the Moon*. Visually, almost everything remains shadowy, creating an atmosphere of threatening gloom: the vague spectacle of a huge cavern seen by match light, the indistinct bloody carcass on a dining table, faint silhouettes of gigantic machines, Morlocks lurking in shadows cast by a single match. There is no photographic clarity to this picture of the Underworld, nothing like the cinematic splendors of "In the Saddle." Wells's storytelling interest here lies elsewhere.

As the Traveller journeys into and through the Underworld, the account becomes intensely tactile, and both physical and psychological pressures are emphasized: the weight of the Traveller's body on the fragile ladder rungs, the oppressive throbbing of the air pumps below, his aching back, his claustrophobia, his fear of falling, the stuffiness of the air, his violent fit of shivering, the lit match that falls "wriggling" into the blackness like a thing alive (6, 55). The climactic moments all involve the Morlocks, hands plucking at the Traveller's clothes, the "lank fingers" running over his face and "gently" disengaging the matchbox from his hand, his violent kicks as he makes his escape, and the yank of "one little wretch" who nearly gets the Traveller's boot as he hurries back up the shaft (6, 56–57). It is a felt more than a seen horror that Wells's story evokes.

What may be most striking about chapter 6 is that in detailing the journey below, Wells leaves the narrative utterly free from interpretive commentary. In the chapter preceding the descent, when the existence of an underworld first becomes apparent to him, the Traveller expatiates on his upstairs-downstairs theory of a split between capital and labor that has been enshrined, biologically and geographically, in the two vertically arranged cultures of the Eloi and the Morlocks. And in the chapter following the descent, the Traveller resumes theorizing, interpreting what he has seen as an instance of devolution. But the chapter in which the descent is narrated is untouched by theory or speculative analysis. The Morlocks are monsters, not symbols, and the Traveller is no cultural anthropologist or political scientist, but a primitive sort of heroic adventurer. He entered this Underworld, he points out, without the defenses or the luxuries of Victorian civilization: arms, medicine, tobacco, or camera. "I stood there," he says, not without a touch of braggadocio, "with only the weapons and the powers that Nature had endowed me with—hands, feet, and teeth; these, and four safety-matches" (6, 55). The Traveller's braving of the subterranean world is one that he barely survives, and when he surfaces, he collapses—as he did at the end of the time-travelling episode—in a "deadly nausea" (6, 57).

What makes the chapter work so effectively as story is not simply the rich sensuousness of the account—although Wells has described it with extraordinary skill while once again invoking the inexpressibility topos. "The sense of these unseen creatures examining me," the Traveller says squeamishly, "was indescribably unpleasant" (6, 56). The genius of the episode lies in the long buildup to this brief moment, which is similar to the way (as Brian W. Aldiss has pointed out) Wells delays for half the novel the first close-up description of a Martian in *The War of the Worlds*.[17] A significant element in the pleasure of a rereading of *The Time Machine* is our anticipation of this long-postponed and greatly desired descent and our gathering up all the hints—which Wells has artfully scattered along the narrative's path—of what is to come.

Bernard Bergonzi, always intensely alert to the romancer in Wells, was right to understand the trip down the well as "a parody of the Harrowing of Hell" operating with "an almost undisplaced mythical significance."[18] But the episode also goes beyond parody and links Wells's Traveller to other fabled travellers from the great book of story. He recapitulates the journeys of Ulysses and Aeneas, of Christ and Dante, and of little Alice into underworlds that are simultaneously terrifying, educative, and liberating. In describing the great struggle of descent and ascent, unburdened and unassisted by the tools of modern civilization, the Traveller to the imagined future joins the company of the fairy tale heroes of the imagined past.

When Wells sends his Traveller down the well, he calls on the same linguistic powers that animate the earlier account of the Traveller in the saddle of the time machine. But here he goes further in linking this episode to some of the most durable conventions and archetypes of romance. If we take it as a story, the descent into the habitat of the Morlocks is both novel and familiar, a Wellsian "invention" that is yet a variation on a central episode of the heroic adventure story.

On the Beach

I come, finally, to what many readers and commentators have understood as one of the great chapters in modern fiction.[19] For the last stage of his recorded journey into the far future, the Traveller is back in the saddle again, though now sidesaddle and loose in his seat, a result of his hasty escape from the Morlocks after the fight inside the pedestal of the sphinx. His journey—and the story—come full circle in the year 30 million. We make the circuit from Genesis to Revelation. In both 802,701 and 30 million we are invited to see how in our beginnings are our endings. Among the Eloi the Traveller found a pleasure ground reminiscent of the mythical Eden from which, in the scriptural reading of the past, life with a soul emerged; the civilization that began in a garden, in the Wellsian reading of the future, will end in one. Now in the year 30 million, the Traveller has gone beyond the end of human culture, but his setting suggests an equally distant past when the human presence on the earth had not yet emerged. He sits on a beach where living organisms, according to the book of science, long ago struggled heroically to move from aquatic to terrestrial status. In Wells's book of science fiction, life will also play out its last inglorious inning on a beach, this one not fronting an ocean teeming with life but a biblically named "Dead Sea," dark and icing over as entropy makes its relentless imprint on the planet (11, 83).

As the narrative in chapter 11 unfolds, we see not the first amphibian, but the anachronistic last man on earth gasping for breath on the shore, trying to process a rarefied air no longer fit for human lungs. The nearly featureless beach bordering a nearly motionless ocean swarms with giant predatory crabs. As the Traveller shivers and clings to his seat, he gazes in dismay on what his world has become. "I cannot convey," the Traveller worries, "the sense of abominable desolation that hung over the world" (11, 83). Yet in echoing the Book of Daniel and the Gospels he succeeds, by allusion, in expressing the inexpressible.[20] The biblical "abomination of desolation" that heralds the end of the world and the Last Judgment becomes the humanist blasphemy of "the stony beach crawling with these foul, slow-stirring monsters." Suddenly, he feels his cheek and ear tickled by a thread and turns to see at his back one of the giant crustaceans, its antennae aquiver, its eyes "wriggling on their stalks," its mouth "all alive with appetite" (11, 83). We know this story. The Traveller is recapitulating his earlier descent into the cavern full of hungry, touchy-feely Morlocks. Just as he had earlier raced up the ladder of the well, so now he pushes the lever of the time machine in order to move vertically up through time, trying to escape this last recrudescence of the Morlocks' Hell. Some of the imagery and phrasing Wells had used to evoke the darkened infernal Underworld of the Morlocks—the stars barely visible through the mouth of the well and the "rayless obscurity" below—appear again in the climactic solar eclipse witnessed by the Traveller at the world's endtime: "I saw the black central shadow of the eclipse sweeping towards me. In another moment the pale stars alone were visible. All else was rayless obscurity. The sky was absolutely black" (11, 85).

But what draws readers again and again to this chapter of *The Time Machine*, what makes it most fully satisfy Lewis's test of rereadability, is not the recurrence of the Morlockian leitmotif, but the power of Wells's litany of things falling apart, falling down, growing dim, going quiet. As the twilight of the planet deepens, everything turning bloodred and black, the air thinning toward vacuum, the cold intensifying, the sun eclipsed, life reduced to a twitching tentacular blob on the terminal beach, the Traveller is overcome with nausea for the third time in the story. And a reader is in the grip of a definitive story of last things. For all his disclaimers of artistry, Wells, I would like to think, might have been amused, at least, by this reader's assessment. For this chapter of *The Time Machine* is more memorable and more rereadable, though only slightly less incredible, than the vision offered in the Book of Revelation. Taken as a story, it beats the Word of God handily.

But I mean to be more than flippant about what Wells has accomplished in the chapter he once called "The Further Vision."[21] A comparison with Milton is not inappropriate. Just as Book VII of *Paradise Lost* turns a bare listing of facts about the six days of Creation in Genesis 1 into gorgeous and vital poetry, making an account of creation into a demonstration of creativity, so Wells has mated the Last Judgment to the second law of thermodynamics and generated neither science nor theology but pure story. In the famous account of his youthful impiety in *Experiment in Autobiography*, Wells says that all he got from his mother's earnest Christianity was "the forms and phrases of it."[22] It is not a negligible legacy; the forms and phrases of biblical texts infuse Wells's imagination and emerge in often wonderfully metamorphosed fictional shape. Conversely, Wells was fascinated by the questions and paradoxes of modern physics, but irritated by physicists' incapacity for forms and phrases that would make sense out of the science: "The more brilliant investigators rocket off into mathematical pyrotechnics and return to common speech with statements that are, according to the legitimate meaning of words, nonsensical. [. . .] Ordinary language ought not to be misused in this way. Clearly these mathematical physicists have not made the real words yet, the necessary words that they can hold by, transmit a meaning with and make the base of a fresh advance."[23] It is precisely this imaginative and linguistic defect, remedied by Wells's eschatological imagery and narrative power in "The Further Vision," that have made this chapter of *The Time Machine* the single most accessible and powerful illustration in the past hundred years of the second law of thermodynamics in action—at least until the publication of Pamela Zoline's story "The Heat Death of the Universe" in 1967.

Chapter 11 of *The Time Machine* can claim the status of a secular scripture. Lord Kelvin's thermodynamics, like all good formulations in physics, has the power of elegantly quantitative abstraction, but the second law can neither visualize entropy nor reconcile us to it. Matthew's report of Jesus' vision of the end of the world offers incomparable pictures of stars falling from the heavens, trumpeting angels, and the Son of Man arriving in thunderclouds for judgment. The gospel narrative is a splendid melodrama, powerful in image, movement, and hortatory rhetoric, but its mythology belongs to a prescientific age. In offering his story about the endtime—a vision which is also a judgment on mortality, on finitude, on the vanity of anthropocentrism—Wells fuses scientific understanding with spiritual catharsis. If, as I once proposed, the Traveller's sojourn in the Palace of Green Porcelain, the run-down museum where he finds the decayed and useless remnants of human culture, represents a *memento mori* for our species, the scene in the year 30 million may be Wells's *memento mori* for the entire terrestrial habitat.[24]

In "On the Beach" Wells has succeeded in fashioning the most beautiful of all lies—a new myth. It does not simply subvert the New Testament Apocalypse, it replaces it with language and invention, images and fabrications that articulate the mysteries of time, change, death, and destiny. It does not simply gloss the second law of thermodynamics, it orchestrates it. The Traveller several times calls his final moments on the beach indescribable—but it is precisely Wells's extraordinarily exact descriptions of the signs and portents of the world's end that call readers and writers back to this story. This, says Warren Wagar in his history of eschatological visions, is "the one passage that sticks in everyone's memory."[25] It is the archetype behind the terminal beaches of Olaf Stapledon and J. G. Ballard and Nevil Shute and Brian W. Aldiss. It looms behind the final shot in the film of *Planet of the Apes* and, in a splendid metamorphosis, the cold beauty of the last scene in Kim Stanley Robinson's *Blue Mars*. The beach Wells's Time Traveller surveys is sterile and comfortless, but over the past century it has proved a fertile and grimly pleasurable locus for imagination. In this climactic vision's capacity to stimulate memory, invite rereading, and inspire new creations is the clearest evidence that the beautiful lie of *The Time Machine* continues to ring true.

Notes

1. Cited in *The Definitive Time Machine: A Critical Edition of H. G. Wells's Scientific Romance with Introduction and Notes*, ed. Harry M. Geduld (Bloomington: Indiana University Press, 1987), p. 171.

2. *H. G. Wells's Literary Criticism*, ed. Patrick Parrinder and Robert Philmus (Sussex: Harvester Press, 1980), pp. 75, 61.

3. Review of *The Time Machine*, by H. G. Wells, *Saturday Review* (20 July 1895), p. 87.

4. H. G. Wells, preface to *The Time Machine: An Invention* (New York: Random House, 1931), p. ix.

5. H. G. Wells, *Experiment in Autobiography: Discoveries and Conclusions of a Very Ordinary Brain (since 1866)* (New York: Macmillan, 1934), p. 417.

6. *Experiment in Autobiography*, p. 422.

7. J. R. Hammond, *H. G. Wells and the Modern Novel* (New York: St. Martin's, 1988), p. 80. Patrick Parrinder has pointed out to me, however, that Wells dropped the subtitle in later editions of *The Time Machine*. For the Miltonic equation of fable with erroneous invention, see the famous description of the fall of Mulciber in *Paradise Lost*, I, lines 730–51.

8. Cited in Geduld, ed., *The Definitive Time Machine*, p. 163.

9. C. S. Lewis, "On Stories," in *Of Other Worlds: Essays and Stories*, ed. Walter Hooper (1966; reprint, New York: Harcourt, 1975), p. 13.

10. "On Stories," pp. 17, 18.

11. I have adopted a different understanding of the effects of a "tale told in quotation marks" from that put forward by Northrop Frye in *Anatomy of Criticism* and applied to *The Time Machine* by Bernard Bergonzi in *The Early H. G. Wells: A Study of the Scientific Romances* (Manchester: Manchester University Press, 1961), pp. 42–43.

12. For a rewarding discussion of Wellsian narrators, see Hammond, *Wells and the Modern Novel*, esp. chapter 3.

13. Review of *The Time Machine*, p. 87.

14. Ernst Robert Curtius, *European Literature and the Latin Middle Ages*, trans. Willard R. Trask (1953; reprint, New York: Harper and Row, 1963), pp. 159–60.

15. T. S. Eliot, "Wells as Journalist," in *H. G. Wells: The Critical Heritage*, ed. Patrick Parrinder (London: Routledge, 1972), p. 320. In his introduction to *The Definitive Time Machine*, Geduld suggests that Wells "concentrates on *undermining disbelief* rather than on creating plausibility" (p. 15).

16. Patrick Parrinder, *H. G. Wells: Shadows of the Future* (Liverpool: Liverpool University Press, 1995), p. 37.

17. Brian W. Aldiss, "Wells and the Leopard Lady," in *The Detached Retina: Aspects of SF and Fantasy* (Liverpool: Liverpool University Press, 1995), p. 117.

18. *The Early H. G. Wells*, p. 52.

19. For a recent example, see Edward James, *Science Fiction in the Twentieth Century* (New York: Oxford University Press, 1994), p. 30.

20. See Daniel 11:31, 12:11; Matthew 24:15; Mark 13:14.

21. Wells had given titles to each chapter in the first British edition of *The Time Machine* but removed them from later printings.

22. *Experiment in Autobiography*, p. 44.

23. *Experiment in Autobiography*, pp. 176–77.

24. Robert Crossley, "In the Palace of Green Porcelain: Artifacts from the Museums of Science Fiction," in *Fictional Space: Essays on Contemporary Science Fiction*, ed. Tom Shippey (Oxford: Blackwell, 1991), p. 86.

25. W. Warren Wagar, *Terminal Visions: The Literature of Last Things* (Bloomington: Indiana University Press, 1982), p. 93.

Was the Time Machine Necessary?

PAUL ALKON

 My concern in this chapter is primarily with the time machine itself, the vehicle that transports the Time Traveller to and from his destinations. I want to invite reconsideration of its role in Wells's story and in science fiction more generally. It has received little attention, and that mainly in the form of perfunctory praise, the effect of which is dismissive if not damning. Most often the time machine is regarded merely as one among several props that create a specious plausibility.[1] As such it seems nice but hardly necessary. Gary K. Wolfe, for example, in his excellent study of science fiction's iconology, devotes only three sentences to the emblematic role of time machines without any mention there of H. G. Wells as the inventor of this kind of vehicle. For Wolfe, the major icons of science fiction, to each of which he devotes a fine chapter, are the barrier, the spaceship, the city, the wasteland, the robot, and the monster. Wolfe only discusses Wells's tale of time travel as a commentary on the fate of cities, without any mention of the time machine itself.[2]

Among passing tributes to the time machine, Frank McConnell's praise is the most perceptive and the least dismissive. He remarks that the novella achieves great power "because it is such a finely fashioned aesthetic machine for producing ambiguity (much like the Time Machine)"; and he insists too that "Invention of the Eloi and the Morlocks is finally not as central to the brilliance of *The Time Machine* as is the invention of the machine itself, and the consequent imagination of time in its fullest, largest, and most challengingly inhuman dimensions."[3] The machine as an example and emblem of ambiguity is, as McConnell suggests, a crucial analogue of the novella as a whole and, as this implies, also an important instrument of its characteristic self-reflexivity.[4] As a means of imagining the alarming magnitude of cosmological timescales, however, the time machine plays a role that is mainly qualitative. By means of a dream vision, an inexplicable time slip (the device of a whole category of time-travel romances), or even mesmeric or cryogenic sleep, a protagonist might *plausibly enough* have been transported to contemplate the final horrors encountered by the Time Traveller on the terminal beach. And readers *could* have travelled along in imagination without inhibiting objections. But it would have been a different *kind* of trip, because it would not have been affiliated with the instruments of scientific investigation.

Robert Scholes and Eric Rabkin almost get it right by remarking in their history of science fiction that the time machine's importance is not in its "vague pseudoscientific rationale [. . .] but in the fact that it was [. . .] a new mechanical agent, a time *machine*," which therefore "changed the whole footing of time travel, opening up the past as well as the future, for imaginative investigation."[5] The past, however, had previously been opened up (in 1889), without recourse to a time machine, by Mark Twain in *A Connecticut Yankee in King Arthur's Court*— and opened up very influentially, too, as Bud Foote has shown in *A Connecticut Yankee in the Twentieth Century: Travel to the Past in Science Fiction*.[6]

Mark Rose notes that "The presence of the machine, the symbol of science and rationality, points to the fable's central concern with power: through science man may be able to dominate time. But what the novel finally reveals is that any such hope is false: not man but time is the master of the universe."[7] This specifies an important symbolic function of the time machine but only hints at how Wells puts the machine to use throughout the tale as a symbol of science and rationality. Nor does Rose say anything of the machine's aesthetic dimension as a marvelously *appealing* vehicle—surely no less so than devices like Nemo's *Nautilus*, Robur's aeronef, or the starship *Enterprise*. For many readers, the time machine may be far more appealing because they can easily imagine themselves in the saddle, zooming off to high adventure. It is a means of fast solo travel whose absurdly simple controls are easily managed by one person without any of the technical skills, discipline, and leadership ability necessary to command more imposing vehicles. The time machine is science fiction's sexy little sports car. Its charms as such, however, have attracted scant admiration from academics, perhaps because, as Stanley Fish remarks, they have a joyless collective preference for the "unbearable ugliness of Volvos."[8]

In the 1970s, Darko Suvin proposed Wells's novella as a paradigm of subsequent science fiction on the basis of a structuralist analysis that ignored the machine per se and any frivolous appeal it might have. Suvin nevertheless acknowledged the time machine's novelty by remarking that Wells "invented a new thing under the sun in the story of time traveling without the help of dreams."[9] This is unequivocal. It is generous. And most of those reading it in the 1970s might well have thought it definitive. Now, however, the issue is in doubt. In his article "Time Travel: Future" for the 1994 *Encyclopedia of Time*, John Clute states that "It will be convenient to treat as functionally almost identical various literary devices that, during the nineteenth century, accomplished the goal achieved by time travel as a device. The notion of an actual time machine, as immortalized in H. G. Wells's *The Time Machine* (1895), came surprisingly late. [. . .] But all of these devices—however simply or elaborately they may be described in any one text—are formally very similar: they are all time machines."[10] If it is true that *all* literary devices for narrative displacement in time are so "formally similar" that they are best lumped together as "time machines," it follows that Wells's originality, the "new thing under the sun" that he introduced to literature, amounts to little more than a "convenient" term for referring to a class that includes dream visions, waking visions, mesmeric trances, suspended animation of other kinds, and even sharp blows to the head like that which sends Twain's Connecticut Yankee to the court of King Arthur. If this leveling is accepted, Wells's claim to novelty dwindles to that of someone who has done critics the favor of providing yet another handy technical term. For Wells this is what Edward Gibbon would surely have called a sufficient humiliation. But there is more at stake than Wells's posthumous dignity and reputation.

To appreciate the larger issues involved, it will be helpful to start by revisiting the time machine's initial manifestation over a century ago. Wells's vague description of the device itself, as critics have remarked, is a tour de force of suggestion.[11] On the basis of his text, no one could make an accurate drawing even of the machine's external shape, which is to say that every imaginative reader is invited to appropriate it psychologically by attempting to envision it by mentally connecting the dots, as it were. Here, as he so often does, Wells invites active rather than passive engagement. His method is concision rather than expansion. His masterpiece is mercifully free of that elephantiasis that afflicts so many of his successors these days.

That said, however, we should also recall that as part of an important pattern of doublings in the novella there are *two* initial descriptions of the machine: first of a model that the Traveller displays and demonstrates to his skeptical friends, and then of the full size vehicle. They are duplicates of one another, differing only in scale. The model is a working model: a real but tiny time machine that vanishes into the future or, as the Traveller admits, possibly into the past, but at any rate away from the moment of its demonstration. In Wells's story there are thus *two* time machines that (from our point of view) share the same fate of mysteriously vanishing, never to return. This doubling invites sustained attention to the machine.

The model that "the Time Traveller held in his hand was a glittering metallic framework, scarcely larger than a small clock, and very delicately made. There was ivory in it, and some transparent crystalline substance" (1, 8). This vague description tantalizingly combines the ordinary with the exotic, the known with the unknown: ivory and small clocks with a metallic framework of undisclosed dimensions and of an unknown material that is transparent but not necessarily glass or crystal. Perhaps the framework is in part actually crystal (one meaning of *crystalline*), but perhaps it is something else that is *like* crystal (another meaning of *crystalline*). Now you see it, now you don't. The Medical Man responds by pronouncing it "beautifully made" (1, 9).

Of its further particulars we have only the Time Traveller's baffling invitation to "notice that it looks singularly askew, and that there is an odd twinkling appearance about this bar, as though it was in some way unreal. [. . .] Also, here is one little white lever, and here is another" (1, 9). The machine's illusive appearance is on Wells's part, though not the Time Traveller's, a deliciously ironic reminder that we are reading a story that is, like all fiction, unreal. Small wonder then that the time machine has an air of unreality. This observation is part of a pattern of self-reflexivity culminating in the Time Traveller's later invitation to judge his tale "as a story" rather than as truth (12, 87). The two little white levers controlling forward and reverse motion in time are the most distinct and therefore the only easily recalled features of the model time machine.

But it is by recollecting the vaguely described small time machine that readers try—and inevitably fail—to envision exactly what the full-sized one looks like. The device on which the Time Traveller makes his journey is "a larger edition of the little mechanism. [. . .] Parts were of nickel, parts of ivory, parts had certainly been filed or sawn out of rock crystal." To the narrator, its "twisted crystalline bars [. . .] seemed to be quartz" (1, 11). Later the Time Traveller mentions (unhelpfully) that it has ivory bars, a brass rail, nickel bars, a quartz rod that for unspecified reasons needs oiling, and a saddle on which he sits while en route. There are four dials to record traversed time in "days [. . .] thousands of days [. . .] millions of days, and [. . .] thousands of millions" (11, 80). The detachable control levers, which fit over (not into) "studs," play an important role in the drama of his escape from the Morlocks, who have "carefully oiled and cleaned" and perhaps even partially disassembled then reassembled the time machine (10, 79). Why it should need or benefit from oiling remains unclear because no moving parts are described except for the dial hands and the two control levers that must be pushed one way or another.

Our final glimpses of the time machine are through the narrator's eyes, first as it appeared to him travel-worn after the voyage: "squat, ugly, and askew; a thing of brass, ebony, ivory, and translucent glimmering quartz. Solid to the touch—for I put out my hand and felt the rail of it—and with brown spots and smears upon the ivory, and bits of grass and moss upon the lower parts, and one rail bent awry" (12, 88). Ugliness is of course not an attribute of the machine but a projection of the narrator's unhappy mood after hearing the Time Traveller's disturbing tale of utopia lost and monsters that will inherit a dying planet. In calling the time machine "a thing," the narrator echoes the Time Traveller's reiterated description of that final low-slung monster on the terminal beach as a "moving thing [. . .] the size of a football perhaps, or, it may be, bigger [. . .] hopping fitfully about" (11, 85). The (now) "squat" and "ugly [. . .] thing" that the time machine (after *its* fitful hopping about) has become in the narrator's view may for readers, too, seem a sinister mechanical doppelgänger of the monstrosities that shall inherit the earth.

But of course readers do not have to share the narrator's gloomy mood, which is, after all, merely one of several possible responses to the story told by the Time Traveller. For more optimistic readers, the machine's "translucent glimmering quartz" may stand out most prominently in a way that retains its aesthetic appeal, and the Time Traveller's tale may seem more marvelous than depressing. The machine is described with sufficient ambiguity to serve as an instrument and emblem of chilling apocalyptic visions and also as an appealing marvel offering novel prospects of adventure and escape. As the narrator remarks in his epilogue, the time machine's final voyage may, for all he (and we) know, have carried its inventor back in time to some grisly doom "among the blood-drinking, hairy savages of the Age of Unpolished Stone" or forward to refuge in some truly utopian age "with the riddles of our own time answered and its wearisome problems solved" (E, 91). Wells's open-ended conclusion invites each reader to imagine a sequel according to his or her taste and temperament, and of course, in a sense, science fiction writers have been doing just that for over a century. Here I want only to stress that how the machine is described within the text and how it is accordingly envisioned by readers—as squat and ugly, or beautifully glimmering, or both—plays an important role in the tone, and therefore the hermeneutics, of Wells's novella.

The last description of the time machine comes just after the Time Traveller's final departure, when the narrator "*seemed* to see a ghostly, indistinct figure sitting in a whirling mass of black and brass for a moment [. . .] . The Time Machine had gone. Save for a subsiding stir of dust, the further end of the laboratory was empty. A pane of the skylight had, apparently, just been blown in" (12, 90; italics added). Here, too, Wells is brilliantly evocative by withholding precise details: rapid temporal motion is suggested by the settling dust and empty sky-light frame that remain following a dubious hallucinatory vision of the Time Traveller sitting amid a strange indeterminate swirl of "black and brass." No explanation is given for the apparent spinning motion of the time machine, a phenomenon never described by the Time Traveller. In his accounts of the eerie sensations experienced during voyages through time, he dwells mostly on subjective impressions of "helpless, headlong motion," "the feeling of prolonged falling," and even "a kind of hysterical exhilaration" (3, 19–20). Of his vehicle's actual behavior he only mentions "a clumsy swaying of the machine for which [he] was unable to account," reiterating "the sickly jarring and swaying of the machine" and the fact that "it swayed and vibrated" (3, 20; 11, 80). Whatever the impression of an outside observer, no spinning motion was apparent to the vehicle's occupant. As critics have remarked, those few features of the machine and its behavior en route that *do* stand out with some clarity allow for easy identification with the voyager's bizarre experience because his descriptions recall nothing so much as travelling upon a bicycle while perched in its seat (and perhaps while learning to ride) as it jolts and sways along an uneven path. A familiar thing is made strange and a very strange thing indeed is thus made familiar without losing anything of its strangeness. Wells has it both ways.

Take away the time machine thus presented, and there would be a very different story: arguably not anything so good, and certainly not the same. The time machine here is not functionally the equivalent of travel via magic, dream vision, mesmeric sleep, telepathy, hallucination, or being hit on the head. Mesmeric sleep and other forms of suspended animation are one-way trips to the future, which will not allow, among other things, the frame narrative that so much enriches, and in many crucial respects creates, the meanings of Wells's tale. A time traveller on a one-way trip could not report his experiences to colleagues living in the era of his departure, nor could such a story depict their responses. Two-way trips allowed by magic, dream visions, and similar devices, including inexplicable time slips like that experienced by Twain's Yankee, could accommodate a frame narrative with *The Time Machine*'s self-reflexivity and other features but would preclude the firm placement of the story as a fable about science. At issue is the creation of symbolism rather than, as is usually argued, the establishment of plausibility, verisimilitude, and suspension of disbelief.

Mary Shelley's *Frankenstein* is our archetypal fiction of science because unlike Faustus, Victor Frankenstein dabbles in chemistry and biology, not demonology. Via imaginary science, Shelley invites the reader to consider, among many other topics, our relationship to the destructive potentialities of real science. So too, by making a machine—an artifact of technology, of applied science—the method of time travel, Wells brings his entire fable, not just the parts dealing with geology, astronomy, Darwinian concepts of evolution, and cosmological speculation about the solar system's future, into the realm of scientific discourse.

By later writing far too modestly of his own achievement as merely "an ingenious use of scientific patter" that "might with advantage be substituted" for "the usual interview with the devil or a magician," Wells was unfair to his younger self and ironically guilty of sanctioning the misleading tradition of dismissively equating the time machine with other forms of time travel.[12] I am not the first to remark that his artistic instincts were better than his critical afterthoughts, interesting as the latter always are. It was Wells the supreme artist, not H. G. the critic and educator, who, while making other masterful revisions to "The Chronic Argonauts," replaced that clumsy title with *The Time Machine*—not, be it noted, *The Time Traveller*, or (worse yet) *The Time Trip*.

By naming his story after the machine—which proves he thought the machine necessary enough—Wells turns the readers' attention to the machine before they even arrive at the tale's first sentence. It is the machine as much as, or perhaps more than, the Traveller that must be regarded as protagonist. The story is as much about *it* as it is about *him*—as much about what it does and symbolizes as about what he stands for and accomplishes, although of course the two are closely related. The time machine is an emblem both of science and the scientist, and of their dubious role in modern life. Although not physically joined, machine and inventor are at a symbolic level as inextricably combined in this tale as any cyborg with its mechanical parts in later science fiction. As in tales of cyborgs or cyberspace jockeys, it is precisely the marriage for better or for worse of human and machine that the novella invites us to contemplate as one of its major themes and as one of humanity's most dire predicaments.

Without his machine, the Time Traveller is almost helpless, nearly stranded in a dangerous future. With it, he gets into trouble and is the bearer of bad tidings. Had he not invented the machine he would, so far as we are concerned, not even have a name, much less be of any interest, for we only know him as the Time Traveller. No machine means no travel and no story—at least not this story. The time machine ultimately carries the scientist to a doubtful destiny: perhaps good, perhaps bad. To others, to the Time Traveller's friends and to readers of the novella, it brings knowledge but hardly unalloyed happiness. To know the future revealed, thanks to the time machine (and its inventor), is not necessarily to be any wiser about how to live in the present. Within the story, the dystopian and apocalyptic futures visited via the machine appear to be fixed, unalterable. For those living in the Time Traveller's era *without* a time machine on which to escape (or at least to distract themselves by finding out more about the future and the past), the only response to a horrifying prospect of planetwide catastrophes that cannot be averted is the narrator's far-from-comforting existentialist suggestion that "If that [future] is so, it remains for us to live as though it were not so" (E, 91).

But for readers, the encounter with the Eloi and the Morlocks is a cautionary tale with a clear, compelling, and very different moral: we *can* and *should* act now to meliorate the condition of the underclass before they start preying upon *us*, and before humanity is irrevocably divided against itself in ways that spell the end of intellect. This moral has not lost any urgency over the years since Wells published his story, but today neither science, the time machine, nor the story itself is able to provide a solution to the problems it discloses. Of course we must act to eliminate social inequities, but *how*? Scientific knowledge, Wells reminds us, is not necessarily power. Thanks to the scientific (not magical or visionary) instrument that is its central device and unifying symbol, his story provides an elegant corollary to Mary Shelley's fable by showing that even if science doesn't *create* difficulties of the kind symbolized by Victor Frankenstein's monster, science may destroy happiness by *revealing* more problems than it or we can solve. Wells also unforgettably suggests, via the Eloi's plight, that discarding science is no solution. Ignorance is neither bliss nor strength.

Veronica Hollinger is right to suggest that despite the plot's apparent grounding in ideas of absolute, not relativistic, time, both the time machine and the novella named after it covertly undermine Newtonian concepts of time and Enlightenment faith in science.[13] Nevertheless, the tale also revives a large measure of that faith by the sheer allure of its glittering, glimmering, translucent, oddly twinkling, beautifully made instrument of scientific investigation and by its fascinating narrated *and potential* adventures which that instrument, the time machine itself, makes possible by opening imaginative vistas of scientifically controlled mobility through the most mysterious dimension. The adventures may be dangerous and depressing to those protagonists who undertake them, but to readers they offer safe excitement together with rare intellectual stimulation and the promise of using science to pierce the veil of the unknown. Without the time machine to serve not only as instrumentality of plot but as a focus of symbolism concerning the role of science, Wells's novella could not have been as powerful and coherent as it is. Nor would its meanings be the same. In this respect the time machine was indispensable. No other means of travelling through time could have done its work in that story.

It is harder to decide with equal certainty whether the time machine was necessary for twentieth-century literature, even science fiction. Wells himself, after all, got along very nicely after 1895 *without* any more time machines. So have many other science fiction writers, even those of time-travel tales. Here we enter the intriguing but doubtful realm of alternative history—in this case alternative literary history. If Wells had not invented the time machine, would someone else have done so? Who? Why? Why does it matter? Was his particular time machine necessary, or would *any* kind of time machine do as well?

The last question is the easiest to answer because the proliferation of variously configured time machines in literature after 1900—ranging from Asimov's kettles in *The End of Eternity* to the temporal hot rod in *Back to the Future*—shows that the bicycle-like shape and simplicity of Wells's machine was not necessary. What matters is that time machines are *machines*, that is, like other machines, they are assumed to operate on the basis of natural rather than supernatural laws even if, as in the case of computers, jet aircraft, and most other machines encountered in everyday life, the inner workings remain mysterious to most observers or even to most users. It is quite enough to know that the Boeing 747 does not stay aloft thanks to the whim of some inscrutable genie or for reasons known only to God. Arthur C. Clarke's too famous dictum that "Any sufficiently advanced technology would be indistinguishable from magic" only holds true for observers who themselves believe in magic. So too for time machines of the Wellsian variety: because they *are* machines, they imply principles—even if unexplained—that bring readers into the arena of the natural rather than the supernatural, of rational, scientific discourse (although other features of a story may take it outside that arena again). Given the development of twentieth-century science, especially in the areas of relativity theory and related mathematical concepts, and given too the pronounced tendency of twentieth-century literature to echo scientific developments in its forms and themes, time machines have, in retrospect, an air of inevitability.

If not Wells, then very likely someone else would have invented one. Clute says that the time machine was discovered "surprisingly late," but it could equally or better be regarded as surprisingly early, coming as it did a decade before Einstein published his special relativity theory in 1905, and of course even longer before that theory's implications and those of its sequel became widely diffused in general culture. Wells did not anticipate relativity, nor was his machine at all based upon a relativistic model of space-time relationships, as Paul Nahin explains in his remarkable book *Time Machines: Time Travel in Physics, Metaphysics, and Science Fiction*.[14] But understanding and (even more often) misunderstanding Einstein's theories stimulated modern and postmodern literary experimentation with temporal discontinuities of many kinds, including time travel.[15] In that Zeitgeist, surely some kind of time machine would have been invented sooner or later, even if Wells had never existed.

I will leave to my readers the pleasures of speculating on who might have invented the time machine in the absence of H. G. Wells. The high concentration of time machines in the pulp era from Hugo Gernsback through John W. Campbell Jr., science fiction's Golden Age, makes the 1920s and 1930s or, in a slightly more sluggish alternate universe, the early 1940s, the likeliest eras for the invention of the time machine in a world without Wells or his story.[16] Not coincidentally, the interval between the 1920s and Hiroshima is in science fiction the period of greatest technophilia, an attitude very much reflected by the proliferation of time machines.[17] From the New Wave starting in the 1960s through the present heyday of postmodernism, there has come not just a turning away from Enlightenment values underlying technophilia in its benign as well as rabid forms, but a variety of explicit and persistent assaults on science and on reason itself. Neo-Luddites are a sign of our times, a portent of sinister reversion to a new age of unreason whose inhabitants, however technophobic, have available for every irrational use the sophisticated machinery provided by advanced science.[18]

It is in this dismal context, and perhaps as another symptom of cultural regression to prescientific modes of thought, that much science fiction is reverting to the conventions of sheer fantasy and far beyond the Swiftian model of fantastic voyage that inspired Wells's more distinctively *scientific* romances. It is in this context too that we find a blurring of what had once seemed a clear and significant distinction between time machines and nonscientific ways of moving protagonists between eras. Literary critics, fortunately, have little influence one way or another on far-reaching cultural trends of which the critics themselves are sometimes minor manifestations. But insofar as critical terms may play some role in shaping attitudes toward science and reason, it matters very much whether time machines are conflated with magical or otherwise inexplicable modes of transportation—hallucinations, dream visions, and the like devices of fantasy. Such conflation furthers the dismissal of science and reason, even in their symbolic forms, from our lives. Time machines of the Wellsian model remain an important concept whose abolition by equation with nonscientific modes of temporal motion in literature advances, however innocently, unintentionally, and minutely, the agenda of those who would send science itself down the memory hole to which Big Brother consigns politically undesirable entities. In 1895 Wells's time machine was necessary for illustrating what is gained and lost by applying science to achieve knowledge of possible futures. Now the time machine remains necessary for those who would think rationally about science with the help of fables like the magnificent one to which we pay homage in this volume.

Notes

1. Mark Hillegas, for example, remarks that whereas in earlier time-travel stories "the visitor arrives in the future by means of such clumsy devices as dream, hypnosis, accident, or trance," Wells's time machine "is considerably more suitable, given the sophisticated requirements for plausibility of a new scientific and mechanical age" (Mark R. Hillegas, *The Future as Nightmare: H. G. Wells and the Anti-Utopians* [New York: Oxford University Press, 1967], p. 27).

2. Gary K. Wolfe, *The Known and the Unknown: The Iconography of Science Fiction* (Kent: Kent State University Press, 1979), pp. 18, 94–98.

3. Frank McConnell, *The Science Fiction of H. G. Wells* (Oxford: Oxford University Press, 1981), pp. 81, 88.

4. The wider significance of *The Time Machine*'s self-reflexivity is nicely explained by comparison with Lem's work in Robert M. Philmus, *"Futurological Congress* as Metageneric Text," *Science-Fiction Studies* 40 (November 1986), 313–28.

5. Robert Scholes and Eric S. Rabkin, *Science Fiction: History, Science, Vision* (Oxford: Oxford University Press, 1977), p. 19.

6. Bud Foote, *The Connecticut Yankee in the Twentieth Century: Travel to the Past in Science Fiction* (New York: Greenwood Press, 1991).

7. Mark Rose, *Alien Encounters: Anatomy of Science Fiction* (Cambridge, Mass.: Harvard University Press, 1981), p. 101.

8. Stanley Fish, "The Unbearable Ugliness of Volvos," *There's No Such Thing As Free Speech And It's A Good Thing, Too* (New York and Oxford: Oxford University Press, 1994), pp. 273–79.

9. Darko Suvin, introduction to *H. G. Wells and Modern Science Fiction*, ed. Darko Suvin and Robert M. Philmus (Lewisburg: Bucknell University Press; London: Associated University Presses, 1977), p. 28. See also in this volume Suvin's "A Grammar of Form and a Criticism of Fact: *The Time Machine* as a Structural Model for Science Fiction" (pp. 90–115); and the chapters on Wells in Darko Suvin, *Metamorphoses of Science Fiction: On the Poetics and History of a Literary Genre* (New Haven and London: Yale University Press, 1979).

10. John Clute, "Time Travel: Future," in *Encyclopedia of Time*, ed. Samuel L. Macey (New York and London: Garland Publishing, Inc., 1994).

11. Bernard Bergonzi applauds the description while explaining it mainly as a clever way for Wells to avoid the trouble of being more specific: "The account of it is a brilliant example of Wells's impressionistic method. [...] The assemblage of details is strictly speaking meaningless but nevertheless conveys very effectively a sense of the machine without

putting the author to the taxing necessity of giving a direct description" (Bernard Bergonzi, "*The Time Machine*: An Ironic Myth," in *H. G. Wells: A Collection of Critical Essays*, ed. Bernard Bergonzi [Englewood Cliffs: Prentice-Hall, 1976], p. 42). Frank McConnell praises Wells's "brilliant and brilliantly vague paragraph" describing the model time machine, finding in the method of that paragraph a paradigm for science fiction aiming at "just enough convincing hardware" to facilitate speculation about "the human implications of possible technological advances" rather than about technology per se (McConnell, p. 82).

12. H. G. Wells, "Preface to the Scientific Romances," in *H. G. Wells's Literary Criticism*, ed. Patrick Parrinder and Robert M. Philmus (Sussex: Harvester Press; New Jersey: Barnes & Noble, 1980), pp. 241–42.

13. Veronica Hollinger, "Deconstructing the Time Machine," *Science-Fiction Studies* 42 (July 1987), 201–21.

14. Paul J. Nahin, *Time Machines: Time Travel in Physics, Metaphysics, and Science Fiction* (New York: American Institute of Physics, 1993).

15. For some examples, see George Slusser and Danièle Chatelain, "Spacetime Geometries: Time Travel and the Modern Geometrical Narrative," *Science-Fiction Studies* 66 (July 1995), 161–86.

16. On the proliferation of time machines during and after the Golden Age of pulps, see Paul A. Carter, *The Creation of Tomorrow: Fifty Years of Magazine Science Fiction* (New York: Columbia University Press, 1977), pp. 89–113.

17. On the history and implications of technophilia in science fiction during its Golden Age, see Andrew Ross, "Getting Out of the Gernsback Continuum," *Critical Inquiry* 17: 2 (Winter 1991), 411–33.

18. See, for some examples of current anti-Enlightenment attitudes, Paul R. Gross and Norman Levitt, *Higher Superstition: The Academic Left and Its Quarrels with Science* (Baltimore and London: The Johns Hopkins University Press, 1994).

The Rebirth of a Scientific Intelligence

Or, From "Traveller" to "Travailer"
in *The Time Machine*

FRANK SCAFELLA

 Wells tells us that during his student years in South Kensington (1884–87), "A vision was being established, in the grey matter of my brain, of the world in which I was to live for all the remainder of my years."[1] At the core of this vision was the idea of man's "mental emancipation" from Reason, an idea embodied in the whole of Wells's work, fiction and nonfiction, as "the upward struggle of the human intelligence" out of

> that blind confidence in Providence, that implicit confidence in the good intentions of the natural order of things, no matter what were our mistakes and misdeeds, characterizing the human mind in the nineteenth century, to that startled realization of the need for men to combine against the cold indifference, the pitiless justice, if you will, of nature, which is our modern attitude.[2]

Experiment in Autobiography Wells called not the story of his life but "the history and adventures of a brain."[3] Thus the H. G. Wells of the autobiography, like Trafford in *Marriage* (1912), "is not so much a solid man as a scientific intelligence."[4]

The same not only can, but must, be said of the protagonist of *The Time Machine*: the Time Traveller is not so much a solid man as a "scientific intelligence" in quest of mental emancipation from Reason. In this light, Bernard Bergonzi's proposal that Wells's early romances are "symbolic—even if not specifically allegorical"[5] appears far too tentative on this aspect of Wells's works, *The Time Machine* in particular. In *The Time Machine*, it may well be, we have to deal not with an occasional romance that inclines toward the allegorical, but with a full-blown allegory of the making of a scientific intelligence—perhaps the first full realization in dramatic form of that vision which was being established in the gray matter of Wells's brain during his student years in South Kensington.

In the intellect's struggle for emancipation from Reason, a man's "reasoning powers are about as much a truth-seeking tool as the snout of a pig," Wells asserts in "The Rediscovery of the Unique."[6] Four years later, this same critical insight into the "history and adventures" of the human brain achieves expression as a judgment on his own existential predicament by the Time Traveller himself, in these words:

> "Patience," said I to myself. "If you want your machine again you must leave that sphinx alone. If they mean to take your machine away, it's little good your wrecking their bronze panels, and if they don't, you will get it back as soon as you can ask for it. To sit among all those unknown things before a puzzle like that is hopeless. That way lies monomania. Face this world. Learn its ways, watch it, be careful of too hasty guesses at its meaning. In the end you will find clues to it all. (5, 39)

In these words a scientific intelligence is reborn.

What is the nature of this new intelligence? How does it differ from the mindset that characterizes the Time Traveller at the beginning of his story? For one thing, this new scientific intelligence can assume nothing of the "real" world to which it awakes. It can propose nothing but patience. It stands face to face, existentially, with the "cold indifference" and "the pitiless justice" of a nature that would, quite literally, devour the "Traveller" body and soul. Second, this new scientific intelligence operates without fear and beyond dread. It has nothing to fear but its own impatience. For nature that, at an earlier time, was thought to be alive and active in the life of man, now presents itself as inanimate and brutally indifferent. We see this indifference in the presence of the Sphinx. Whereas for Oedipus (to whom the Time Traveller bears many resemblances) the Sphinx posed riddles of nature and man that Oedipus could unravel only by exercise of Reason, for the Time Traveller she has become a mute monument and mausoleum, an implement for imprisonment of the active force of "brain" in the world, as the Time Traveller will learn in time.

Third and most important, however, is the transformation in mental attitude within the Time Traveller, which takes place in the above quoted dialogue with himself even as he conducts it. He enters time as a "traveller"; he finds himself in time a "travailer." He sets out for the future on his time machine as a voyager, merely a journeyer, in time conceived as spatial; but here in the midst of that journey, he finds himself a travailer, one whose very own intellectual labor, toil, and suffering will in fact *make* "time" a condition and circumstance of his active brain. With that "work" in time, the bulk of *The Time Machine* concerns itself. There is no going back to time "travel" for the "Travailer" unless and until the work he performs intellectually in this new "real" world permits him to realize Wells's own lifelong desire "to get to close quarters with Madame Fact even if it meant a scuffle with her," thus to "get hold of Fact, strip off her inessentials and, if she behaves badly put her in stays and irons."[7]

This is a very different attitude toward the world than the one with which the Time Traveller launches himself into the future. He sets out on his travels as an experimental investigator. He carries in his mind a fully formed idea for which he seeks verification.

> "Then there is the future," said the Very Young Man. "Just think! One might invest
> all one's money, leave it to accumulate at interest, and hurry on ahead!"
> "To discover a society," said I, "erected on a strictly communistic basis." [. . .]
> "Yes, so it seemed to me, and so I never talked of it until—"
> "Experimental verification!" cried I. "You are going to verify *that*?" (1, 7–8)

Yes, he is. And experimental verification remains his primary intention. But as we learn subsequently, and as the Time Traveller himself finds out the hard way, there are at least three things wrong with his reading of his "future world" as at once the fulfillment of the communistic idea and an instance of the subjugation of nature by a growing scientific knowledge of the world and man.

First, his theory, exclusively contemplative and rationalistic in nature, does not account for the dominating presence of the White Sphinx. The Time Traveller ignores the Sphinx, as have most critical readings of *The Time Machine*. Yet there is the White Sphinx alone to greet the Time Traveller on his arrival in 802,701. It is also ironic that he is seated on the bench of griffin's heads (a mythical monster closely associated with the sphinx) when he spins out the initial theory of this world of his future.[8]

Second, the Time Traveller's initial interpretation of the world of 802,701 is factually wrong. Sheer rational contemplation has no need for confirmation of reality. It is only later, under the sobering prospect of losing himself forever to the timespace of 802,701, that the Time Traveller experiences, with "startled realization," Wells's own lifelong desire "to get to close quarters with Madame Fact."

Third, the Time Traveller's interpretation founders because it is a perfect reenactment of the old Aristotelian, rather than of the new, intellectual science. "Communism" (4, 29) is the immediate inference to which the Time Traveller leaps rationally. He does not earn this idea through inquiry into the state of things as he finds them. But, one might object, he has not had time for inquiry into things as they actually are in 802,701. Indeed! Yet it is not that he has not had time for research; it is that he experiences no need for it until the theft of his time machine renders him Travailer rather than Traveller. Inquiry into the state of things as they really are always appears superfluous to the supreme rationalist. He assumes that the real is ultimately to be tested by rational and deductive, rather than sensory, methods: he regards "reason" as a separate source of knowledge, in no way dependent upon experience. Hence the Time Traveller, in his initial theory, reasons inferentially from a category of mind rather than experientially from evidence gathered by firsthand investigation into things as they actually are. Given the idea of "communism," the Time Traveller rests confidently in knowing the most important thing there is to know about this new Time into which his machine has ushered him. Working deductively from the communistic idea, everything fits.

It is not surprising that Wells began his story with a Time "Traveller" rather than a "Travailer." As H. Bruce Franklin has recently pointed out in an essay on time travel in the work of Mark Twain, "Time travel is a peculiarly modern form of exploration" with which H. G. Wells and the major thinkers of his time would have been intimately familiar. The possibility of "travel" in time became plausible, Franklin points out, only

> when science and technology began to induce changes in material existence so rapid that people could perceive them in a single lifetime . . . [and] the fundamental conditions in other "times" began to seem qualitatively different from those of the present. These ever swifter changes effected by science and technology led inevitably to the remembrance of time past and the anticipation of future time when life was and would be different from the present—in ways determined by science and technology. . . . Science conceptualized cosmic time, within which it located geological time, within which it designed a history of the human species.[9]

This "scientific design" of human history had become clear to the leading thinkers of Europe and the United States by the second half of the nineteenth century, and it is this confidence in history as progressive that emboldens the Time Traveller to launch himself into the future as an experimental investigator. He buys into this "scientific design" of history, as Wells himself bought into the scientific mind-set of man in the modern world, not to present it experientially as a formulation of an inquiring intelligence, but to confirm it experimentally by use of a technology that promised access to truth. Yet something wholly unexpected happened to Wells and to his Traveller on their way to experimental verification: namely, Wells's story itself became for him (and for his Time Traveller) a laboratory in which he actually discovered and confirmed the full and spontaneous emergence of a truly intellectual science in the mind and actions of the

Time Traveller. This turn in the Traveller's journey takes by surprise both Wells and his hero in the very writing of *The Time Machine*.

"I still remember writing that part of the story in which the Time Traveller returns to find his machine removed and his retreat cut off," Wells recalled in 1934.

> I sat alone at the round table downstairs writing steadily in the luminous circle cast by a shaded paraffin lamp. . . . It was a very warm blue August night and the window was wide open. The best part of my mind fled through the story in a state of concentration before the Morlocks . . . My innate impulse, when I am at the writing desk [is] to let statement and story rip, to put me quite openly where I was.[10]

This final sentence contains an interesting locution for the writer: "to put *me* quite openly where *I* was." Clearly, "me" is H. G. Wells himself, who sits at his desk writing in nineteenth-century London; the "I" is Wells as Time Traveller in the world of 802,701. For Wells the writer, the story comes to serve the same function as the time machine for the Traveller: writing puts the nineteenth-century writer mentally and intellectually quite openly at the foot of that hill in 802,701 where "I," in sheer panic from the loss of his machine, flails about madly in early recognition of the gravity of his loss. There, at the foot of that hill and facing his loss in a panic, "I" and "me" become existentially one. When this happens, there is nothing "I" can do for "me" but to follow "me" back to "my" own time. For it is in this moment of panic that the Traveller—possessed of fear, in dread and anguish of mind, overcome by fatigue and despair, cursing aloud, sobbing and bawling like a child, blundering about, faint and blind with anger, screaming, calling helplessly on God—becomes the Travailer, the "me" who has been put by the story itself quite openly where "I" was in 802,701. This "me" has lost his own time mentally as fully as "I" has lost his technologically. The two become one in travail. It is now only by intelligent work of the brain that either or both will make his way back to his own time. It is significant that both *travel* and *travail* carry the same sense of torment, distress, affliction, labor, toil, and suffering. But sense development has not followed the same course in English as in French. English has not developed the simple sense "work" for which the Old English word *travail* lives on. On the other hand, French has not evolved the sense "journey" that appeared early in Anglo-French and has become the main sense in English (and is differentiated by the spelling "travel") while the more original senses, so far as they continue in use, retain the earlier spelling "travail."

Here is the point: if, as Time "Traveller," Wells in his hero had thought to take an exploratory excursion into the future in the interest of verifying experimentally the fate of communism as the dominant social idea of his time; and if he thought to confirm the future of communism experimentally by use of the great faith he and others of his time invested in the revelatory promise of modern technology, then suddenly and quite unexpectedly, in the midst of this experimental "voyage," Wells, in his hero, finds himself on a major adventure into the unfathomable in quest of the unknown. His midcourse transformation of mind and heart signals a change that renders his hero fellow "Travailer" with Bunyan's Pilgrim and with all those knights of medieval romance who precede him. Perhaps the last thing Wells anticipated was to find his hero and himself on an intellectually perilous journey. Yet perilous the Traveller's journey becomes with the swiftness of the dread that seizes him when the Morlocks steal his machine. In "time" he gets it back, as we know, but the thing we have not yet articulated is the peculiar kind of "work" Wells's hero performs as "Travailer" in time, how that "work" differs intellectually from the mental operations that prevail early in the Time Traveller, and how the workings of "intellectual versatility" in the Time Traveller replicate the modern intellect's great and perilous struggle for emancipation from Reason.

To the Time Traveller initially, as we have seen, the time machine serves principally as a means to an end. By means of the machine he proposes to determine that things are thus and so in a future that he conceives of as a spatiotemporal continuum. Not just anyone can make a time machine, however. It takes the driving force of intellectual versatility to conceive and accomplish this feat.

The making of a time machine is not simply a matter of gathering together the necessary materials. The machine can be conceived and constructed only by a man within whom there resides an all-consuming desire for exploring the future in person. This desire must be coupled with a strong wish to become something other than what one at present is. These twin compulsions from within the Time Traveller are not primarily of the character of curiosity; they come from so deep within him as to render the future more real to him than the present. He is a man out of his time long before he climbs into the saddle of his machine, and the wishful longing that renders him anachronic also makes him "responsible" (in Martin Heidegger's sense of this word) for the technological means by which he acts to start himself on his way to his own time.[11]

This is to say that the creation of the time machine is by no means a simple matter of applying technical expertise to the construction of a technological instrument. Rather, the machine materializes from hope that resides deep within the Time Traveller. In his creation of the machine, he reveals hope for the future. The materialization of the machine forms the Time Traveller's deepest wish and promises to carry that wish forward into realization. And what is that wish? "I knew I was an Anachronic Man," says Dr Nebogipfel, ancestor and progenitor of the Time Traveller; "my age was still to come."[12]

How does the Anachronic Man know this about himself and his true age? Not by Reason. Not by looking about him and seeing what is factually the case. But by a sudden and total recognition of his truest and deepest self in the mirror of a fairy tale. "The Ugly Duckling" awakens in the Anachronic Man something he had known from beyond knowledge, prior to thinking:

> The ugly duckling that proved to be a swan, that lived through all contempt and bitterness, to float at last sublime. From that hour forth, I *dreamt* of meeting with my kind, dreamt of encountering that *sympathy* I knew was my profoundest need.[13]

Given this fairy-tale grounding of his wish, the Anachronic Man (or Time Traveller) feels himself committed from beyond Reason to thirty years of toil to produce his machine, not a production of technical expertise and mere factual knowledge alone, but of hope:

> One filmy hope alone held me to life, a hope to which I clung until it had become a certain thing. Thirty years of unremitting toil and deepest thought among hidden things of matter and form and life, and then *that*, the Chronic Argo, *the ship that sails through time*, and now I go to join my generation, to journey through the ages till my time has come.[14]

Of particular interest in this description of how the Chronic Argo, or Time Machine, came to be is its salient congruence with the insights of Martin Heidegger into the essence of modern technology. As Heidegger might say of Wells's time machine, its origin is not in technical expertise but in the dream, hope and expectation from deep within the Time Traveller himself, who "gathers together in advance the aspect and the matter" of the technological instrument. This gathering together of hope and expectations in advance of the making of the actual machine occurs

> with a view to the finished thing envisioned as completed, and from this gathering determines the manner of its construction. Thus what is decisive in *techne* does not lie at all in making and manipulating nor in the using of means, but rather in the aforementioned revealing [of hope and dream]. It is as revealing, and not as manufacturing, that *techne* is a bringing-forth.[15]

In this view, the time machine functions less as an instrument of means and ends than as a realization—an "unconcealment" and "presencing"—of the dream that makes a future, and hence a material realization of personal history as vision from the realm of hope in a human soul. The time machine embodies the nature of dream and hope rather than of technical know-how. Its use leads to apprehension of *aletheia*, of truth. We should experience no surprise, therefore, when the time machine, employed as a means of travel on a space-time continuum, works only to throw the Time Traveller back upon himself, rendering him "travailer" in addition to "traveller."

The loss of the Time Traveller's machine to the Morlocks results in a sudden presencing of hope and profound desire for his own time. He points to nothing other than this when he tells his tale to the company gathered in his home on his return and speaks of what happened in 802,701 as having occurred "during my time in this *real* future":

> In some of these visions of Utopias and coming times which I have read, there is a vast amount of detail about building, and social arrangements, and so forth. But while such details are easy enough to obtain when the whole world is contained in one's imagination, they are altogether inaccessible to a *real* traveller amid such *realities* as I found here. (5, 41; emphasis mine)

A "real" future as distinct from an "imaginative" one? What makes it "real"? And what are the "realities" among which he finds himself in "my time"? One thing is certain: of those "realities" that constitute "my time," the Time Traveller must form his own theory if he is to regain possession of his machine and recover his lost world.

What can the Time Traveller mean by "real" and "realities" in the context of his narrative? Is not *The Time Machine* itself a full-blown Utopia in which the words "real" and "realities" function as they would for Sir Thomas More? It would seem so to the outsider. But *The Time Machine* can be regarded as a Utopia only if we conceive of the machine itself as an essentially technical means to an imaginary end. There is nothing imaginary, however, in what happens to the Time Traveller once he loses his machine. For that which becomes "real" to the Time Traveller is "intellectual versatility" driven by hope of regaining his own world which he now recognizes as that "time"—the time in which he must live *by exercise of* intellectual versatility itself. When he feels himself thrown back on intelligence and constrained by circumstance to exercise versatility of mind as his primary mode of disclosing truth, the Traveller becomes Travailer. He has his work cut out for him.

By the "real" future the Time Traveller now means that world in which things become present by the exercise of intelligence and by that alone. Intelligence exercised in the interest of discovery breaks the tether of the Time Traveller's mind to Reason. Where he experiences a disclosure of the "real," he also apprehends the necessity for the exercise of intellectual versatility to appropriate the "real" to man's use. Just here science comes directly into play, for "Science is a theory of the real," says Heidegger.[16] Here in a nutshell is the Time Traveller's theory of the real:

> It is a law of nature we overlook, that intellectual versatility is the compensation for change, danger, and trouble. An animal perfectly in harmony with its environment is a perfect mechanism. Nature never appeals to intelligence until habit and instinct are useless. There is no intelligence where there is no change and no need of change. Only those animals partake of intelligence that have to meet a huge variety of needs and dangers. (10, 78)

No longer do the Time Traveller's words reflect the supreme confidence of the rationalist; here, instead, we witness an action of intellectual versatility as mental acuity and poise that knows that it does not know, yet knows that it can do nothing but seek knowledge or die. Of his theory of "intellectual versatility" he observes, immediately after articulating it, that "It may be as wrong an explanation as mortal wit could invent. It is *how the thing shaped itself* to me, and as that I give it to you" (10, 79; emphasis mine).

"It is how the thing shaped itself to me:" what or whom is doing the thinking here? Not the Time Traveller himself by exercise of Reason but "the thing" that is real even as it shapes itself "to" the brain. That which is "real" presents itself to the Time Traveller of itself. It is what can be grasped and held by intelligence alone. For the Time Traveller's uncertainty about his theory is not about the thing that shapes itself to him; uncertainty is not a manifestation of Cartesian doubt. It is rather a factor of intellectual versatility itself which knows that it does not and cannot know fully or absolutely. Intelligence forms a theory of the real by letting the thing shape itself to mind. It figures itself to Wells's Time Traveller as a "reverent paying heed to the unconcealment of what presences," as Heidegger would express it, as that "beholding that watches over truth."[17] Intellectual versatility, forming itself as theory, is not a looking-at that sunders and compartmentalizes things; it is that in the Time Traveller that *observes*, that *considers*, that presences. This is the peculiar job of work that the loss of his machine makes necessary for Wells's hero and renders him "Travailer." Knowing that intellect is thus and so is itself a work of intelligence in the Time Traveller. And by this power, he turns to face the White Sphinx one final time in an act of self-sacrifice that stands as the nineteenth century's supreme example of intellectual versatility at work in a human brain.

Wells speaks often of "intelligence" in *The Conquest of Time* (1942). It now appears that *The Time Machine* was no small step in the direction of "intelligence" as he understands and articulates it in this later book. The conquest of time, Wells proposes in 1942, is accomplished by "the dawning human intelligence," which emerges in the brain (as he had discovered in the "travails" of the Time Traveller) from a man's "assembled mental complex in a human body" that was, for a time in man's history (as in the person of the Time Traveller), stampeded by ego, personality, and Reason.[18] In what becomes the "ever-expanding Now"[19] of 802,701 Wells finds himself, in the Time Traveller, quite decisively beyond the tyranny of ego and personality, acting intelligently in his own "person" because he is constrained to act spontaneously, not in full freedom from past and future, but in full freedom of a newborn intellectual versatility.

By means of his "intelligence"—as he experiences it fully at work in the travails of the Time Traveller—Wells comes to understand, as does the American philosopher John Dewey, the active capacity of mind born of those "great and ever-growing methods of observation, experiment and reflective reasoning which have in a very short time revolutionized the physical and, to a considerable degree, the physiological conditions of life."[20] As Wells discovers in the "travails" of his Traveller, intelligence inheres in

> a method of inquiry so inclusive in range and so penetrating, so pervasive and so universal, as to provide the pattern and model which permits, invites and even demands the kind of formulation that falls within the function of philosophy. It is a method of knowing that is self-corrective in operation; that learns from failures as from successes. The heart of the method is the discovery of the identity of inquiry with discovery.[21]

The "identity of inquiry with discovery" characterizes perfectly the new scientific intelligence born in Wells's Time Traveller. The Chronic Argo and the Time Machine, conceived by Nebogipfel and the Time Traveller alike as a means of conveyance from present to future and used as such, become in midcourse a way of revealing the new scientific spirit of intellectual versatility. Wells discovered this truth in the very writing of his stories, a truth that Martin Heidegger puts as follows: "Technology is a way of revealing," a way of "bringing-forth," of "poiesis."[22] Man appears to exercise control in the making of the means but he has no control over that which the means brings forth: "man does not have control over unconcealment itself, in which at any given time the real shows itself or withdraws [. . .] itself in the light of ideas."[23] The Traveller can only respond to whatever addresses itself to him, and in that response he becomes a travailer, a worker in the field of inquiry, on a quest into the unfathomable in search of the unknown.

Notes

1. H. G. Wells, *Experiment in Autobiography: Discoveries and Conclusions of a Very Ordinary Brain (since 1866)* 2 vols. (1934; London: Gollancz and Cresset Press, 1966), 1: 266.

2. Ibid., 1: 332.

3. Ibid., 1: 337.

4. Ibid., 2: 497.

5. Bernard Bergonzi, *The Early H. G. Wells* (Manchester: Manchester University Press, 1961), p. 18.

6. H. G. Wells, "The Rediscovery of the Unique," *The Fortnightly Review,* 1891. Reprinted in H. G. Wells, *Early Writings in Science and Science Fiction,* ed. Robert M. Philmus and David Y. Hughes (Berkeley: University of California Press, 1975), p. 25.

7. *Experiment in Autobiography,* 453.

8. Frank Scafella, "The White Sphinx and *The Time Machine,*" *Science-Fiction Studies* 25 (1981), 255–64.

9. H. Bruce Franklin, "Travelling in Time with Mark Twain," in *American Literature and Science,* ed. Robert J. Scholnick (Lexington: University Press of Kentucky, 1992), 157, 158.

10. *Experiment in Autobiography,* 2: 518, 482.

11. See Martin Heidegger, "The Question Concerning Technology" and "Science and Reflection" in *The Question Concerning Technology and Other Essays,* trans. with an introduction by William Lovitt (New York: Harper and Row, 1977).

12. H. G. Wells, "The Chronic Argonauts," *Science Schools Journal,* reprinted in Bergonzi, *The Early H. G. Wells,* pp. 187–214; quote is from p. 209.

13. "The Chronic Argonauts," p. 208; emphasis mine.

14. "The Chronic Argonauts," p. 209.

15. Heidegger, "The Question Concerning Technology," 13.

16. Heidegger, "Science and Reflection," 171.

17. Ibid., 164, 165.

18. H. G. Wells, *The Conquest of Time* (London: Watts, 1942), p. 43.

19. Ibid., p. 2.

20. John Dewey, *Reconstruction in Philosophy* (Boston: Beacon Press, 1957), viii–ix.

21. Ibid., xxix–xxx.

22. Heidegger, "The Question Concerning Technology," 10, 11.

23. Ibid., 18.

Time Before and After
The Time Machine

W. M. S. RUSSELL

In about A.D. 100, Plutarch wrote his dialogue *On the Face that Appears in the Disc of the Moon*, which I have called "the most important of all precursors of science fiction."[1] It so impressed Johannes Kepler that he learned Greek well enough to translate it into Latin, and it stimulated his own *Somnium* (*Dream*) of 1609, widely considered the first modern science fiction story.[2] But in spite of these pioneers and the dozens of authors and works between Kepler and H. G. Wells, *The Time Machine* of 1895 is rightly given a very special place in the history of science fiction, so that Edward James has even called it "the great Founding Text of our field."[3] But *The Time Machine* was not only a benchmark in the history of literature. Through its treatment of time as a fourth dimension, the novel opened up an exciting new chapter in the history of ideas. In order to understand Wells's achievement, we must begin with a brief history of the concept of the fourth dimension.

When he introduced special relativity in 1905, and for three years after, Einstein wrote in terms of the conventional three spatial dimensions and time. But by showing that different observers have different timelines and by using time as a fourth coordinate to "locate" events, he discarded the absolute time and space of Newton. In the words of his colleague Peter Bergmann, "the special theory of relativity replaces 'absolute length' and 'absolute time' [...] by a new 'absolute,' often called the invariant space-time interval."[4] In 1908, the year before his death, Einstein's old teacher, Hermann Minkowski, took the logical next step: he reformulated the theory in terms of a space-time continuum, with time as the fourth dimension.[5] Einstein remarked, surely with his tongue in his cheek, "Since the mathematicians have invaded the theory of relativity, I do not understand it myself any more." But he soon adopted Minkowski's formulation and used it in all his later work, including general relativity, for which it was essential.[6] Ever since then, time has been regarded as the fourth dimension, and a higher spatial dimension as the fifth.[7]

But in earlier times, the term "fourth dimension" was very confusingly used for *both* time and a higher spatial dimension. The concept of a fourth spatial dimension was suggested by August Möbius in 1827 and worked out in detail by Georg Riemann in 1854. In 1877, a number of distinguished scientists were taken in by the medium Henry Slade, who claimed to send objects into the fourth spatial dimension so that he could make a knot in a closed loop or transform a right-handed into a left-handed shell.[8] In 1884, Charles Howard Hinton published his influential work, *What Is the Fourth Dimension?*, and Edwin Abbott his very successful satire, *Flatland*, about a two-dimensional world visited by a being from the mysterious third dimension.[9] The concept of an infinite number of parallel universes, so useful for science fiction, goes back to Leucippus and Democritus in the fifth century B.C., but the fourth spatial dimension provided a new rationale for this idea.[10] H. G. Wells was perfectly aware of all this. As he wrote in 1942, discussing the fourth spatial dimension, "I exploited this idea of endless Newtonian worlds side by side in a story called 'The Plattner Story' (1896) and also in a book, *Men Like Gods*, where a carful of people skidded [. . .] into an adjacent world lying like another page in a book, side by side with ours."[11]

But of course Wells's great achievement was to discuss time as the fourth dimension. This concept was much less well known in the later nineteenth century, though it does have a long history. Aristotle related time closely to motion, and therefore to space.[12] J. B. Priestley quotes Aristotle's remark that "if there were more heavens than one, the movement of any of them equally would be time, so that there would be many times at the same time"; "and for a moment," adds Priestley, "we feel as if Einstein may be just around the corner."[13] At about the same time, two rather scientific schools of Chinese philosophy conceived of space and time as virtually equivalent. Summing up their views, Joseph Needham suggests they "envisaged something like [. . .] a universal space-time continuum within which an infinite number of local reference frames coexist." Said Hui Shih, "Going to the State of Yüeh today, one arrives there yesterday."[14]

The first person to express time as the fourth dimension was an unknown Frenchman. In 1754, in his article on "Dimension" in the *Encyclopédie*, Jean D'Alembert wrote as follows: "An intelligent man of my acquaintance believes one could regard duration as a fourth dimension, and that the product of time by solidity would be in some way a product of four dimensions. This idea can be contested, but it has, I think, some merit, if only that of novelty" (my translation).[15] In 1846, the idea was taken up again by Gustav Fechner. According to

J. W. Dunne, even Hinton, at least once, referred his fourth dimension to time.[16] But by the 1880s, the idea was completely overshadowed by that of a fourth spatial dimension. On 14 January 1887, a student called E. A. Hamilton-Gordon read a paper on the fourth dimension at the Debating Society of the Normal School of Science. It was published later that year in the *Science Schools Journal*. Bernard Bergonzi plausibly suggests this was the debate that first interested Wells in the subject. As examples of things the fourth dimension could *not* possibly be, Hamilton-Gordon listed "Life," "Heaven," "Velocity"—and "Time."[17] Nevertheless, Wells wrote casually in 1942 of these early student discussions, "one or two of us concluded definitely that this fourth dimension of the mathematicians was duration."[18] Well, one of them did anyway, and that same year he wrote "The Chronic Argonauts." One interesting fact throws a brilliant light on Wells's originality and vision. In 1909, the year after Minkowski's classical work on space-time, the *Scientific American* offered a prize for an essay on the fourth dimension.[19] Not one of the entries addressed the fourth dimension as time or duration.

There were something like eight versions of *The Time Machine*, including the famous "Universe Rigid," a nonfictional article vandalized by Frank Harris.[20] But all seem to have contained the essence of Wells's idea. It is summed up in a sentence used in several of them, including the final Heinemann book version of *The Time Machine*: "*There is no difference between Time and any of the three dimensions of Space except that our consciousness moves along it*" (1, 4). With this sentence, as I put it earlier, Wells opened up an exciting new chapter in the history of ideas.

In Paris, Alfred Vallette's journal, the *Mercure*, gave an immediate warm welcome to *The Time Machine*.[21] The book was noticed in 1896, and in 1898–99 the *Mercure* published Henry Davray's translation. There followed no less than three commentaries in the *Mercure*. The first, in February 1899, was by Rachilde (Marguerite Vallette), but she left all discussion of time travel to others concentrating on the sociological predictions. In May, Paul Valéry gave a vague philosophical disquisition on symbols as time machines. But the really interesting contribution, also in February, was by Alfred Jarry: "Commentaire pour servir à la Construction Pratique de la Machine à explorer le Temps" ["Commentary to Serve for the Practical Construction of the Time Machine"], characteristically attributed, not to Jarry himself, but to Dr. Faustroll of the College of Pataphysics.

Alfred Jarry, though the author of many respectable works, is unique in literary history in owing all his renown to a plagiarism. His name was made by the Ubu plays, which were actually written by Charles and Henri Morin, two schoolfellows of Jarry's at Rennes in the 1880s, about a deservedly unpopular teacher.[22] The trouble with plagiarism is that like the boy who cried "Wolf," one is never quite trusted again. However, it does seem, even from the evidence of the Morins, that Jarry himself invented the spoof science of Pataphysics, which is sufficiently like the real thing to be interesting. In his *Commentary*, Jarry sets out, half seriously, one feels, to describe an actual time machine. He defines time as succession and space as simultaneity. He observes that we move in the direction of time and with the same speed. If, he continues, "we could stay motionless in absolute space, along the course of time, that is, suddenly shut ourselves into a machine which isolates us from time, [. . .] all future and past instants would be explored successively." A machine isolating us in this way from duration would make us transparent to physical phenomena, through which we could move unaffected by them. The machine would have to be absolutely elastic, nonmagnetic, subject to gravity but sufficiently independent of Earth's motions to conserve an invariable direction in absolute space. All these contributions are satisfied by the *luminiferous ether*. Jarry then refers to the gyrostatic composition of the ether worked out (to meet all these requirements) by W. Thomson [Lord Kelvin] in 1890 and duly constructs his machine (with a very impressive nonsense diagram) out of rods and wheels making up three rotating gyrostats.[23]

The ether, which plays so important a part in Jarry's scheme, was a central concept of nineteenth-century science. At one time, Newton thought he had disproved its existence, but he finally had to accept it.[24] As the medium of the propagation of electromagnetic waves, including light, the ether was supposed to be solid, but this peculiar substance was also believed to permeate all space and matter and to have all the properties mentioned by Jarry. The ether is generally supposed to have been eliminated by the famous Michelson-Morley experiment of the late 1880s, which Stephen Baxter has suggested may have been known to Wells,[25] but various attempts were made to save it, and J. B. Priestley was being taught it in school in 1907.[26] However, "with the formulation of the special theory of relativity, ether hypotheses lost much of their attractiveness" (Bergmann), and "in modern physics the expressions 'light ether' (divested of its alleged mechanical properties) and 'physical space' are considered synonymous" (Gamow).[27] In 1919, Theodr Kaluza suggested electromagnetic waves were actually vibrating in a fifth (fourth spatial) dimension.[28] It might be worth looking at Jarry's paper again from this point of view. Certainly it is a thought-provoking essay, and by no means is it all nonsense. Equally certainly, it could never have been written without first reading Wells.

In Vienna, *The Time Machine* evoked an equally interesting response from the versatile Jewish actor-writer-translator-journalist, Egon Friedell, who was born in 1878 and committed suicide in 1938, when the Nazis acquired Austria. At some unknown time, Friedell wrote a book called *Die Reise mit der Zeitmaschine* [*The Journey with the Time Machine*]. This was published in Munich in 1946, after the fall of the Nazis, and in 1972 Donald Wollheim published an English translation by Eddy C. Bertin, entitled *The Return of the Time Machine*. Although often entertaining, Friedell's book is hardly a novel, but rather a compendium of paradoxes, or of everything that could go wrong with time travel. It is especially travel to the past that creates problems. Since the earth is itself a time machine moving forward, the resistance of the time energy must be overcome by travelling first to the future and then using the acquired momentum to drive into the past. Then there is the problem of arriving at a time before the machine itself has been invented, and so before it exists. Perhaps the most interesting thing in the book is a throwaway line. Friedell observes that the Time Traveller could always return "exactly at the same moment he left. To spectators here he wouldn't have been away at all, or at most only *during the unimportant time-lag which his machine would need to pass through the needed time-planes*" (my emphasis). It is just this fact, that time travel would take time, unnoticed by everyone else including Wells, that gave J. W. Dunne the starting point for his serial analysis of time.[29]

In Britain, Wells's friend and fellow Fabian Edith Nesbit introduced time travel into children's literature in 1905, with *The Story of the Amulet*.[30] The novel contains a graceful tribute to Wells when the children visit a much improved future London, where he is revered as a great reformer who helped to make the improvements possible. Nesbit has a delightfully cavalier way with time travel paradox: "'And if you hadn't told Caesar all that about how things are now, he'd never have invaded Britain,' said Robert to Jane as they sat down to tea. 'Oh , nonsense,' said Anthea, pouring out; 'it was all settled hundreds of years ago.'"[31] Since *The Amulet* there have of course been many time travel stories for children. John Masefield's *The Box of Delights*, published in 1935, contains the interesting idea, also mentioned by Friedell, that a traveller to the past would cast no shadow there "because," as Friedell notes, "we humans throw our shadows forward, but never backward."[32]

But the most astonishing feature of Wells's ideas about time is their anticipation of modern physics. As we have seen, in 1908 Minkowski reformulated special relativity theory in terms of a space-time continuum, with time as the fourth dimension, and Einstein accepted this and used it when he developed the theory of general relativity. Let me repeat again the words of the Time Traveller: "*There is no difference between Time and any of the three dimensions of Space except that our consciousness moves along it.*" And here is Hermann Weyl, summing up relativity theory in 1922: "Only the consciousness that passes on in one portion of this world experiences the detached piece which comes to meet it, and passes behind it as history, that is as a process that is going forward in time and takes place in space."[33] Minkowski's space-time continuum is very precisely Wells's universe rigid.

There is no evidence that Minkowski, or even Einstein, read *The Time Machine*. In 1930, Einstein was at a banquet with Bernard Shaw and Wells and expressed sympathy with their "conceptions of life," but he was obviously referring to their social and political views.[34] But what is so amazing is that Wells, with his writer's imagination, predicted with such accuracy one of the central principles of modern physics. I find it equally amazing that so few physicists have given his vision the appreciation it deserves. I have only been able to find two. J. W. Dunne refers to the Time Traveller outlining Wells's case "with a clearness and conciseness which has rarely, if ever, been surpassed." He gives Wells credit for being the first to see that time *must* be regarded as a fourth dimension and also, by using the plural phrase "our mental existences," anticipates the multiple observers of relativity theory.[35] The other physicist to give Wells due honor is L. Silberstein, in his book *The Theory of Relativity*, published in 1914. Writing of Minkowski's concept, Silberstein observes: "There is thus far an intrinsic similarity [. . .] between space and time, or as the Time Traveller, in a wonderful anticipation of Mr Wells, puts it 'There is no difference between Time and Space except that our consciousness moves along it.' It is interesting that even the terms used by Minkowski to express these ideas, as 'three-dimensional geometry becoming a chapter of the four-dimensional physics,' are anticipated in Mr Wells's fantastic novels." He quotes the Time Traveller's interpretation of portraits or statues of the same man at different ages: "'All these are evidently sections, as it were, Three-Dimensional representations of his Four-Dimensional being, which is a fixed and unalterable thing.' Thus Mr Wells seems to perceive clearly this absoluteness, as it were, of the world tube and the relativity of its various sections." This generous tribute seems to me perfectly justified.[36]

As Milic Capek has shown, some physicists, contrary to the Time Traveller, have given time a special status, and therefore do not accept the equivalence of Minkowski's four dimensions. In spite of the neglect of Wells's work by most physicists, we may divide them, for convenience, into Wellsians, Anti-Wellsians, and Fence-Sitters.[37] The first Wellsian was Minkowski. "Space of itself," he wrote, "and time of itself will sink into mere shadows and only a kind of union between them shall survive."[38] He was supported in his Wellsian view by William Quin, O. C. de Beauregard, Adolf Grünbaum, evidently Silberstein,[39] and, above all, the great mathematician Kurt Gödel, writing in 1949. Gödel's starting point was the relativity of simultaneity. Einstein himself lists as the first of the "insights of definite nature which physics owes to the special theory of relativity," that "there is no such thing as simultaneity of distant events."[40] If one observer claims event A happened before event B, declares Gödel, another observer may claim the opposite. He proceeds to show that, in certain kinds of universes satisfying Einstein's equations, it would be theoretically possible to travel to the past, including one's own past, though only by using virtually impossible velocities and fuel loads. Moreover, even without such high speeds and loads, "for *every* possible definition of a world time one could travel into regions of the universe which are passed according to that definition."[41]

The Anti-Wellsians, who regarded time as essentially different from the three spatial dimensions, included Émile Meyerson, Paul Langevin, Sir Arthur Eddington, Capek, and A. N. Whitehead. Finally, there were the Fence-Sitters, who "shifted their views on this subject, sometimes even within one and the same book"; these included Sir James Jeans, Hermann Weyl, Hans Reichenbach—and Einstein.[42] In 1922 and again in 1928, Einstein expressed agreement with Meyerson "that in the four-dimensional continuum all dimensions are not equivalent."[43] But in 1949 he expressed cautious approval of Gödel's ideas.[44] And four weeks before his death in 1955, he wrote in a letter of condolence to a friend: "For us believing physicists, the division into past, present and future has merely the meaning of an albeit obstinate illusion."[45] So (to misquote Sir Walter Scott) Einstein's self a Wellsian died.

Of course no account of time after *The Time Machine* would be complete without a detailed discussion of J. B. Priestley and J. W. Dunne. J. B. Priestley was brought up on Wells's writings, and in his autobiographical book *Margin Released,* he gave perhaps the warmest and fairest account ever given of Wells's personality.[46] No other writer has had such a lifelong interest in time. His "Time Plays" are both fine works for the stage and fine thought experiments.[47] In *Dangerous Corner* (1932), in Priestley's own words, he used "the device of splitting time into two, thus showing what *might* have happened."[48] *Johnson over Jordan* (1939) is ostensibly about the experience of the protagonist immediately after his death, in which, like the proverbial drowning man, he is brought face to face with episodes of his whole past life. But Priestley notes that it "must not be regarded as a play about life-after-death"; he was trying "to create as it were a four-dimensional drama," showing what the Time Traveller would have called the hero's four-dimensional being.[49] *I Have Been Here Before* (1937) is based on the peculiar kind of reincarnation favored by the mystic P. D. Ouspensky (presumably suggested by the phenomenon of *déjà vu*), in which a person lives his or her life over and over again, until he or she gets it right—or hopelessly wrong. But the play can equally be interpreted as a case of precognition being used to avert disaster. The most interesting of the plays, *Time and the Conways* (also 1937), was stimulated by reading Dunne. The second act is a vision of a pretty dismal future seen by the heroine. In the third act she returns to the present, with only the vaguest relics of her vision in her mind. At the end of the second act, she has been cleared by her wise brother with a lecture on time and the promise of a loan of a book, which is clearly Dunne's *An Experiment with Time*. Finally, Priestley's book *Man and Time* (first published in 1964) is easily the best popular book on the subject. If it seems a little inconclusive and to contribute little to the theory of the subject, it is only fair to add that Priestley never claimed to be either a physicist or a writer of Wells's imagination.

J. W. Dunne certainly did add more than a little to the theory of the subject, especially in his two great books, *An Experiment with Time* (1927) and *The Serial Universe* (1934). He served in the army in the Boer War and left his important aeronautical research notes with Wells for safety at that time;[50] he was, of course, one of the greatest of all aircraft designers. When *An Experiment* appeared, it was greeted with enthusiasm by both Priestley and Wells.[51] In spite of his generous tribute to Wells, quoted earlier, Dunne states categorically that "It was not Wells's *Time Machine* which provided my starting-point." He dates his own special approach to the subject to his childhood. He was born in 1875, thirteen years before publication of "The Chronic Argonauts." His real starting point, overlooked as he notes by Wells, is "that anything which moves in Time must *take Time* over its movement" (his italics).[52] This leads him eventually to his serial conception of time, which can be oversimplified to mean that time itself has many, even an infinite number of dimensions. Whether Dunne's theory is or is not eventually accepted, *An Experiment* will always remain a major contribution to the theory of time, and *The Serial Universe* one of the most important commentaries on relativity and quantum theory. But both books are heavy going. Priestley tells of the occasion when Dunne gave a talk to the cast of *Time and the Conways*:

> With that innocence which seems to belong to mathematicians and engineers [...] he covered a blackboard with mathematical formulae and threw over his shoulder various references to Minkowski and the Michelson-Morley experiment. [...] Pretending to know what he was talking about, the players gave a magnificent performance.[53]

I end with a little book called *The Conquest of Time*, published in 1942 by one Herbert George Wells. It is sad reading. The author mentions discussions of four-dimensional geometry among the South Kensington students half-a-century earlier: "One or two of us," he writes, "concluded definitely that this fourth dimension of the mathematicians was duration." And he continues:

> I don't remember that we followed up the consequences of that conclusion with any severity. Later on I wrote a fantasy called *The Time Machine*. [. . .] It was entirely fantasy, and the reader was bluffed past the essential difficulties of the proposition entirely for the sake of the story. . . . [54]

Yes, these are the actual words, in 1942, of the author of the "Universe Rigid." In spite of Dunne's firm disclaimer, already published by then, Wells accuses him of taking *The Time Machine* too seriously. True, ten pages later, he somehow manages to return to the fourth dimension and even the universe rigid.[55] But he never withdraws his explicit dismissal of Dunne, or his implicit dismissal of the young Wells.

I sympathize with Wells's loyal admirer Priestley when he writes:

> I find myself regretting deeply, for his sake as well as ours, his later attitude toward the Time problem. [. . .] He was irritable when the subject came up. He pooh-poohed Dunne [. . .] and although he was never rude about it he deplored the way in which I was bothering my head about Time in the '30s. He was like a man who, having wrongly given up playing an instrument for which he had a flair, then refused to listen to anybody else playing it.[56]

Max Beerbohm hit the nail on the head in his time travel cartoon of 1929, in which a pontificating elder Wells confronts his shy and enthusiastic young doppelgänger.[57] In the words of the Time Traveller, the four-dimensional being of Herbert George Wells may be a "fixed and unalterable thing," but we are free to choose our section, or "Three-dimensional representation" (1, 5). More than a century after his most wonderful achievement, let us be remembering, not the disillusioned elder, but the young creator of *The Time Machine*.

Notes

This is a somewhat modified version of the paper presented at the Symposium. For a longer version, see W. M. S. Russell, "Time Before and After *The Time Machine*," *Foundation* 65 (1995), 24–40.

1. W. M. S. Russell, "Life and Afterlife on Other Worlds," *Foundation* 28 (1983), 34–56. Quotation from p. 38.

2. Ibid., 36–37.

3. Edward James, "Editorial," *Foundation* 65 (1995), 3–5. Quotation from p. 5.

4. P. C. Bergmann, *The Riddle of Gravitation* (London: John Murray, 1969), p. 33; for

a lengthy and very clear exposition of this, see G. Gamow, *One Two Three . . . Infinity* (New York: New American Library, 1953), chaps. 4 and 5. For Newton's absolute space and time, see Gamow, p. 93 and R. S. Westfall, *The Life of Isaac Newton* (Cambridge: Cambridge University Press, 1993), p. 166.

5. Bergmann, op. cit., pp. 41, 51; P. Coveney and R. Highfield, *The Arrow of Time* (London: Flamingo, 1991), p. 82; A. Einstein, "Autobiographical Notes," in *Albert Einstein: Philosopher-Scientist*, ed. P. A. Schilpp (La Salle, Ill.: Open Court Publishing, 1970), pp. 1–94, esp. p. 15.

6. A. Sommerfield, "To Albert Einstein's Seventieth Birthday," in Schilpp, op. cit., pp. 97–105, esp. p. 103.

7. M. Kaku, *Hyperspace* (Oxford: Oxford University Press, 1994), pp. 10, 100.

8. Ibid., pp. 37–43, 49–53.

9. Ibid., pp. 68–75, 55–58; B. Bergonzi, *The Early H. G. Wells: A Study of the Scientific Romances* (Manchester: Manchester University Press, 1961), p. 32.

10. W. M. S. Russell, "Folktales and Science Fiction," *Foundation* 25 (1982), 5–30, esp. p. 12.

11. H. G. Wells, *The Conquest of Time* (London: Watts, 1942), p. 79.

12. O. C. de Beauregard, "Time in Relativity Theory Arguments for a Philosophy of Being," in *The Voices of Time*, ed. J. T. Fraser (London: Allen Lane, 1968), pp. 417–33 and 668–72, esp. p. 668; H. D. Zeh, *The Physical Basis of the Direction of Time* (Berlin: Springer-Verlag, 1992), p. 8.

13. J. B. Priestley, *Man and Time* (New York: Dell, 1968), p. 138.

14. J. Needham, "Time and Knowledge in China and the West," in Fraser, op. cit., pp. 92–135, 608–25, esp. pp. 92–96.

15. For the attribution of the article to D'Alembert, see J. W. Dunne, *An Experiment with Time* (London: Faber and Faber, 1939), p. 112; P. de la Cotardière and P. Fuentes, *Camille Flammarion* (Paris: Flammarion, 1994), p. 319.

16. Dunne, op. cit., pp. 112–13, 119.

17. Bergonzi, op. cit., pp. 31–32.

18. Wells, *The Conquest of Time* (London: Watts, 1942), p. 71.

19. Kaku, op. cit., p. 75.

20. R. M. Philmus and D. Y. Hughes, eds., *H. G. Wells: Early Writings in Science and Science Fiction* (Berkeley: University of California Press, 1975), pp. 4–5, 47–49; Bergonzi, op. cit., pp. 38–40.

21. J. H. Sainmont, ed., *Dr. Faustroll: Commentaire pour servir à la Construction Pratique de la Machine à Explorer le Temps* (Chalons-sur-Marne: Collège de Pataphysique, 1976), pp. 7–12.

22. N. Arnaud and H. Bordillon, eds., *Alfred Jarry: Ubu* (Paris: Gallimard, 1978), pp. 7–23.

23. Sainmont, op. cit., pp. 29–59. My translations.

24. Westfall, op. cit., pp. 148, 154, 183, 254, 257–58, 297.

25. S. Baxter, "1880s Science and *The Time Machine*," *H. G. Wells Newsletter* 3: 9 (1995), 3.

26. Priestley, op. cit., pp. 61–62.

27. Bergmann, op. cit., p. 247; Gamow, op. cit., pp. 93–94; Kaku op. cit., pp. 8, 263; Einstein, op. cit., pp. 19, 25; L. de Broglie, "A General Survey of the Scientific Work of Albert Einstein," in Schilpp, op. cit., pp. 111–12; I. Asimov, *Understanding Physics: Light, Magnetism and Electricity* (New York: American Library, 1969), chap. 6.

28. Kaku, op. cit., pp. 99–104.

29. D. A. Wollheim, ed., *Egon Friedell: The Return of the Time Machine*, trans. E. C. Bertin (New York: DAW, 1972), pp. 11–16, 28, 64–68, 89, 106–8; Dunne, op. cit., p. 121.

30. J. Briggs, *A Woman of Passion: The Life of E. Nesbit 1858–1924* (Harmondsworth: Penguin, 1989), pp. 245, 297.

31. E. Nesbit, *The Story of the Amulet* (Harmondsworth: Penguin, 1959), pp. 193, 231.

32. J. Masefield, *The Box of Delights* (London: Heinemann, 1991), p. 192; Wollheim, op. cit., p. 112.

33. Cited by G. J. Whitrow, "Time and the Universe," in Fraser, op. cit., pp. 580, 165.

34. R. W. Clark, *Einstein: The Life and Times* (London: Hodder, 1979), p. 399.

35. Dunne, op. cit., pp. 119–20.

36. Cited by M. Capek, "Time in Relativity Theory: Arguments for a Philosophy of Becoming," in Fraser, op. cit., pp. 434–35.

37. Ibid., pp. 434–39.

38. Cited by R. Fischer, "Biological Time," in Fraser, op. cit., p. 366.

39. Capek, op. cit., p. 437.

40. Einstein, op. cit., p. 61.

41. K. Gödel, "A Remark about the Relationship between Relativity Theory and Idealistic Philosophy," in Schilpp, op. cit., pp. 555–62; cf. Capek, op. cit., pp. 436–37 and Whitrow, op. cit., pp. 573, 681.

42. Capek, op. cit., p. 437; for H. Reichenbach, see his paper "The Philosophical Significance of the Theory of Relativity," in Schilpp, op. cit., pp. 287–311, esp. p. 305, and for Jeans, see also P. T. Landsberg, ed., *The Enigma of Time* (Bristol: Adam Hilgerm, 1984), pp. 27–28.

43. Capek, op. cit., pp. 434–37.

44. A. Einstein, "Remarks to the Essays Appearing in this Collective Volume," in Schilpp, op. cit., pp. 663–88, esp. pp. 687–88.

45. Zeh, op. cit., p. 164.

46. J. B. Priestley, *Margin Released* (London: Reprint Society, 1963), pp. 8, 164–67.

47. J. B. Priestley, *The Plays*, vol. 1 (London: Heinemann, 1948); V. Brome, *J. B. Priestley* (London: Hamish Hamilton, 1988), chap. 15.

48. Priestley, *The Plays*, p. vii.

49. Ibid., pp. ix–x.

50. Wells, *The Conquest of Time*, p. 71; Priestley, *Man and Time*, pp. 265–66.

51. Dunne, op. cit., quotations on jacket.

52. Ibid., pp. 121, 211.

53. Priestley, *Margin Released*, pp. 202–3; cf. *Man and Time*, p. 266 and Brome, op. cit., p. 200.

54. Wells, *The Conquest of Time*, p. 71.

55. Wells, *The Conquest of Time*, Appendix 2, pp. 71–86.

56. Priestley, *Man and Time*, p. 167.

57. Ibid., p. 101; Landsberg, op. cit., pp. 17–18.

PART 2

Currents of Its Time

Neoteny, Anthropology, Society,
Numerology, Imperiality

Wells and Neoteny

KIRBY FARRELL

Among other things, the Victorian reception of Darwinism is a record of cultural efforts to come to terms with death. Besides controverting traditional religious doctrine, Darwinism disrupted the magic circle of personal and cultural narcissism by situating humankind among the animals in an adaptive struggle doomed to end in meaningless extinction. *The Time Machine* represents one effort to assimilate this cognitive shock. Victorian culture vigorously rationalized the threat. Some openly repudiated Darwinism, while others massaged it into conformity with existing verities and consolations. Some agile churchmen tried to maintain that natural selection was only a technical term for the benevolent hand of God. But philosopher-scientists could be limber, too. From "the survival of the fittest," Social Darwinism recuperated old-fashioned notions of hierarchy and warrior-heroism and mated them with modern enthusiasms for progress and productivity.

Conservative tamers of Darwin minimized the role of chance and the play of genetic possibilities in evolution while promoting a reassuring sort of determinism. "Survival" became an absolute value, for example, and "proved" the absolute worth of the "fittest." Andrew Carnegie used this rhetoric to praise millionaires in his "Gospel of Wealth," raising a cathedral of sanctimonious capitalism that is still defying the laws of gravity in Washington and elsewhere today.[1] As R. A. Rappaport succinctly puts it, "Sanctification transforms the arbitrary into the necessary, and regulatory mechanisms which are arbitrary are likely to be sanctified."[2]

Pseudo-Darwinian determinism implicitly sanctified the status quo, grounding society's inconsistencies and irrationality in a new conviction of national authority. The varieties of pseudo-Darwinism, that is, worked to rebuild cultural morale and to substantiate puny humans—especially rich puny humans—in the world. In this sense the theories were a cultural technology for converting survival-anxiety into a new robust conviction of power and symbolic immortality.[3] For example, Andrew Carnegie ends his sermon on wealth by rhapsodizing about the rich man's ability to squeeze through the eye of the needle into heaven. From the biblical text, Carnegie extracts—I am tempted to say "extorts"—the faith that the rich will be accepted into God's neighborhood and live forever. Even the upbeat plutocrat needed to warp Darwinism away from death.

But determinism could console the poor, too, even as fatalism supported the immemorial Egyptian peasant. Even painful destiny may be co-opted to serve an apparently submissive human will. This was Queen Victoria's strategy of controlling death-anxiety and crushing grief when she sacralized and fixated on Albert's death. And it was a characteristic maneuver of the age. It is a subtle step from accepting God's will to identifying with—sharing in, codirecting—God's will. Emulating the queen, even dressing like her, Wells's mother, Sarah, managed adversity by trying to spy out divine necessity and conform herself to it. And in a different but related way, so did her ostensibly rebellious son H. G. The essence of the behavior is passive assertion or even passive aggression. It is evident in the way the prophetic Wells submitted to an apocalyptic vision and used it to support messianic fantasies of saving the world through his superior insight. One model for this imaginative maneuver is of course the idea of Christ the crucified son submitting to, and sharing in, the will of the Father, so that by his self-sacrifice he comes to command and deliver humankind. Almost always in Wells, meditations on extinction are matched by fantasies of self-aggrandizement. Even his most rigorous thinking about evolutionary possibility usually reveals some sort of determinism at work, and the vestigial outlines of Victorian ideologies. His distortions matter because half-unwittingly they anticipate many of the twisted shapes science and evolution took in the twentieth century.

One way of getting at these distortions is to look at the evolutionary concept of neoteny. Wells alludes to neoteny in the final pages of *The Shape of Things to Come* (1933), one of his later prophecies of world catastrophe and therapeutic scientific despotism. As first defined by J. Kollmann (1884), neoteny is the evolutionary process in which the regulatory system retards ancestral developmental rates so that in humans—in fact, in the whole primate order—neotenates still look and act like juveniles when they are reproductively adult. The process of retarded allometric development produces adult animals that retain the increased adaptive flexibility of the young.

The Shape of Things to Come pretends to be a dream diary kept by a League of Nations official. Like the time machine, the dreams supposedly have penetrated time. The dreamer has been able to read a future textbook that recounts history from the actual early twentieth century through a calamitous world war, a reconstructive period of "Puritan Tyranny," and, finally, a sort of millennial near utopia. This future advertises Wells's cranky fervor for eugenics and a familiar Lamarckian wishfulness about the heritability of desirable cultural traits. With artistic sleight of hand, he salts his visionary rhetorical stardust with daring statistical nuggets—"The Behavior Control Report for [the year] 2104," his dreamer tells us, "records 715 cases of stealing for the whole world." With an old man's doggedness, he revisits his favorite themes: the menacing "abyss of extinction,"[4] deliverance by an oligarchy of military-scientific wise men, integrated world government, a world encyclopedia even more promising than the internet,[5] and a revolutionary "new pattern of living" to be "imposed" upon "our race."[6]

Where the sibylline exercise turns a fresh corner is near the end, when the narrator describes near-utopian humankind as neotenic. He announces a "difference in the age cycle between ourselves and our ancestors, which has prolonged the youthful phase and shifted on the valid years towards the thirty-five to eighty period." Where in the remote past our ancestor "was as solitary an animal as the tiger," he passed "through stages of increasing sociability. The onset of these stages was made practicable by the retention of immature characteristics into adult life. The same thing is happening to the remnant of lions today. They remain cubbish and friendly now to a much later age." "What has happened during the past three and a half centuries to the human consciousness has been a sublimation of individuality."[7] By contrast, "adult" characteristics are the hallowed virtues of Victorian ideology and the stuff of masculine survival fantasies: individual fitness, competitive strength, discipline, fixity of purpose, and the like.

Neoteny means that regulatory system genes delay the onset of adult characteristics. As a result, adult animals retain youthful physical proportions—of brain weight to body weight, say—but they also demonstrate youthful behaviors such as curiosity, ease of learning, social cooperativeness, and submissiveness. Unlike sociobiology and orthodox psychoanalysis, neoteny assumes that humans inherit "the extremely social instincts of youthful primates" rather than "typical adult animal behaviors such as territoriality or dominance hierarchy."[8] Neoteny selects for traits that may have fitted early humans for their migratory way of life during the last few million years. The same qualities have probably brought about the loss of much species-specific recognition behavior and the youthful care-soliciting behavior, which has since the last Ice Age brought humans and all their various domesticated animals into an alliance so prolific that it is "threatening the extinction of all wild species that are habitat-specific, highly specialized and independent."[9]

Throughout his life, Wells's interests kept bringing him close to the idea of neoteny. The Eloi and Morlocks have many juvenile traits, for example, but the novel scorns them as maladaptive. In the 1930s, Wells wrote *The Science of Life* with Julian Huxley at a time when Huxley was exploring neoteny. Yet he only began to grasp the concept at the close of *The Shape of Things to Come*, the year after Huxley's *Problems of Relative Growth* came out. To ask why he missed or resisted the idea is to unpack some of Wells's distinctive prejudices, but also some of the major cultural shifts of his lifetime.

For the early Wells, neotenic traits signify not adaptive advantage, but liability. With "their little pink hands," hairless faces, "little chins," and "large and mild" eyes, the Eloi present conspicuously juvenile proportions (4, 24). But the Eloi are helpless, and the Morlocks rigidly predatory, each imprisoned in a specific environmental niche. The Eloi's "social paradise" (4, 32) disguises nature red in tooth and claw. In part this is Wells the susceptible young journalist echoing Max Nordau (*Degeneration*, 1892) and other fashionable Jeremiahs. But his conception of Darwinism reflects a much wider array of influences. His teacher, T. H. Huxley, carefully preserved a moral dimension in evolution. For Huxley, intelligence and culture placed humankind "as on a mountain top, far above the level of his humble fellows, and transfigured from his grosser nature by reflecting, here and there, a ray from the infinite source of truth."[10] Such tacitly religious rhetoric grounded the new science in the ancient hierarchy of patriarchal values. He modifies Christianity's dualism and conviction of cosmic purposes without really repudiating them. For all his iconoclasm, Huxley's mountaintop rises into a Victorian Christianity sky, lifting his superior humans toward symbolic immortality.[11]

Where neoteny finds adaptive value in juvenile traits, many Victorian Christians and Darwinians shared ancient prejudices about childhood.[12] Augustinian theology saw the child as a chaotic, excremental creature akin to the brutes and in need of firm adult discipline. The Augustinian child is close to the lowly origins that Christians—and even the skeptical Huxley—sought to transcend. Social Darwinism especially resonated with Augustinian fantasies by making virtues out of supposedly "adult" traits such as competition, self-discipline, tenacity, muscular strength, and individualism—characteristics that in neotenic terms are fixed and potentially maladaptive. Only in 1902 did Peter Kropotkin make his famous case for the adaptive benefits of cooperation in his book *Mutual Aid*.

As James Kincaid has pointed out, adult projections and the internal contradictions of the period made childhood endlessly plastic.[13] Like Victorian religion, medical commentaries tangle the child in a net of prescriptive controls. Doctors medicalized cultural alarm over defective training and infantile rebelliousness. They wrote morally charged treatises on bed-wetting and devised harnesses to restrain or punish erotic behaviors in children. Economic life stressed not the fluent give and take of children's play, but mechanistic efficiency, bureaucratic order, and above all profit. On yet another level, racial chauvinism identified "lesser breeds" both with children and with the apes popularly imagined to be our ancestors. Late-Victorian Britain and America worried volubly about a fatigued white race "falling back" into the "beautiful, futile" childishness that debilitates Wells's Eloi.[14]

Victorian fantasies about childhood and race are unthinkable apart from assumptions about gender. Wells's audience would have classified most neotenic characteristics as feminine, subject to the culture's ambivalence toward women. As the model of respectability and domestic management, the revered mother scarcely exemplifies neotenic qualities. If anything, those qualities were probably most evident in girlhood, in courtship behaviors, and in relations among women, where culturally sanctioned "adult" characteristics were less important than sociability, care-soliciting play, and the like. The coquettish, pathetic Weena exhibits some excusable care-soliciting behaviors in coaxing the Time Traveller into "a little rubbing of the limbs" (5, 43). By comparison, neotenic traits actually signal danger as stereotyped in the seductive aggression of the femme fatale. But then, to explain Original Sin, Augustinian tradition focused on juvenile qualities in Eve—on her curiosity, impulsiveness, and indiscriminate sociability, especially toward strangers.

In *The Time Machine*, pseudoneoteny reflects many Augustinian assumptions about childhood and gender, all of them intensified by apocalyptic dread that owes much to Sarah Wells's religious zeal. Wells stressed the Morlocks' morphological changes and adaptation to meet material needs. Why then should they become fixed in such inefficient predation?[15] The Time Traveller moralizes their behavior as revenge, evoking Cain and Abel. "[G]enerations ago, man had thrust his brother man out of the ease and the sunshine. And now that brother was coming back—changed!" (7, 58). The fantasy of revenge owes its power to conflicts over competition, injustice, and status, which the novel assumes its readers will share. At the same time, these distressing adult issues are displaced onto ancient "brothers," and the Morlocks are characterized as half-civilized and immature "things." As abused, angry inferiors, the Morlocks fill an ideological niche in Victorian culture, which had been inhabited by rioting apprentices in early modern London and is inhabited in today's media and film lore by depraved juvenile gangs, neo-Nazi skinheads, and drug-crazed teenage psychopaths.

The Time Traveller's pity for the victimized Eloi and outrage at the predatory

Morlocks expresses parental ambivalence toward the young. Unlike their forebears, Victorian parents were increasingly concerned not to break the spirit of the child in order to extinguish "the Old Adam." The Eloi reflect anxieties about the dangers of inculcating too much submissiveness or not enough self-discipline, just as the Morlocks suggest fears of arousing uncontrollable hatred through too much severity. Which is to say that the novel imagines a parent-figure among pseudochildren who are beyond his control. Authority and nurture are alike in crisis. Even in depicting Weena's childish female dependency, the Traveller makes affection a liability. The Eloi indulge in erotic dalliance, but they pay for it on Morlock dinner tables.

The Traveller's obsession with parental authority signals anxiety about regulating competition within, as well as between, families. He has landed in a world in which individual autonomy is dangerously scarce, where the Victorian parent has to strike out at alienated children to recover the stolen time machine that stands for adult authority and freedom to move. With Morlocks constantly menacing him for food, the Traveller defends his desire "to go killing one's own descendants! But it was impossible, somehow, to feel any humanity in the things" (8, 67). The parent-child competition here expresses a wide range of generational, class, and gender conflicts.

To complicate matters, while the Traveller rages at hostile youth, the child in him fears shadowy hostile parents. When he first sights "white, ape-like creature[s] [. . .] carrying some dark body," he feels premonitory dread and thinks of them as ancestral "ghosts" (5, 45).[16] A moment later his anxiety about predatory parents reminds him that, as "the younger Darwin" speculated, "the planets must ultimately fall back one by one into the parent body," the Sun (5, 46). Like the shafts that house the Morlocks and can suck in a scrap of paper, these images suggest parental resorption or cannibalism. But this infanticidal idea is also compatible with the late-Victorian trope of vampirism. The vampire usurps the victim's will and dramatizes the dread that in a world without enough autonomy to go around, powerful others may capture you. A parent or parent-figure may usurp or "take back" the child's will. The Time Traveller fears that the Morlocks probe and, in effect, master him as he lies sleeping like a child, feeling "drowned" (5, 44). During the climactic mayhem, he experiences the Morlocks as vampire-children, their "little teeth nipping at my neck" (9, 74). But it is significant that the minute he recovers from his ordeal, the Traveller attacks his dinner with "the appetite of a tramp" (2, 16), smacking his lips over "good wholesome meat" (12, 87).

As Robert Pattison points out, English culture has balanced Augustinian pessimism about the child with a tradition it derives from Pelagius, which centered on Christ the wise child teaching in the temple.[17] This tradition expands the trope of the sacrificial innocent lamb and supports a nurturant parenting ethos. It is symptomatic of conflicted Victorian attitudes that Wells shifts Pelagian traits onto the feeble, beautiful Eloi with a mixture of pathos and scorn. Though he chivalrously defends them, the Time Traveller is nonetheless ambivalent toward the Eloi, rather as public opinion was toward "degenerate" hippie "flower children" in the 1960s.[18]

In disparaging children's' fascination with toys, the Traveller perpetuates older ideas of children as economic instruments to be harnessed into social fitness. He never recognizes that play is the human's basic developmental process, important to adults and children. The hostility to play is revealingly keyed to the Traveller's fear of the Eloi's dependency, his resentment of their lack of productivity, and to his fear of their defenselessness. Although he is an inventor, he shows no appreciation of the heuristic, improvisatory nature of play as a means of mastering an environment. On the contrary, childhood means loss of self-control, as when the Traveller reacts to the loss of the time machine by "bawling like an angry child" (5, 36). Loss of autonomy also figures in his fear of being "examined" in his bed while asleep—like a child under parental gaze—a fear that accords with the proverb that "children should be seen and not heard." Indirectly, the child's diminished autonomy helps to account for the Eloi's alarming loss of individuality and gender difference as well as their "communism."[19]

By the 1930s, other voices were qualifying Victorian Darwinism by emphasizing the adaptive values of cooperation and social life. To Freud's argument in *Civilization and Its Discontents* that aggression is an original, instinctual disposition in man, Havelock Ellis replied, echoing Peter Kropotkin, "As regards the primary impulse of aggression, I would not object to this if you insisted equally on a primary impulse of mutual help. If the primary aggressive impulse was predominant,—we should not be here! A species can only survive by the predominance of the impulse of mutual help."[20]

As Wells tried to come to terms with old age in the 1930s, he began pushing the consoling idea of "collective immortality." The fantasy tacitly draws on neotenic social bonding. Given his lifelong anxiety about extinction, Wells may have been attracted to neoteny partly because it enabled him to rationalize an existential refusal to accept the finality of fixed roles and ultimately death itself. In *The Time Machine,* pseudoneoteny focuses Wells's fear of death on decadence and compensatory fantasies of heroic aggression. By contrast, neotenic socialization and plasticity offered Wells in his last years a consoling vision of cooperation, nurture, and symbolic immortality.

In addition, because juvenile behavior relies so much on play, it implies a value system that may have given Wells some relief from the grimly competitive—"predatory"—values of the young man who had struggled up from poverty half a century earlier. In glancing at neoteny, he may have been trying to get beyond the workaholic survival motives of his youth. Perhaps it would be more accurate to say that Wells periodically rebelled against "adult" fixity all his life—not only in his self-renewing love affairs, but even in the irresolute retreat from the discipline of laboratory science at South Kensington that turned him into a journalist and indirectly brought *The Time Machine* into being. In this sense, neoteny provided a "scientific" justification for his characterological need for gregarious, heuristic play. It offered him a means to rethink and resist the obsessive, traumatic doctrines that had formed him, from apocalyptic entropy to chivalric violence.

It is symptomatic of Wells and of his time that he was unable to make more of neoteny. *The Shape of Things to Come*, after all, enlists the concept to serve a familiar prophetic program. Its rhetorically driven arguments are closed to the sorts of insights that have led to post-Victorian Darwinism: specifically, to the new skepticism that a particular gene produces a particular cultural effect; and to the shift in emphasis away from biological determinism to biological potentiality.[21] Perhaps most threatening of all to an animal that substantiates itself in the world through symbolic order and meaning, post-Victorian Darwinism is open to the role of chance in evolution. More than a century after *The Time Machine*, evolutionary theories make more room for stochastic change. Eric White puts it succinctly: "The 'postmodern' stance toward the natural world [. . .] entails an alternative emplotment of evolutionary history. If themes of *intelligibility, transcendence*, and *purpose* are prominent in narratives based on the Modern Synthesis, many recent evolutionists, from the 1970s at least, would sooner highlight in their depictions of the course of biological evolution themes of *complexity, finitude*, and *free play*. These critics of the Modern Synthesis have argued that Darwin did not himself support what Stephen Jay Gould and Richard Lewonthin have labeled the 'Panglossian paradigm' of adaptive optimization."[22]

Recent humanistic analyses of Darwinism have stressed its historical particularity and its constructedness. Every generation faces the problem of how to find language and theory more adequate to the ineffable complexity of evolution. But there is a second problem, too, as Wells's use of neoteny illustrates: how to overcome the creaturely denial that defends us against death-anxiety and the world's overwhelming complexity at the cost of half blinding us. The idea of intelligibility is a consoling anodyne, as handy and irresistible today as a Victorian headache powder. Even now, as in Wells's day, science readily devises intellectual maneuvers that attempt, in Davydd Greenwood's words, "to domesticate Darwinism's randomized, liminal world in motion and render it less fearsome."[23]

In *The Shape of Things to Come*, Wells cannot see that his prophetic dream of an oligarchy of wise men is in fact retrograde. Nor does he recognize the need for a revolution in feeling away from sadistic-triumphal themes of punishment and industrial might that shaped his culture—as they continue to distort ours. After all, we too obsessively overestimate our "adult" traits. Modern industrial warfare herds masses of obedient young men together like sheep and then describes the killing with a heroic vocabulary borrowed from Homer.

In a perverse way, despite its transparent sentimentality, Wells was not merely shrewd, but emotionally coherent in the speech he gave at a seventieth birthday dinner organized by PEN to honor him in October 1936. After the guests' tributes, Wells said he felt like "a little boy at a lovely party, who has been given quite a lot of jolly toys and who has spread his play about on the floor. Then comes his Nurse. 'Now Master Bertie,' she says, 'it's getting late. Time you began to put away your toys.'" Wells added: "I hate the thought of leaving. [. . .] Few of my games are nearly finished and some I have hardly begun."[24] This valediction catches some of the great themes of his life, including his transformation from below-stairs poverty to "Master Bertie" of the jolly toys and doting Nurse. But it also sums up his intellectual life as child's play, with a sort of humility and candor that puts in a healthy perspective some of the anxious distortions of his prophetic self.

Notes

1. Andrew Carnegie, *The Gospel of Wealth and Other Timely Essays* (New York, 1900), chap. 2.

2. R. A. Rappaport, "The Sacred in Human Evolution," *Annual Review of Ecology and Systematics* 2 (1971), 23–44.

3. Ernest Becker understands cultures as historically particular symbolic action systems that generate a conviction of heroic immortality. See *The Denial of Death* (New York, 1973), and *Escape from Evil* (New York, 1975).

4. H. G. Wells, *The Shape of Things to Come* (New York, 1936), pp. 422, 426.

5. "The Encyclopaedic organization, which centres upon Barcelona, with its seventeen million active workers, is the Memory of Mankind. Its tentacles spread out in one direction to million of investigators, checkers and correspondents, and in another to keep

the educational process in living touch with mental advance." (Wells, *The Shape of Things to Come*, p. 420). In Wells's *The Anatomy of Frustration* (London and New York, 1936), the encyclopedia is tacitly a heroic protagonist, the "hope of our species." Concepts like a "world brain" make the encyclopedia a cosmic Sherlock Holmes and presage the messianic coloring of some panegyrics about computers in the late twentieth century.

6. Wells, *The Shape of Things to Come*, p. 431.

7. Ibid., pp. 426, 427, 428.

8. Raymond P. Coppinger and Charles Kay Smith, "Neotenic Evolution and the Origin of Human Nature: An Abstract," *Cybernetics* 1: 1, 38. I am deeply indebted to Kay Smith for exploring cultural implications of neoteny with me. Stephen Jay Gould explains neoteny in *Ontogeny and Phylogeny* (Cambridge, Mass., 1977).

9. Coppinger and Smith, pp. 37–38. This domestic alliance "now amounts to about twenty percent of the total biomass of terrestrial earth" (p. 39).

10. This is the final flourish of Huxley's "On the Relations of Man to the Lower Animals" (1863), in *Darwin*, ed. Philip Appleman (New York, 1979), p. 241. Cf. Sherlock Holmes's allusion to Hamlet's definition of man as "like a god," yet also "the paragon of animals" in *The Sign of Four*.

11. Cf. Matthew Arnold, who "argued in his most popular work, *Literature and Dogma* (1873), we must read the God of the Bible 'in a scientific way,' that is, as an impersonal natural force, a 'not ourselves, which is in us and in the world around us.' But he needed to add that this was a natural force which 'makes for righteousness,' thus at a stroke deconstructing his painstaking 'scientific' case against anthropomorphism. He had to keep the human spirit at the center of things; Arnold was not alone in his moralization of the god nature." Peter Allen Dale, "Realism Revisited: Darwin and Foucault Among the Victorians," *Review* 12 (1990), 311.

12. For a controversial but unflinching account of the projective aggression evident toward children in western cultures, see "The Evolution of Childhood," in *The History of Childhood*, ed. Lloyd deMause (New York, 1975), pp. 1–79.

13. James Kincaid, *Child-Loving: The Erotic Child and Victorian Culture* (Berkeley, 1993).

14. See Gail Bederman, *Manliness and Civilization* (Chicago, 1995), esp. chaps. 1 and 2.

15. David J. Lake highlights some of the inconsistencies in Wells's understanding of evolution: "if the Eloi are made decadent by a too easy life, why should the subterranean workers be made decadent by a hard one? Would not their grim conditions in fact lead to selection for intelligence, for survival of the cunningest?" See "The White Sphinx and the Whitened Lemur: Images of Death in *The Time Machine*," *Science-Fiction Studies* 17 (1979), 81.

16. Cf. Small's flight from and repressed anger at his family, and Holmes's identification with Hamlet, who is oppressed by a parental ghost. Rider Haggard's *She* depicts the discovery of—and flight from—an underground world of mummified, ghostly parents.

17. Robert Pattison, *The Child Figure in English Literature* (Athens, Ga., 1978), pp. 11–20. Pattison considers Victorian childhood in chaps. 4–6.

18. An even more exact analogy would be the way popular American magazines in the 1990s such as *Vanity Fair* and *Time* sentimentalized the sorry fates of self-indulgent and self-destructive celebrities, the decadent "aristocrats" of consumer democracy.

19. Androgyny had fashionable esoteric meanings in the 1890s. Compare Wells's use of the sphinx in *The Time Machine* with Josephin Peladan's novel *L'Androgyne* (1891), which fantasizes about evolution: "Esoterically, he [the androgyne] represents the initial state of man, which is identical to his final state. [...] The sphinx incarnates the complete theology with the solution of origins and finalities. [...] The sphinx smiles at his divine enlightenment; he will reconstitute a day of his original unity, because he is man and god, in the same measure of involution and evolution." Painters commonly used the sphinx to stress the spiritual significance of androgyny and to link that with religion and mysticism. See Shearer West, *Fin de Siècle* (Woodstock, N.Y., 1994), chap. 5, esp. pp. 81–82. Peladan's theory is ultimately misogynistic and homosexual—interesting in light of Wells's angst about homosexual decadence.

20. Ellis added: "You quote the saying of Hobbes, 'Homo homini lupus.' But as Shaftesbury pointed out two centuries ago, the saying is not valid, since we cannot compare the attitude of an animal to its *own* species with that to *another* species. If man is like the wolf, then, said Shaftesbury, we have to remember that 'wolves are to wolves very kind and loving creatures.' the impulse of aggression is, fundamentally, a manifestation of the impulse of mutual help. We are aggressive towards those whom, we think, threaten those we love. If we view aggression biologically, this seems to me its only explanation." See Phyllis Grosskurth, *Havelock Ellis* (New York, 1980), p. 393.

21. These are Stephen Jay Gould's terms in *Ever Since Darwin* (New York, 1977).

22. Eric White, "The End of Metanarratives in Evolutionary Biology," *Modern Language Quarterly* 51, no. 1 (1990), p. 71.

23. Davydd Greenwood, *The Taming of Evolution: The Persistence of Nonevolutionary Views in the Study of Humans* (Ithaca, 1984), p. 69.

24. Quoted in Norman and Jeanne Mackenzie, *The Time Traveller: The Life of H. G. Wells* (New York, 1973), p. 395.

The Time Machine
and Victorian Mythology

SYLVIA HARDY

In her article "The Death of the Sun: Victorian Solar Physics and Solar Myth," Gillian Beer claims that H. G. Wells's *The Time Machine* is a solar myth, one of many varied responses in the late nineteenth century to what appeared to be a contradiction between the "progressive" implications of evolutionary theory and the anxieties generated by discoveries in solar physics, which predicted the cooling of the sun. "Physics, mythography, and the ordinary fear of death," Beer suggests, "converged in late nineteenth-century imagination. Such condensations form most readily at a point of contradiction."[1] In this study, I argue that although it is clear that the theories of solar physics—with their inevitable outcome of extinction—are central to *The Time Machine*, there is also evidence that Wells draws on mythology to a greater extent and with more positive effect than has yet been recognized, and that in this respect the story can be considered a solar myth.

The word *myth* has, of course, a number of connotations. In modern literary criticism, *The Time Machine* has often been described and interpreted in mythical terms. In 1946, V. S. Pritchett commented that, "like all excellent works it has meaning within its meaning,"[2] and Bernard Bergonzi, in his 1961 study *The Early H. G. Wells*, defined a myth as a story that "can be interpreted in many ways, none of them quite consistent, all of them more alive and fruitful than the rigid allegorical correspondence." The term "myth" has "a peculiar applicability to Wells's romances," Bergonzi suggests, because they "possess a wide relevance but nevertheless have a particular historical point of departure."[3] The historical point of departure for Wells in 1895 was an impatience with what he saw as a smug progressionism in contemporary thought; as he later wrote, his aim in *The Time Machine* had been to provide "a glimpse of the future that ran counter to the placid assumption of that time that Evolution was a pro-human force making things better and better for mankind."[4] Peter Bowler claims, in *The Invention*

of Progress, that contrary to popular belief, Darwinism played a crucial role in nineteenth-century thinking not because it convinced everyone of the power of natural selection—the full implications of this idea were too disturbing—but because it fed into ideas about progress.[5] This is exactly the point Wells makes in his 1891 paper, "Zoological Retrogression," where he insists on the contingent nature of natural selection, which entails a branching process of development and not an assured ascent: "there is, therefore, no guarantee in scientific knowledge of man's permanence or permanent ascendancy."[6]

In this paper I am concerned with the approaches to myth that developed in the second half of the nineteenth century, when the object of study was not, as in earlier periods, the interpretation of individual myths,[7] but a scientific exploration of the ways of thinking of mankind's prehistoric ancestors. Dominated by comparative studies of early language and of early man, mythography after 1856 played an important part in what has been described as an obsession with origins in the nineteenth century.[8] As Janet Burstein points out in "Victorian Mythography and the Progress of the Intellect," "As eloquent fragments of an irrecoverable past, myths seemed to offer access to a phenomenon that was otherwise unknowable, and thus constituted the best, if not the clearest, evidence of the genesis and development of human thought."[9]

It is clear from Wells's writings that he was familiar with the work of the two schools of mythography that were most influential in the second half of the nineteenth century.[10] It would, in any case, have been impossible for anyone as interested in ideas and in the possibilities of language as Wells certainly was in the 1880s and 1890s not to have been aware of the controversy between two rival groups of theorists—the solarists and the anthropologists—which began in 1873 and continued unabated, in books, newspapers, and in popular as well as scholarly journals, until the death of Friedrich Max Müller in 1900. "The protagonists of these systems," writes Richard Dorson, "engaged in a duel which occupied the last three decades of the century, and attracted the attention of the English nation and the outside world."[11] Solar mythology came first and held undisputed sway for two decades. It was introduced by Müller, a Sanskrit scholar from Germany who came to England in 1846 and spent most of his life as Professor of Comparative Philology at Oxford. In 1856, his essay on comparative mythology outlined his theory of solar mythology and reoriented all previous thinking on myths. Müller was certainly concerned with origins because his comparative study of the Aryan (or Indo-European) languages convinced him that these languages derived from a common source, and his great discovery was that the names of Vedic gods were etymologically related to those of their Greek and Latin counterparts. Mythology was an important part of his overall conceptual system—in every edition of his frequently revised *Lectures on the Science of Language*, five chapters were devoted to mythology—and he considered it to be an inherent part of language itself.[12] "Nothing is excluded from mythological expression," Müller wrote, "neither morals, nor philosophy, neither history nor religion, have escaped the spell of that ancient sybil."[13] What is more, he argues, solar myth affects our everyday lives, and in a Cambridge lecture Müller asserted that, given the centrality of the "solar drama" in the lives of men and women of all periods, it was inevitable that this should be reflected in their language and culture:

> What we call Morning, the ancient Aryans called the Sun or the Dawn. [...] What we call Noon, and Evening, and Night, what we call Spring and Winter, what we call Year, and Time, and Life, and Eternity—all this the ancient Aryans called Sun. And yet wise people wonder and say, How curious that the ancient Aryans should have had so many solar myths. Why, every time we say "Good morning," we commit a solar myth. Every poet who sings about "the May driving the Winter from the field again" commits a solar myth. Every "Christmas number" of our newspapers— ringing out the old year and ringing in the new—is brimful of solar myths. Be not afraid of solar myths.[14]

And there is no doubt that for a considerable period, ideas about solar myths were enormously influential. In 1870, the reviewer of George W. Cox's *Aryan Mythology* commented: "Mr Matthew Arnold, indeed, speaks of the set of modern mythological science towards atmospheric and solar myths as so irresistible 'that we can hardly now look up at the sun without having the sensation of a myth.'"[15] The coexistence of solar physics—the work of Hermann von Helmholtz, Lord Kelvin, and John Tyndall—with solar mythology in the second half of the nineteenth century is not without significance. Beer suggests that "Max Müller's solar mythography was so powerful because it gave expression to covert dreads then current; it cast itself as past enquiry, but expressed present fears."[16] Stephen Toulmin, making a similar point in his paper "Contemporary Scientific Mythology," warns his reader against feelings of superiority on this score: "The attempt to explain natural phenomena by personification may be dead or moribund. But many of the motives which produced the myths of the Greek and Northern peoples remain active in us still." One of these motives, he maintains, is anxiety; he points to the way people coped with the fears aroused by Copernican cosmology: "reasons had to be found for thinking that the Sun was a worthy centre of things and its being the source of light and heat was argued, even by such men as Kepler, as showing that the Sun rather than the Earth was the true House of

God." In time, he suggests, people began to see astronomical questions as separate from their feelings of security and dignity, but, until they did, "myth and theory were not clearly distinguished, and the quest for knowledge remained entangled with the quest for security." What is more, "Things which once were fused can be again confused"[17]—a comment particularly applicable to the late nineteenth century, a period when, as one recent writer puts it, "the laws of thermodynamics give modern specificity and focus to myth, to the ancient myth of the death of the sun."[18]

Max Müller was well aware of the connections between science and myth and, in fact, always insisted that his own approach to language and mythology should be seen as a branch of science.[19] Writing in 1891, he suggests that the most persuasive explanations of solar physics are unable to account for the deep-rooted feelings that the sun has aroused in mankind throughout the centuries:

> Not even the most recent scientific discoveries described in Tyndall's genuine eloquence—which teach us how we live, and move, and have our being in the sun, how we burn it, how we breathe it, how we feed on it—give us any idea of what this source of light and life, this silent traveller, this majestic ruler, this departing friend or dying hero, in his daily or yearly course, was to the awakening consciousness of mankind. [...] The names of the sun are endless and so are his stories; but who he was, whence he came and whither he went, remained a mystery from beginning to end.[20]

Müller's ideas about language and myth were in accord with the spirit of the age insofar as they fed into the nineteenth-century fear of degeneration, a concomitant of the belief that the earth's energy was "running down."[21] He maintained that there had been, at the early stages of Aryan culture, a "mythopoeic" age, a period when the conception of gods first arose. When language was at its material stage, the names of the sun, the sky, the dawn, and so on had a direct relationship to the phenomena to which they referred. With the passage of time, as language grew by metaphorical extension to express abstract meanings, the metaphorical words became "appellatives" and formed the substance of myths. As the original meanings were forgotten, the gods were seen first as persons, then as deities.[22] Müller saw both metaphor and mythology, therefore, as a "disease of language."[23]

For Müller, all myths were a product of the rules governing the use of language; for the rival anthropological evolutionist school of mythography, in contrast, myths were explanatory, the outcome of primitive man's attempt to make sense of the world. In *The Time Machine*, the Eloi's assumption that the Time

Traveller has arrived out of the sun in a thunderclap at first shocks him —"were these creatures fools?" (4, 24)—but he soon realizes that not only in size, but in moral sense and intellectual grasp, the Eloi have regressed to what appears to be a childlike stage of cultural development where they explain what they cannot understand by recourse to myth—an attitude of mind, of course, which the positivist, scientific Time Traveller regards as ludicrous. Anthropological mythography, which rapidly became influential in the 1870s, arose partly as a response to Darwinian theory—in the closing chapter of *The Origin of Species*, Darwin had expressed the hope that when evolutionary principles are applied to the study of mankind, "Light will be thrown on the origin of man and his history"[24]—and partly as a reaction against Müller and his fellow solarists. The anthropological approach was essentially developmental. E. B. Tylor, in *Primitive Culture*, outlined his belief in a universal pattern of development across all cultures but stressed that there had been very different rates of progress: "To the human intellect in its early childlike state may be assigned the origin and first development of myth." Tylor regards "the savage" as "a representative of the childhood of the human race."[25]

Andrew Lang, the best-known and most vociferous protagonist of the anthropological school, claimed that his interest in mythology began when he first read Müller and became impatient with the exclusive focus on the myths of Aryan races. Lang never denied the presence of solar and star myths across the world but insisted that they were the product of the animistic stage of culture, not of any disease of language.[26] Both Tylor and Lang pointed to the fact that the same myths were to be found all around the world, in Mexico, in Africa, in Australia, and among the Eskimos, where there could have been no opportunity for interchange, linguistic or otherwise. The conclusion must be, Lang claims, that "Similar conditions of mind produce similar practices, apart from identity of race, or borrowing of ideas and manners." In *Primitive Culture*, Tylor had argued that primitive tribes pass through the same stages of cultural progression. If this is so, asks Lang, "May not similar explanatory stories have occurred to the ancestors of the Australians, and to the ancestors of the Greeks, however remote their home, while they were still in the savage condition?"[27] Anthropological mythography, therefore, did not restrict itself to Aryan sources but studied the customs and myths of the primitive peoples ("savages") still existing in various parts of the world. As Bowler points out, for anthropological mythologists "Savages are fossilized relics of human evolution in the biological as well as the social sense; they illustrate the 'missing links' in the ascent of humankind."[28]

The solar theorists and the anthropologists battled over their respective approaches with tenacity; both saw their fields of study as important contributions to science, and both defended their methods of approach as the only ones capable of establishing the truth about early man. By the end of the century, it was generally assumed that solar myth had become a joke, and that the anthropologists had won the argument. But more recently, folklorists and linguists have reassessed the issues. Richard Dorson, for instance, in his history of British folklorists, argues convincingly that Müller had been right in many of his criticisms of the anthropological approach,[29] and in his 1978 *Explorations in Language and Meaning*, Malcolm Crick hails Müller as a forerunner of semiotics and claims that time has vindicated him: "He tried to express some very important ideas before an adequate language was available to frame them, and his consequent eclipse has hidden much of value from our view."[30]

Wells did not fully subscribe to either view. In the early chapters of *The Outline of History*, he draws on the work of a number of writers on the subject but shows himself to be impatient of any theory, anthropological or solarist, that claims to provide a blanket explanation for all mythology and primitive culture. In the chapter on early religions he writes:

> It is necessary to lay some stress upon this confusion and variety of origin in gods, because there is a very great literature now in existence upon religious origins, in which a number of writers insist, some on this leading idea and some on that—we have noted several in our chapter XII on "Early Thought"—as though it were the only idea. Professor Max Müller in his time, for example, harped perpetually on the idea of sun stories and sun worship. He would have had us think that early man never had lusts or fears, cravings for power, nightmares or fantasies, but that he meditated perpetually on the beneficent source of light and life in the sky. Now dawn and sunset are very moving facts in the daily life, but they are only two among many.[31]

Wells is, however, equally dismissive of the anthropologists' claims that late-nineteenth-century "primitives" can be studied as representatives of stone-age man, and here he expresses what was also Müller's view. "Early men, three or four hundred generations ago," he insists, "had brains very like our own."[32] But although Wells may not have been convinced by the mythographers' theories and is often scathing about their conclusions, a number of their arguments, as well as the controversial issues raised in mythology during the last three decades of the nineteenth century, find their way into *The Time Machine*, his own solar myth.

Wells uses the anthropological mythologists' methods—while subverting their assumptions—in his story because the Time Traveller's problem in his exploration of the future is very similar to theirs. How is it possible to construct a coher-

ent and authentic picture of an era that has left no clear or complete record?[33]
The Time Traveller's first attempts to explain "the condition of ruinous splendour
in which I found the world—for ruinous it was" (4, 28–29) are, in fact, an inversion of the method Andrew Lang proposes in *Custom and Myth*. One way of
interpreting primitive myth, Lang suggests, is to start from existing folklore, which
"represents, in the midst of a civilised race, the savage ideas out of which
civilisation has been evolved. The conclusion will usually be that the fact which
puzzles us by its presence in civilisation is a relic surviving from the time when
the ancestors of a civilised race were in the state of savagery."[34] Thus, as he attempts to understand the Eloi, the Time Traveller again and again bases his hypotheses on "survivals" (4, 33)[35] from what he sees as trends and incipient developments of his own time—although he, of course, is operating in reverse, seeking
for what has survived of civilized culture in a primitive society. Thus, the lack of
differentiation between the sexes in the Eloi, he speculates, stems from the fact
that the need for such specialization had ceased to exist: "We see some beginnings of this even in our time, and in this future age it was complete" (4, 30).
Similarly, his discovery of the subterranean Morlocks leads him to speculate about
contemporary London. "Even now," he asks, "does not an East-end worker live
in such artificial conditions as practically to be cut off from the natural surface of
the earth?" (5, 49).

The epistemological challenge faced by the Time Traveller derives, above all,
from the lack of language in the world of 802,701, and here again he is in a position similar to the Victorian anthropologists. But while the anthropologists could
sometimes rely on the testimony of missionaries or travellers, the Time Traveller
is only too aware that one of *his* major problems is the lack of a guide or "convenient cicerone in the pattern of the Utopian books" (5, 50), and he compares his
situation in this world of the future with that of a traveller from a wholly different
culture who arrives in England: "Conceive the tale of London which a negro,
fresh from Central Africa, would take back to his tribe!" (5, 41).[36] The Eloi do
have a language, of course, and the Time Traveller is eager to learn it as quickly
as he can, but he finds it inadequate as a means of discovering any of the things
he wants to know:

> Either I missed some subtle point, or their language was excessively simple—al-
> most exclusively composed of concrete substantives and verbs. There seemed to
> be few, if any, abstract terms, or little use of figurative language. Their sentences
> were usually simple and of two words, and I failed to convey or understand any but
> the simplest propositions. (5, 39–40)

The decadence and evolutionary regression of the Eloi (and presumably of the Morlocks as well, although we cannot be sure of this because the Time Traveller does not even begin to decipher their language) is evidenced by the inadequacy of their language to deal with anything beyond present experience at its most rudimentary level. Wells's description of the Eloi language shows it, in fact, to be an ironic parallel of what Müller extols as the clarity and purity of the material stage of language that served man's immediate needs—"the practical requirements it was originally intended to answer"—before the disease of mythology began.[37]

The significance of language in understanding the remote past was, then, a crucial aspect of Victorian mythography and an important bone of contention.[38] Language was central for solar theorists, because they saw mythology as a product of language, and the meaning of myths as recoverable only by the methods of comparative linguistic analysis;[39] the anthropologists, on the other hand, were prepared to base their conclusions on observation and comparison. Our assessment of the Time Traveller's attempts to make sense of the remote future is bound up with this issue. When his time machine disappears, he struggles to find an explanation based on what he has deduced about the Eloi from observation and bemoans the difficulties of "reading" the future through physical phenomena alone:

> I felt I lacked a clue. I felt—how shall I put it? Suppose you found an inscription, with sentences here and there in excellent plain English, and interpolated therewith, others made up of words, of letters even, absolutely unknown to you? Well, on the third day of my visit, that was how the world of Eight Hundred and Two Thousand Seven Hundred and One presented itself to me! (5, 42)[40]

Victorian mythographers were often obliged to derive their source material from oral traditions in cultures that had not yet acquired writing. *The Time Machine* reverses this situation. In the Palace of Green Porcelain, the Time Traveller discovers only the decaying vestiges of books in what had once been an extensive library: "They had long since dropped to pieces, and every semblance of print had left them" (8, 68). The world of the future appears to have no surviving written records; history in its historiographical sense has ceased to exist. Even when written language *has* been preserved, it no longer signifies. The Time Traveller notices an inscription "in some unknown character" on the face of the Palace of Green Porcelain and tells us: "I thought, rather foolishly, that Weena might help me to interpret this, but I only learned that the bare idea of writing had never entered her head" (8, 64). Time and again he searches for confirmation of the clues and traces he observes but, ultimately, has to acknowledge that he is left with an unprovable hypothesis. When the Time Traveller gives his final explanation of the world of the Eloi and Morlocks he comments: "So I say I saw it in my last view of the world of Eight Hundred and Two Thousand Seven Hundred and One." But he warns his listeners that "It may be as wrong an explanation as mortal wit could invent. It is how the thing shaped itself to me, and as that I give it to you" (10, 79). The methods he has available to him enable him to construct a posthistory but provide no way of testing its validity. As I have already indicated, in *The Outline of History* Wells rejects theories in mythography that claim to offer an all-embracing interpretation of all myths and primitive cultures, and in a book review of 1898 he challenges Grant Allen's theory that all gods were the apotheosis of dead ancestors and all sacred stones were sepulchral. There must, he argues, have been a vast number of reasons why men made use of such stones, but we have no way of knowing what they were: "Only with the coming of organized tradition and complex powers of language, only when savagery was over and the barbaric stage reached, when men talked freely and the Word grew potent, only then would the treatment of the remarkable stone grow at all uniform." Quite possibly, he argues, what Grant Allen suggests did occur, but "his unauthenticated evidence in the matter proves nothing but that. It barely proves that. It does not prove that all other possible interpretations did not also occur."[41] For Wells, as for Müller, language is a *sine qua non* of recoverable meaning.

Perhaps the most important aspect of the mythographers' disagreements so far as *The Time Machine* is concerned is their diametrically opposed views on the significance of language to man's place in nature. The whole question of what it meant to be human was a controversial issue throughout this period because it was inseparable from questions of descent. T. H. Huxley begins his lecture "On the Relations of Man to the Lower Animals" with the assertion that "The question of questions for mankind—the problem which underlies all others, and is more deeply interesting than any other—is the ascertainment of the place which Man occupies in nature and of his relations to the universe of things."[42] It is an issue, I would suggest, that is central to an interpretation of *The Time Machine*, and in particular to our assessment of the Time Traveller's judgments. There seems little doubt that Wells's lifelong convictions about language as a defining human characteristic were initially derived from Huxley, who maintained that although man "is, in substance and structure, one with the brutes," he is nonetheless distinguished from them because "he alone possesses the marvellous endowment of intelligible and rational speech."[43] In *The Time Machine*, however, the Time Traveller is faced with particular problems of definition—problems that were regarded as of fundamental importance by both schools of mythology. In *The Descent of Man* (1871), Darwin argued that articulate language arose out of the instinctive cries, especially "the musical tones and rhythm [...] used by our half-human ancestors, during the season of courtship."[44] This was the interjectionist theory of language origins, which, though by no means new, nonetheless carried considerable weight in its association with evolutionary theory.

The idea of language as an evolutionary product was, in general, accepted by the anthropologists, because it fit with their developmental approach.[45] Max Müller, on the other hand, emphatically rejected the idea that language could have evolved in this way, although he accepted Darwinian theory so far as human bodily attributes were concerned. Such emotional interjections exist in every language, he asserts, but they can never be any more than "the outskirts of real language. Language begins where interjections end."[46] Basing his argument on the symbolic, generalizing system of language, he asserts that language cannot be seen as part of the evolutionary process because it is the sole preserve of the rational animal—the human:

> Where then is the difference between brute and man? What is it that man can do, and of which we find no signs, no rudiments, in the whole brute world? I answer without hesitation: the one great barrier between the brute and man is *Language*. Man speaks, and no brute has ever uttered a word. Language is our Rubicon, and no brute will dare to cross it.[47]

The Time Traveller finds it difficult to come to terms with the idea of the Morlocks as his descendants and is both troubled and confused by his reactions to them. From his arrival he takes it for granted that the Eloi, for all their shortcomings, are human, but the Morlocks are at first seen, unequivocally, as animals—their footprints are "sloth-like," and his first view of them is as "ape-like figure[s]" (5, 46). Later, when he catches sight of them in the distance, they are categorized as "vermin" (6, 52), having "the half-bleached colour of worms" (6, 51), as "ant-like" (7, 60), and so on. In fact, the Time Traveller is horrified by the realization that "this bleached, obscene nocturnal Thing [...] was also heir to all the ages" (5, 47)—the reference to Tennyson's "Locksley Hall" introducing another level of irony.

It is, however, clear throughout his narrative that the Time Traveller likes to see himself as a civilized man, capable in his enforced role as an anthropologist and ethnographer of making objective, enlightened, and just decisions. He is only too aware of the unfairness of his widely different responses to the Morlocks and the Eloi but is nonetheless unable to counter the instinctive loathing he feels for the former, feelings he knows to be irrational. Significantly, his encounter with the Morlocks in the darkness of the well is described in sensory terms of touch and smell. But he is uneasily aware, too, that his reactions derive from what he has seen of them—their color, their shape—and are, in fact, based on appearances. The Morlocks *look* "nauseatingly inhuman," and he *senses* in them "a something inhuman and malign" (7, 57). Meanwhile, he acknowledges that "However great their intellectual degradation, the Eloi had kept too much of the human form not to claim my sympathy, and to make me perforce a sharer in their degradation and their Fear" (7, 63). If Max Müller's and T. H. Huxley's views are accepted, if language *is* the defining characteristic of human beings—and the Time Traveller is in no doubt that the Morlocks too have a language[48]—then the Time Traveller's attitude must be seen as irrational as well as immoral. It is clear that he realizes this. When he describes his preparation of a mace sufficient to crush any Morlock skull he might encounter, he tries to preempt an anticipated response from his listeners—also enlightened, educated, professional men of "this ripe prime of the human race" (7, 58). "And I longed very much to kill a Morlock or so," he acknowledges, but goes on, "Very inhuman, you may think, to want to go killing one's own descendants! But it was impossible, somehow, to feel any humanity in the things" (8, 67).

Anthropological mythographers considered themselves to be scientists with a detached and objective approach to primitive cultures, but Wells's glimpse of the future is presented through the eyes of an archetypal nineteenth-century figure of science, who has not only been shaped but also misled by the myths of his own culture. Admittedly, his complacent belief in progress—his initial assumption that he need not equip himself with a camera, for instance, because "the men of the Future would certainly be infinitely ahead of us in all their appliances" (6, 55)—is soon dispelled, but nonetheless he continues for a long time to overvalue his own rationality and detachment. What is more, he appears to have repressed, or at least to have lost touch with, his own basic emotions and instinctual reactions: "However helpless the little people in the presence of their mysterious Fear," he boasts, "I was differently constituted. I came out of this age of ours, this ripe prime of the human race, when Fear does not paralyse and mystery has lost its terrors" (7, 58). These passages are, of course, heavily ironic; in one sense they are a comment on the prevailing view that "Evolution was a prohuman force making things better and better for mankind," and in another they constitute an attack on the developmental assumptions of progressionist mythographers such as Tylor, who, in the final paragraph of *Primitive Culture*, presents the "science of culture" as "a reformer's science" that can help society in two ways, by promoting progress and removing hindrance:

> To impress men's minds with a doctrine of development, will lead them in all honour to their ancestors to continue the progressive work of past ages, to continue it the more vigorously because light has increased in the world, and where barbaric hordes groped blindly, cultured men can often move onward with a clear view. It is a harsher, and at times even painful, office of ethnography to expose the remains of crude old culture which have passed into harmful superstition, and mark these out for destruction.[49]

Tylor's aims seem particularly ironic when considered in relation to the future as revealed in *The Time Machine*. The way in which the Time Traveller's judgment is held up to question, and often undermined, in this section of the narrative is important for our reading of his further visions of the future.

Another way in which Victorian mythography is reflected in *The Time Machine* is in Wells's treatment of time. As the nineteenth century progressed, scientific discoveries in geology and paleontology obliged everyone to think about the nature and extent of time. In "Origins and Oblivion in Victorian Narrative," Gillian Beer maintains that writers in this period "were enforcedly made aware that life had been going on for millions of years before human memory existed: no memory of that state was possible; life and story did not require the human race," and her essay looks at the various ways in which Victorian writers coped with this disturbing notion.[50] In *The Time Machine*, I believe, Wells "coped" not only by employing scientific explanations of time—in the opening paragraphs, for instance, the Time Traveller draws on geometry, mechanics, and psychology when describing his invention—but also by drawing on mythology as a means of structuring his story around the two diametrically opposed ways of looking at time, which the geologist Stephen Jay Gould designates as "time's arrow" and "time's cycle."[51] In relation to this story, these two ways of looking at time can be categorized as linear (scientific/chronological/historical) time and cyclic (mythic) time. In *Time's Arrow, Time's Cycle*, Gould suggests that what he calls "deep time"—the vast, seemingly illimitable expanses of time uncovered by geological discoveries and presupposed by Darwinian theory—can be comprehended only in terms of such metaphors as arrows and cycles.[52] It is this dual vision of reality that, I believe, gives Wells's first scientific romance its peculiarly ambivalent quality.

At first glance, it seems self-evident that *The Time Machine* is plotted on linear time. The Time Traveller's journey into the future is a clear illustration of time's arrow. It could scarcely be more so, in fact, since it encompasses a sequence of events beginning in the narrative present, moving forward to the year 802,701, and eventually reaching what the Time Traveller assumes to be the final stage of the planet's life. Although Wells is at pains to convince the reader that the journey takes place only in time and not in space,[53] the Time Traveller's account of the sensations evoked by time travel—"There is a feeling exactly like that one has upon a switchback—of a helpless headlong motion!" (3, 18)—and of his own participation—"I flung myself into futurity"—together with phrases like "faster and faster still"; "I put on pace"; "still gaining velocity"—give the reader a sense of movement in space as well as in time (3, 19–20). It is as though the time machine is pursuing a trajectory across the sky, although a closer reading shows that it is the sun, moon, and stars that are hopping, leaping, twinkling, swaying, and so on.

Above all, the fact that the linear, scientifically based progression of events in *The Time Machine* seems to be leading toward universal extinction gives the reader a sense of powerlessness. What can be done to counter the inexorable advance of time's arrow toward the one inevitability of human life, death itself?[54] In a very obvious sense, then, it is undeniable that *The Time Machine* is, as Gillian Beer suggests, a response to the anxieties raised by solar physics. The story envisages a future where the working out of the second law of thermodynamics is shown in operation. Since the second law asserted that energy could never be saved because heat is one-directional in nature and cannot be conserved, the ultimate exhaustion of useful energy is unavoidable; the earth will get colder and colder and eventually will be unable to sustain any life-form. When the Time Traveller reaches the world of 802,701, this change is already in progress; paradoxically, he notes that the sun is markedly hotter, but this is explained in terms of the speculations of "the younger Darwin," that "the planets will ultimately fall back one by one into the parent body. As these catastrophes occur, the sun will blaze with renewed energy" (5, 46), and as he journeys further into the future, the Time Traveller sees the sun "grow larger and duller in the westward sky, and the life of the old earth ebb away." Eventually, only "the pale stars alone were visible. All else was rayless obscurity" (11, 83–85).

But, of course, Wells's scientific romance is not a scientific treatise but an imaginative narrative. The effect of time's arrow that I have outlined is itself achieved by literary means, and an analysis of narrative structure shows that neither the story (sequence of events) nor the discourse (text) of *The Time Machine* is linear.[55] In terms of story, the Time Traveller *returns*, after a few hours, to the

place he started from; in terms of discourse (because the Time Traveller's account of his journey is embedded within a framing story), the whole of the text
that describes his journey is, in Gérard Genette's terms, an anachrony (an external prolepsis because the events occur at a time in the future beyond the time
limits of the framing story). What is more, the narration returns to the first
(extradiegetic) narrator, and we discover for the first time that we are being told
of these events three years after they occurred, and it is, of course, possible, given
the open ending of the story, that the Time Traveller may yet return. The movement of the narrative, therefore, is not linear but circular or cyclic; the effect of
time's arrow in the narrative structure of *The Time Machine* is, in fact, a "sleight-
of-hand."[56]

Another cyclic effect in the text is achieved through the explicit use of myth.
In *Shadows of the Future*, Patrick Parrinder suggests that the implied timescale
of the Time Traveller's journey opens up "unimaginable and almost meaningless expanses of time, yet paradoxically *The Time Machine* renders a thirty million year future thinkable. That is the 'virtual reality' effect of the story's mythical, apocalyptic hold over the reader."[57] This mythical, apocalyptic hold is
achieved, I would suggest, by the coexistence of the two opposed notions of time
within the story. Within the apparently linear framework of this narrative—a sequential account of unique events—Wells introduces a number of devices that
give the reader a sense of time's cycle. His use of classical myth in *The Time Machine* has often been noted, but these mythical references have, I would suggest,
a more fundamental and important function than the universalizing and ironic
ones that have generally been ascribed to them. The references to the Golden
Age and to the sunset of mankind,[58] for instance, function in a variety of ways.
They create a picture of beauty and harmony that contrasts strikingly with the
Time Traveller's later discoveries, and they do, of course, remind the reader of
the ironic contrast between the paradisal period of happiness and nobility celebrated in the Golden Age of Greek myth and the decadent society of 802,701.
But also, when seen in conjunction with the Time Traveller's speculations that
mankind must once have attained a balanced civilization that had "long since
passed its zenith" (5, 50), the references to the Golden Age and the sunset of mankind produce an impression not just of change and contrast, but also of movement around different points of a circle, from a position leading up to what the
narrator in the epilogue calls "the manhood of the race" (E, 91)—the culminating
time when society achieved perfection—to a position that comes after it, a corre-
sponding point on the other side of the circle. A feature of time's cycle, Gould
maintains, is that time has no direction: "Fundamental states are immanent in

time, always present and never changing. Apparent motions are parts of repeating cycles, and differences of the past will be realities of the future."[59]

The parallels that have been drawn between the Traveller and Prometheus,[60] and his descent into the well, which is seen as an ironic parody of Odysseus's visit to Hades (or the associated Christian myth of the Harrowing of Hell), can be said to serve the same function. Perhaps the most prominent and most often analyzed mythical symbol in *The Time Machine* is the Sphinx, whose "white leprous face" (5, 34) is the first thing the Time Traveller sees when he arrives in 802,701 and the last thing he sees as he departs. Patrick Parrinder's claim that "The existence of a future Sphinx is a grotesque repetition implying that what is to come is (like the Sphinx's famous riddle, to which the answer is 'a man') no more and no less than what we already know"[61] encapsulates brilliantly the ways in which the Sphinx, too, contributes to the cyclic view of time.

To what extent, then, can *The Time Machine* be considered a solar myth? The story offers us a scientific view of the future, but it also presents an alternative. From a linear view of history, the sun represents a one-way path to extinction, the thermodynamic "heat death" of the earth, but from a cyclical view, the perspective of myth, it is the ultimate symbol of recurrence and rebirth. The earliest and most fundamental myths, as the solarists point out, are those related to the sun, and in *The Science of Language*, Müller insists that these patterns of recurrence in myth have not only shaped western culture but continue to influence our thinking:

> I look upon the sunrise and sunset, on the daily return of day and night, on the battle between light and darkness, on the whole solar drama in all its details that is acted every day, every month, every year, in heaven and in earth, as the principal subject of early mythology. I consider that the very idea of divine powers sprang from the wonderment with which the forefathers of the Aryan family stared at the bright (deva) powers that came and went no one knew whence or whither, that never failed, never faded, never died, and were called immortal, i.e. unfading, as compared with the feeble and decaying race of man. I consider the regular recurrence of phenomena an almost indispensable condition of their being raised, through the charms of mythological phraseology, to the rank of immortals.[62]

A cyclic view of culture and history was propounded by the eighteenth-century philosopher Giambattista Vico in *The New Science*. He argued that a historical progression governed both language and thought at different stages of cultural development, and that these different stages have their own values and perspectives. This leads him to the relativistic notion of history embodied in his famous principle "that the world of civil society has certainly been made by men, and that its principles are therefore to be found within the modifications of our own human mind."[63] It could be argued, then, that the interpretation the scientifically trained Time Traveller gives to his view of the future cannot but reflect the conceptual system of beliefs, values, and assumptions of the nineteenth century, which he has helped to construct and which has constructed him. Out of this comes his scientific materialism and his unquestioning acceptance of solar physics. But, as I have already suggested, our faith in the reliability of the Time Traveller's judgment has already been shaken—are we to take as final his interpretation of what he sees on his furthest journey into the future? From a cosmic mythical perspective, even the Time Traveller's further visions thirty million years hence, when "the sun had come to obscure nearly a tenth part of the darkling heavens" (11, 83), can be seen as part of this recurrent pattern of decline, death, and rebirth. Is the possible sign of life that the Time Traveller observes—"some black object flopping about" on a sandbank—a rock, as he supposes, or an ammonite (11, 84)? As Gould points out, "time's arrow is the intelligibility of distinct and irreversible events, while time's cycle is the intelligibility of timeless order and lawlike structure. We must have both."[64]

I am not suggesting that Wells himself intended such an interpretation—it seems highly unlikely that he did given what he himself has said about the scientific romances and the thinking that gave rise to them—and it is even less likely that he self-consciously set out, like Thomas Hardy, to conform to the requirements of solar mythology.[65] But as Umberto Eco points out, there is an "intention of the text," which may or may not be the intention of the author.[66] I would maintain, therefore, that the use of myth and mythography in *The Time Machine* contributes a subtext that offers the reader another way of reading, another vision of time, which leads us to question the validity of the Time Traveller's evidence and, ultimately, the truth of his interpretation. It is significant that the first narrator, who accepts the Time Traveller's journey in time, does *not* accept his reading of his experiences: "But to me the future is still black and blank—is a vast ignorance" (E, 91). Upon his return, the Time Traveller challenges his listeners: "No. I cannot expect you to believe it. Take it as a lie—or a prophecy. Say I dreamed it in the workshop. Consider I have been speculating upon the destinies of our race until I have hatched this fiction. Treat my assertion of its truth as a mere stroke of art to enhance its interest, And taking it as a story, what do you think of it?" (12, 87). The dual vision offered by the presence of both science *and* mythology in *The Time Machine* makes it most difficult for the reader to answer this question.

Notes

I would like to thank Dr. Amanda Hodgson, who is engaged in research on solar mythology and Victorian literature, for her help and advice.

1. Gillian Beer, "The Death of the Sun: Victorian Solar Physics and Solar Myth," in *The Sun is God: Painting, Literature and Mythology in the Nineteenth Century*, ed. J. B. Bullen (Oxford: Clarendon Press, 1989), p. 159.

2. V. S. Pritchett, *The Living Novel* (London: Arrow, 1960), p. 125.

3. Bernard Bergonzi, *The Early H. G. Wells: A Study of the Scientific Romances* (Manchester: Manchester University Press, 1961), pp. 61, 19.

4. H. G. Wells, preface to *The Scientific Romances of H. G. Wells* (London: Gollancz, 1933), p. ix.

5. Peter J. Bowler, *The Invention of Progress: The Victorians and the Past* (Oxford: Blackwell, 1989), p. 135.

6. H. G. Wells, "Zoological Retrogression," in *Early Writings in Science and Science Fiction by H. G. Wells*, ed. Robert Philmus and David Hughes (London: University of California Press, 1975), p. 168.

7. See James Kissane, "Victorian Mythology," *Victorian Studies* 6 (1962), 5–28.

8. See Robert Ackerman, *J. G. Frazer: His Life and Work* (Cambridge: Cambridge University Press, 1987), pp. 74–75.

9. Janet Burstein, "Victorian Mythography and the Progress of the Intellect," *Victorian Studies* 18 (1974–75), 309–24. Edward B. Tylor, *Primitive Culture: Researches into the Development of Mythology, Philosophy, Religion, Language, Art and Custom* (London: John Murray, 1871), 1: 275, writes, "this turning of mythology to account as a means of tracing the history of the laws of the human mind, is a branch of science scarcely discovered till the nineteenth century."

10. In 1898 Wells reviewed Grant Allen's *The Evolution of the Idea of God* and an anonymous book on the Cabal for the *Saturday Review*, and here he makes comparisons with Tylor's *Primitive Culture* (1871). See *Early Writings in Science and Science Fiction by H. G. Wells*, pp. 40–46. Wells has direct recourse to mythography in the opening chapters of *The Outline of History* (London: George Newnes, 1920), where he is discussing the beginnings of language and early cultural development. In chapter 9, "The Neanderthal Race," there is a reference to Andrew Lang, Sir John Lubbock, and J. J. Atkinson; in chapter 12, "Early Thought," he refers to the work of Sir J. G. Frazer, Grant Allen, E. B. Tylor, and A. E. Crawley in relation to the origins of religion; and in chapter 19, "Gods and Stars, Priests and Kings," there is a passage on Max Müller. From the frequency with which these names recur in Wells's writing (and the relative paucity of reference to more recent authors in anthropology and mythology) it seems clear that when he addressed this subject in his later work, Wells was drawing on his reading of the 1890s and 1900s.

11. Richard M. Dorson, *The British Folklorists: A History* (Chicago: University of Chicago Press, 1968), p. 160. See also Richard M. Dorson, "The Eclipse of Solar Mythol-

ogy," in *Myth: A Symposium,* ed. T. A. Sebeok (Bloomington: Indiana University Press, 1958), p. 52.

12. F. M. Müller, *The Science of Language: Founded on the Lectures Delivered at the Royal Institution in 1861 and 1863* (London: Longman, 1899).

13. Quoted by Janet Burstein in "Victorian Mythography and the Progress of the Intellect," p. 314.

14. See Dorson, "The Eclipse of Solar Mythology," p. 32.

15. [T. S. Baynes], review of three books by George W. Cox, *Edinburgh Review* 132 (1870), 330–63.

16. Gillian Beer, "Victorian Solar Physics and Solar Myth," p. 165.

17. Stephen Toulmin, *Metaphysical Belief: Three Essays* (London: SCMP, 1957), pp. 15, 78. Toulmin uses the term "myth" in this essay not in the sense of an untruth, but as a way of describing how scientific theories and terminology can be distorted if they are taken out of context and used to support conclusions of a kind to which, as scientific theories or terms, they have no relevance (pp. 15–25).

18. Quoted in J. A. V. Chapple, ed., *Science and Literature in the Nineteenth Century* (Basingstoke: Macmillan, 1986), p. 42.

19. Müller, *The Science of Language*, 1: vii–viii. A number of Müller's major works include the word "science" in their titles.

20. F. M. Müller, *Lectures on the Origin of Religion* (London: Longman, 1891), pp. 213–14. John Tyndall was a physicist who researched heat radiation and became professor at the Royal Institution in 1854.

21. See Bowler, *The Invention of Progress*, p. 195.

22. Müller, *The Science of Language*, 1: 10–11.

23. Müller, *The Science of Language*, 1: 450–56; 2: 525. Müller variously describes mythology as an "affection" or "disorder" of language, which may, he contends, "infect every part of the intellectual life of man." He also points to the dangers of what he calls modern mythology: "I include under that name all those cases in which language assumes an independent power, and reacts on the mind, instead of being, as it was intended to be, the mere realisation and outward embodiment of the mind" (2: 647). This definition is not only very close to Wittgenstein's later notion of the bewitchment of language, but also to Wells's insistence in *The Outline of History* that for early man, language had a dual aspect: "In speech he had woven a net to bind his race together, but also it was a net about his feet" I, 76).

24. Charles Darwin, *On the Origin of the Species by Means of Natural Selection* (London: Ward Lock, 1901), p. 375.

25. Tylor, *Primitive Culture*, 1: 284.

26. Andrew Lang, *Custom and Myth*, 2nd ed. (London: Longman, 1885), pp. 2–3.

27. Ibid., pp. 21–22, 24.

28. Bowler, *The Invention of Progress*, p. 39.

29. Dorson, *The British Folklorists: A History*.

30. Malcolm Crick, *Explorations in Language and Meaning: Towards a Semantic Anthropology* (London: Malory Press, 1976), p. 35.

31. Wells, *The Outline of History*, 1: 138.

32. Ibid., p. 138.

33. This was a problem for many nineteenth-century sciences. In *The Origin of Species*, p. 374, Darwin points to "the extreme imperfection of the record" in geological discovery: "The crust of the earth with its embedded remains must not be looked at as a well-filled museum, but a poor collection made at hazard and at rare intervals."

34. Lang, *Custom and Myth*, p. 25.

35. See Tylor, *Primitive Culture*, 1: 16.

36. See ibid., p. 58.

37. Müller, *The Science of Language*, 1: 8. In his description of the Eloi language, Wells demonstrates an advanced grasp of linguistic development for this period. See Edward Sapir, *Culture, Language and Personality* (Berkeley: University of California Press, 1966), p. 6. Writing in 1933, Sapir insisted that every language is perfect for the culture that produces it.

38. With the exception of Tylor, Victorian anthropologists showed little interest in language per se, but for Müller, language was the basis not only of myth but of human culture in general, and, indeed, of the mind itself. See Malcolm Crick, *Explorations in Language and Meaning*, p. 16: "For him, command of the language of another society was the *sine qua non* of real anthropological work."

39. For a long time, Müller refused to respond to the anthropologists' attacks on him on the grounds that no one ignorant of Sanskrit was entitled to express an opinion of his work. See Dorson, *British Folklorists*, p. 164n.

40. What is fascinating is the frequency with which nineteenth-century writers identify the evidence offered by physical traces of the past with that given in books. Darwin uses an identical metaphor in *The Origin of Species*, p. 242: "I look at the natural geological record, as a history of the world imperfectly kept and written in a changing dialect; of this history we possess the last volume alone, relating only to two or three countries. Of this volume, only here and there a short chapter has been preserved; and of each page, only here and there a few lines. Each word of the slowly-changing language, in which the history is supposed to be written, being more or less different in the interrupted succession of chapters, may represent the apparently abruptly changed forms of life, entombed in our consecutive, but widely separated, formations." H. G. Wells and Julian Huxley, in *Evolution—Fact and Theory* (London: Cassell, 1934), p. 11, describe the different layers of the earth's crust in the same terms: "These sheets of inert matter are the pages of the book of our planet's history. They lie scattered over the globe, often torn, defaced or crumpled. But patience and reason combined have been able to reconstruct whole chapters and sections of that great book."

41. H. G. Wells, "On Contemporary Theology," in *Early Writings in Science and Science Fiction*, p. 41.

42. T. H. Huxley, *Collected Essays* (London: Macmillan, 1894), 7: 77.

43. Ibid., p. 155. Wells asserts categorically in *Mankind in the Making* (London: Chapman & Hall, 1903), p. 121, that "With speech humanity begins."

44. See Chapple, *Science and Literature in the Nineteenth Century*, p. 132.

45. Tylor had reservations. In *Primitive Culture* he gives two lengthy chapters to an exhaustive consideration of the interjectionist theory and concludes that "Valid as this theory proves itself within limits" it accounts for only "a twentieth of the crude forms in any language. [. . .] A key must unlock more doors than this, to be taken as the master-key" (1: 229–30).

46. Müller, *The Science of Language*, 1: 507. In the preface to *The Science of Thought* (London: Longman, 1887), p. xi, Müller stresses that he is a Darwinian but adds that, although man is certainly an animal, "We share everything with animals except language, which is our own."

47. Ibid., 1: 489–90.

48. The Time Traveller tells us that when he first descended into the Morlocks' well, "I tried to call to them, but the language they had was apparently different from that of the Upper-world people" (6, 54).

49. Tylor, *Primitive Culture*, 1: 453.

50. Gillian Beer, "Origins and Oblivion in Victorian Narrative," *Arguing with the Past* (London: Routledge, 1989), p. 13.

51. Patrick Parrinder, in "From Rome to Richmond" (in this volume), suggests that *The Time Machine* is plotted on two different timescales, the evolutionary and the historiographical, but his argument is based on a different premise from the one I advance here.

52. Stephen J. Gould, *Time's Arrow, Time's Cycle: Myth and Metaphor in the Discovery of Geological Time* (Cambridge, Mass., and London: Harvard University Press, 1987), p. 10. Gould cites Freud's claim about the three blows to man's self-esteem and claims that the psychoanalyst omitted one of the greatest steps from his list: "He neglected the great temporal limitation imposed by geology upon human importance—the discovery of 'deep time.'[. . .] What could be more comforting, what more convenient for human domination than the traditional concept of a young earth, ruled by human will within days of its origin. How threatening, by contrast, the notion of an almost incomprehensible immensity, with human habitation restricted to a millimicrosecond at the end!" (pp. 1–2). This, of course, is related to Wells's avowed aims for *The Time Machine*.

53. The Time Traveller assures his guests on his return that his machine which "had started from the south-east corner of the laboratory" is now "in the north-west, against the wall where you saw it. That gives you the exact distance from my little lawn to the pedestal of the White Sphinx, into which the Morlocks had carried my machine" (12, 86).

54. Stephen Toulmin, "Contemporary Scientific Mythology," in *Metaphysical Beliefs*, p. 33, speculates that human ingenuity could come up with a solution: "If need be jet-propelling the orbit of the planet a little nearer the sun. There are countless things they

might do to falsify the prediction, many of them at the moment no more than Science Fiction, but none of them out of the question if you consider the amount of time at their disposal."

55. See Gérard Genette, *Narrative Discourse* (Ithaca, N.Y.: Cornell University Press, 1972). The duration aspect of time in *The Time Machine* presents particular difficulties for narratology because, as Parrinder points out in *Shadows of the Future* (Liverpool: Liverpool University Press, 1995), p. 36, the Time Traveller has aged only a few hours during his journey, which means that it must have taken place within a different time frame from the one he leaves and later reenters.

56. This is the phrase the Medical Man applies to the Time Traveller, whom he suspects of "Some sleight-of-hand trick or other" (1, 8).

57. Parrinder, *Shadows of the Future*, p. 40.

58. In the first, Heinemann, edition of *The Time Machine*, chapters 5 and 6 were entitled "In the Golden Age" and "The Sunset of Mankind."

59. Gould, *Time's Arrow, Time's Cycle*, p. 11.

60. The links between the Time Traveller and his matches and Prometheus the fire-bringer are particularly interesting. Zeus entrusted Prometheus with the creation of mankind and other animals, and the latter initially gave fire to man to make him superior to other animals—an ironic touch given the Time Traveller's response to the humanity of the Morlocks. It is ironic, too—since Prometheus means "forethought"—that the Time Traveller's gift of fire to a culture in which "the art of fire-making had been forgotten" (9, 71) results in so much destruction.

61. Parrinder, *Shadows of the Future*, p. 16.

62. Müller, *The Science of Language*, 2: 639–40.

63. Giambattista Vico, *The New Science*, trans. Thomas Goddard Bergin and Max Harold Fisch (Ithaca, N.Y.: Cornell University Press, 1948), p. 331.

64. See Gould, *Time's Arrow, Time's Cycle*, p. 16.

65. See John Paterson, *The Making of "The Return of the Native"* (Berkeley: University of California Press, 1960). Paterson provides evidence from the manuscript of *The Return of the Native* (1878) that Thomas Hardy set out to incorporate solar theory in his novel. Hardy originally named his hero "Hugh," with a surname beginning with "B." After four chapters, Hardy changed his mind and renamed the character "Clym Yeobright"—a significant change from the point of view of solar theory since Müller was adamant that the hero of any true solar myth must have a name deriving from a word etymologically related to the sun. (The Time Traveller's lack of a name would certainly have ruled him out.)

66. Umberto Eco, *The Limits of Interpretation* (Bloomington: Indiana University Press, 1990), p. 58.

The Time Machine
and Wells's Social Trajectory

JOHN HUNTINGTON

 As Lionel Stevenson observed almost thirty years ago, H. G. Wells "emerged from the lowest stratum of the middle class, which had previously produced only one major English novelist—Dickens."[1] Wells enthusiasts have tended not to make much of that exceptional origin, but we miss something of Wells's accomplishment if we slight the difficulties of his social trajectory. *The Time Machine* is an important book because it manages to voice Wells's social aspirations and his deep social angers, while still maintaining the decorum required for its author to become a successful writer. It is an intricate stylistic feat, not to be accomplished in a single try.

That the Time Traveller "hated to have servants waiting at dinner" (2, 15) is a clue to the complexity of class awareness behind *The Time Machine*. The comment is one of the remarkably few signs in this parable of class difference of an awareness in the present—that is, in the Time Traveller's 1895—of the powerful social distinctions that will become genetic in the next eight hundred millennia. The remark shows that even before he saw the future and the consequences of class oppression, the Time Traveller had a social conscience. Yet, though he feels some unhappiness about the master-servant relationship, the Time Traveller accepts the privileges of the master position. He salves his conscience by keeping the servants out of sight in certain public rituals, such as meals. Before we hastily condemn him as a hypocrite on this account, however, we need to remind ourselves that the delicate subtleties of class awareness and behavior in eras other than our own are very difficult to reconstruct and evaluate. People born into families with servants—and in 1895 this does not mean only the aristocracy but also people of quite modest economic standing—take servants for granted. Indeed, the Karl Marx family had a servant.[2]

I would suggest that at the end of the nineteenth century, unease with servants waiting at dinner is, in fact, not so much a sign of "conscience" as it is a sign of a person who has been in the servant class. Ann Kipps shares exactly the same sentiment, preferring a house that does not require servants at all.[3] The Time Traveller is working out a difficult negotiation with what Pierre Bourdieu would label his *habitus*; a transposable set of expectations and values that one internalizes early in life and which one brings to bear in new social and economic situations.[4] The Time Traveller's upbringing has conditioned him to rise in class, but he has difficulty behaving the way people born to the higher position do. And Wells himself, here in his first published novel, is working out a similar difficulty. The nervousness about how servants should be handled is Wells's as much as the Time Traveller's. The position of privilege, to which Wells very much aspires and ultimately receives due to the success of *The Time Traveller*, is also, thanks to his disadvantaged upbringing, an object of resentment.

For many years it has been commonplace to discuss Wells's hostility toward the working class.[5] The fear of, and antipathy toward, the Morlocks is taken as an expression of this class attitude. But we miss much of Wells's complexity and power if we simplify his attitudes into simple positives and negatives. His attitude toward the Morlocks as expressed in the text itself is a very complicated one, mixed, as I have suggested elsewhere, with sexual and sadistic feelings.[6] Now I want to pursue this question further by asking what "fear of the working class" might mean *socially*. I should note that arguments for Wells's class attitude often refer to the underground servants' quarters at Uppark. But underground is an emotionally double-valued icon: if it identifies a contemptible social inferiority, it also identifies a source of deep and righteous anger. Anthony West speaks of Wells's outrage at first seeing the underground quarters about which his mother had boasted:[7] such rage is evidence of sympathy rather than horror and fear. To settle Wells's attitude by quoting out of context Bernard Bergonzi's statement that he "disliked and feared the working class"[8] is to oversimplify and thereby distort a very intricate and conflicted social moment and to obscure an important aspect of *The Time Machine*'s success.

By turning class difference into species difference, Wells both foregrounds the fact of class separation, making *The Time Machine* one of the great statements of social outrage, and hides the way class actually operates. This contradiction runs through Wells's work and, I would suggest, defines one of the special qualities of his art. It is also a particularly difficult issue to deal with because Wells himself, even as he depicted class issues in his fiction, persistently sought to deny the importance of class as a meaningful analytical category. He repeatedly expressed irritation at Marx for basing his theories on class hostility.[9] We need to realize that Wells's denial of class is itself a social strategy and that at this point Wells himself cannot help us theoretically. In *Kipps*, Arthur Kipps's experience is generalizable: a person coming from low on the social scale, however wealthy he or she may become, can never be comfortable in anything but very modest circumstances. Wells knows from his own experience how class background (*habitus*) complicates success. Yet, if his success is to be rewarding and worth the effort, Wells cannot accept Kipps as his model. His denial of the reality of class may well be a way of assuring himself that it is possible to rise out of his class of origin. In this reading, *Kipps* is an exorcism of sorts, written when Wells himself was safely famous.

In 1894, when he is finishing *The Time Machine*, Wells is in the midst of an enormous social gamble. We should take very seriously his remark to Elizabeth Healey as *The Time Machine* was about to appear in the *New Review*: "It's my trump card and if it does not come off very much I shall know my place for the rest of my career."[10] To "know one's place" conventionally means to accept one's class position and to give up ambitions of rising in class. *The Time Machine* is, in fact, a gambit in Wells's strategy to escape his mother's class. As such, it can never ignore class even as it is careful never to be "vulgar" about class by mentioning it in a resentful way.

Vulgarity is itself a complex and interesting social judgment. It ingeniously turns plain speaking and a refusal to participate in the euphemisms that hide the violence of culture and by which a society rationalizes its structure and distinctions (Bourdieu terms these euphemisms "misrecognitions") into social gaffes.[11] Any analysis of social differences, insofar as it exposes misrecognitions that constitute the language and style with which the game of culture is played, will risk vulgarity. Vulgarity is a social crime not because it is false—quite the contrary!— but because those who employ it bluntly refuse to play the game. Yet the charge of vulgarity is more potent than the accusation of falsehood, and any aspiring writer will take great pains to avoid the charge.

By writing a popular story about class catastrophe, Wells is playing a risky and delicate game. Even as it tells an angry and vengeful parable of the consequences of class division, *The Time Machine* avoids appearing vulgar about class by ignoring—except for the very brief and casual mentions of servants—class division in the present. Paradoxically, by talking about class difference in terms of species, Wells obviates the most subtle dimension of the class issue: style, which would upset his audience and would cause him the most anxiety. The Morlocks may be lower class by their genealogy, but they are identified symbolically rather than realistically. They are creatures from a zoo, not people from a slum. One reason it takes the Time Traveller a while to realize the nature of the situation is that the Morlocks do not immediately suggest a class style. The Eloi, on the contrary, as others have frequently observed, are depicted somewhat more precisely in terms of fin-de-siècle aesthetic icons.[12] The elegant upper class aestheticism is a sign of the mocker's own superiority. If by making the Morlocks inhuman Wells evades the vulgarity of depicting lower-class style, by making the criticism of the Eloi stylistic he avoids the opposite vulgarity of seeming to resent upper-class privilege. *The Time Machine*, thus, may explicitly raise the issue of class division and oppression, but it sanitizes it with an allegory of sorts. It does not commit the vulgarity of showing the lower classes as they are. The actual servants are kept out of sight.

The class awareness that Wells is muffling in *The Time Machine* emerges more directly in *The Wheels of Chance* (1896), written and published the year after *The Time Machine*.[13] Where *The Time Machine* creates a symbolic parable along Darwinian lines and avoids the issues of class style and behavior, *The Wheels of Chance* uses comic realism to show how thoroughly class *style* shapes social relations. The novel's protagonist, Mr Hoopdriver, draper's assistant and cyclist, is clearly a version of Wells himself. The anxiety Hoopdriver represents is one that the success of *The Time Machine* has made acute for Wells: by the time one is an adult, has one's class background (*habitus*) become inescapable?

In *The Wheels of Chance* Wells uses comedy to depict issues of class differences and even to appreciate the disadvantaged point of view. Here he can flirt with an angry realism that would speak of class suffering but remain light. In the following paragraph from early in the novel, Wells threatens to cross the line into vulgarity, but in the end he defuses the threat:

> But real literature, as distinguished from anecdote, does not concern itself with superficial appearances alone. Literature is revelation. Modern literature is indecorous revelation. It is the duty of the earnest author to tell you what you would not have seen—even at the cost of some blushes. And the thing that you would not have seen about this young man, and the thing of the greatest moment to this story, the thing that must be told if the book is to be written, was—let us face it bravely—the Remarkable Condition of this Young Man's Legs.[14]

The teasing threat of vulgarity, of "indecorous revelation," is finally inconsequential. A second level of this joke occurs when it turns out that Hoopdriver's legs are battered not from labor or abuse, as we would expect an "earnest author" to tell us, but from incompetent bicycling. In mocking pretentious literary claims to insight into scandalous truth, the passage nevertheless plays on the reader's anxious awareness that—I will invoke the Bourdievian criterion—"distance from necessity" is what really matters, and Mr Hoopdriver, however distractingly foolish he is on a bicycle, has very little such distance.

This crucial social measure marks the great difference between Mr Hoopdriver and Jessie Milton, the heroine of the tale, and shapes their different and mutually incomprehensible styles. When Jessie complains about how her stepmother has thwarted her resolve to Live Her Own Life, "Mr Hoopdriver was puzzled, but admiring. It was wonderful how clear and ready her words were."[15] Hoopdriver admires Jessie's way of speaking, that is, her class style, but he cannot understand her point, for the very possibilities of middle-class life are baffling to this man who was apprenticed early, who, in his education, has been at the mercy of the firm and a few irrelevant extension courses,[16] and who, despite his pleasure in the escapade, is never free from having to calculate how his money will last[17] or from worrying that he is in possession of a stolen bicycle. One of the signs of Jessie Milton's secure social "place," her assured distance from necessity, is that she doesn't even think about these last matters until they are brought to her attention near the end. Living Her Own Life is not an economic issue.

For Wells, a man rising rapidly on the social scale (from draper's assistant and son of a servant to brilliant novelist who in two years will be commissioning his own house in Kent), the anxiety is that he will not be able to play the part his economic success has earned, that he will stylistically remain a servant even as he succeeds monetarily. In a society very precise about manners and style, such as that of Victorian England, *habitus* is bound to reveal itself in all kinds of situations and in ways that one cannot anticipate. Hoopdriver is terribly aware how hand movements, self-effacing locutions, and embarrassing practical quirks such as collecting straight-pins in his lapel betray his class background. The power of *habitus* is summed up in his nervous question, "Where would the draper break out next?"[18] Luckily for his disguise, Jessie is innocent and is easily convinced that he behaves strangely because he is a colonial, not because he is lower-class. Other, more worldly people, however, know from a single word, gesture, or even just a casual glimpse that they are dealing with what they slightingly call a "greasy proletarian."[19] For Wells, struggling heroically to make a "place," it is important to know how style is read socially. But while class can be a recurrent theme of his work, the difficulties and insecurities involved in it are a secret to be hidden. One can talk about the subject only in a style (usually comedy) that hides one's own involvement in the difficulty.

I recall these aspects of *The Wheels of Chance* to emphasize how aware Wells is of the dynamics of class difference and of how class shapes sensibility. The triumph of *The Time Machine* is that Wells raises the issue of class without being heard as a Mr Hoopdriver, a cockney upstart. Yet, if others did not see it, Wells himself, even as he hides class issues and camouflages himself as a member of the intellectual middle class, is aware of the class differences. Twenty years later, in his friendship-ending criticism of Henry James, the issue returns, and he faults James partly for leaving out politics and "opinions" but also for not writing about "poor people dominated by the imperatives of Saturday night and Monday morning."[20] Saturday night might suggest sexual debauch,[21] but Monday morning recalls the realities of work and money and, in short, distance from necessity. And as he criticizes James, he also mocks himself.[22] Boon himself (that is, Henry James), addressing Bliss (that is, Wells) imagines the ideal novelist for expressing the idea for The Mind of the Race: "Something of your [Wells's] deep moral earnestness, you know, only a little more presentable and not quite so vindictive," said Boon, "and without your—lapses."[23] (*Boon* 60). "Morally earnest," "unpresentable," "vindictive"?—this does not sound like a description of Wells's own writings; I suspect that in this ironic self-denigration we are hearing Wells's confession of what he fears he may sound like. Moral earnestness, as Bourdieu argues in *Distinction*, is commonly a quality of middle- and lower-class art which the dominant fraction, that fraction most removed from necessity, finds "tasteless." The "lapses" Boon hesitantly mentions are not moral (even in this kind of indirect allusion Wells does not discuss his sexual escapades) but stylistic. They represent that quality of vulgar impudence in Wells that would evolve into what Raymond Williams would later term his "bouncing cheeky finally rampant commercialism."[24]

In *Boon*, Wells mocks the posture of aesthetic art. Writing under the elegant name of "Reginald Bliss," he ironically complains, in a passage that is complementary to the mocking declaration that literature is "indecorous revelation" in *The Wheels of Chance*, that "literature" is a trivial discourse of the upper middle class: "Of course, one knows that real literature is something that has to do with leisure and cultivated people and books and shaded lamps and all that sort of thing."[25] The deeper irony is that this bourgeois world of shaded lamps transforms into one of the truly utopian visions that recurs in Wells's fiction. The Time Traveller's parlor is just such a utopian space, a comfortable setting for pure ideas. It is more than a stilted device for exposition; it is a vision of classless male society, a premonition of the society of the Samurai. It is no accident that this kind of vision recurs in *Boon* itself: much of the book recounts a series of conversations "as we sat in the rose-arbour smoking after lunch."[26] This platonic space, free from economic necessity or rivalry, though surrounded by evidence of economic security, is always a happy and stimulating one for Wells. Here one is not with the narrator of *Kipps*, squirming uncomfortably under those "Argus eyes of the social system" and those "innumerable mean judgments" on one's "clothes and bearing, upon [one's] pretensions and movements."[27] Here one is judged not by one's accent, clothing, or manner, one's ambitions or pleasures, but by one's ideas alone. It is a space that allows for a "pure" style.

The utopian space of the Time Traveller's parlor is balanced against the appalling divisions of the grim 802,701 pastoral. This stylistic economy, which involves matching generic styles and narrative oppositions, did not come quickly or easily to Wells. It is an important invention that evolves somewhat awkwardly through the different drafts of *The Time Machine*. In its evolution, we can see Wells the artist solving the problem of how to give voice to his strong class awareness without losing the gamble with fame by becoming vulgar.

A crucial change between Wells's first version of the novel, "The Chronic Argonauts," and *The Time Machine* is in the motive for time travel. Dr Nebogipfel, the Time Traveller in the very first version, is, by contrast, a mad, driven scientist of the Frankensteinian tradition.[28] Time travel is, for him, a desperate necessity. In the midst of his explanations of time, Dr Nebogipfel tells the Reverend Elijah Ulysses Cook the story of "The Ugly Duckling" in pointed detail:

> Even when I read that simple narrative for the first time, a thousand bitter experiences had begun the teaching of my isolation among the people of my birth—I knew the story was for me. The ugly duckling that proved to be a swan, that lived through all contempt and bitterness, to float at last sublime. [. . .] In short, Mr Cook, I discovered that I was one of those superior Cagots called a genius—a man born out of my time. [. . .][29]

The anachronistic man is analogous to the lower-class man who feels his "isolation among the people of [his] birth" and resolves to escape. The anguish we hear in this passage is, importantly, absent from the final version. The Time Traveller is in a utopian situation, and he invents time travel the way an author invents a story, as a display of ingenuity, as a paradox befitting a cultivated parlor. He is motivated by a pure intellectual drive, not the kind of ugly-duckling loneliness of which the Doctor complains. As Wells rewrites the story, the anguishing consequences of class division become distanced (in time and in urgency), and the true utopia of the tale becomes not some future world hospitable to genius but that 1895 parlor in which all men are economically indistinguishable and the only criterion of discrimination is intelligence.

In the *National Observer* version of *The Time Machine* we can see how nervous Wells is about bringing up class at all. It is significant that here, in his first rendering of the Eloi-Morlock split, he explicitly denies its class basis.[30]

> I do not mean any split between working people and rich—families drop and rise from toil to wealth continually—but between the sombre, mechanically industrious, arithmetical, inartistic type, the type of the Puritan and the American millionaire and the pleasure-loving, witty, and graceful type that gives us our clever artists, our actors and writers, some of our gentry, and many an elegant rogue.[31]

In this early version of *The Time Machine*, Wells even goes so far as to suggest that servitude may be a chosen condition, lamenting "the deep reasonless instincts that keep man the servant of his fellow man."[32] Only in the *New Review* version of *The Time Machine* does Wells come out and interpret the split between Eloi and Morlock as originating precisely and explicitly in class exploitation. Such change suggests not intellectual growth or confusion but social anxiety. The point is that Wells is both animated by class anger and unsure about his ability to "pass" as cultivated. The *National Observer* version is an attempt to deny the class anger that has created the fantasy. The great accomplishment of *The Time Machine* we are familiar with is its success in overcoming the inhibitions of the earlier version while maintaining the tone of objective neutrality. That neutrality is the great gamble of *The Time Machine*: Wells puts his success as a science writer, who speaks soberly in that special realm of technical discourse in which class is irrelevant,[33] to work in fiction, a discourse in which issues of class are inescapable. In terms of the traditions of literature, this strategy is the opposite of Poe, whose Dupin aspires to a literary place by emphasizing his extraordinary competence in the art of allusion (think of the importance of his familiarity with Crebillion). Wells, who is well-read in the English and French literary classics, works with a palette almost entirely devoid of explicit allusion. The exception, to be sure, is the White Sphinx. But the final obscurity of that allusion may paradoxically testify to the nonliterary nature of Wells's narrative.

Bernard Loing has described this style well: it is free from specific ideology, a prose that describes physical realities and immediate sensations.[34] What I want to emphasize is the way the style conceals Wells's deepest concerns while rendering a tale that speaks to them with a power and an anger that he himself will publicly deny. It is this style that prevents the descriptions of the Morlocks from being only an expression of hostility to proletarians, even as it prevents the descriptions of the Eloi from being simply a W. H. Hudson–like erotic fantasy. In its striking surface neutrality, so different from Poe's extravagance, this style allows Wells to sympathize with the generally repulsive Morlocks and to feel a profound lack of interest in the Eloi, a lack of interest that becomes contempt.

Despite the openness about class that Wells achieves in *The Time Machine*, there are still moments when he blurs what for a moment seem clear formulations. Bourdieu's "distance from necessity," his measure of economic rank and security, in a rather remarkable way echoes a concern that recurs a number of times late in *The Time Machine*. The Time Traveller explains that it is necessity, that grim grindstone, that keeps us keen. What is telling in the present context is that in his final theory of the *value* of "Mother Necessity" (10, 78), the Time Traveller opens the way to a critique of the dominant and leisure classes and then deflects it. No sooner has he suggested a class criticism than he shifts to apply it to the whole system, to all classes. "I understood now what all the beauty of the Upper-world people covered" (10, 78) might seem an insight into the dialectic of class domination whereby domination weakens the dominators and strengthens the dominated. But instead it turns into a critique of the complacency of the whole culture: "Once, life and property must have reached almost absolute safety. The rich had been assured of his wealth and comfort, the toiler assured of his life and work. No doubt in that perfect world there had been no unemployed problem, no social question left unsolved. And a great quiet had followed" (10, 78).

Despite what he says here, some part of Wells cannot believe this world of the secure rich and the permanently employed toiler is stable and "perfect." Imagine trying to convince Mr Hoopdriver, the draper's assistant yearning to impress Jessie Milton, that unemployment is the only "social question"! At another time the Time Traveller will begin to indulge in a specific criticism of the upper classes:

> Then I tried to preserve myself from the horror that was coming upon me, by regarding it as a rigorous punishment of human selfishness. Man had been content to live in ease and delight upon the labours of his fellow man [here the complacency of "the toiler assured of his life and work" is exploded], had taken Necessity as his watchword and excuse, and in the fulness of time Necessity had come home to him. I even tried a Carlyle-like scorn of this wretched aristocracy in decay. (7, 63)

But again, the class criticism is deflected, this time by sympathy:

> But this attitude of mind was impossible. However great their intellectual degradation, the Eloi had kept too much of the human form not to claim my sympathy, and to make me perforce a sharer in their degradation and their Fear. (7, 63)

In this shift away from class back to species, we see exactly Wells's own double consciousness as he aspires to become a successful writer. He is filled with anger at the inequalities that his mother accepted, but his ambitions are not revolutionary or anarchistic. Success as a writer means becoming a member of the dominant class he condemns, and it is important to his conception of success that the social structure, so offensive at one level, remain in place so that he can secure his "place" in it. The final version of *The Time Machine* and the invention of the Scientific Romance that followed from its success represent as much an accomplishment of "style" as James's masterpieces or the more eccentric modernist texts of a few decades later. In place of the Jamesian nuance so enjoyed by members of the dominant class who take education, leisure, and distance from necessity for granted, is a more risky artfulness, which puts into question the very bases of "civilization" while still struggling within that questioned world. Adorno's profound insight into the paradox of the cultural critic recognizes that commentators cannot usefully analyze and critique culture except from within culture itself.[35] With this paradoxical social dynamic in mind, we can read the stoic end of Wells's novel as about not just cosmic hope, but social ambition. The Time Traveller, we all remember, "thought but cheerlessly of the Advancement of Mankind, and saw in the growing pile of civilisation only a foolish heaping that must inevitably fall back upon and destroy its makers in the end" (E, 91). This "falling back" is not a description of decline but of the dialectic of domination. The narrator's famous response—"If that is so, it remains for us to live as though it were not so" (E, 91)—is then a statement of Wells's resolve to find a "place" in the "meanly conceived" world[36] that he hates: that is, it states his resolve to become a successful novelist despite all the complexities that such an ambition entails.

Notes

1. Lionel Stevenson, *The History of the English Novel,* Volume 11, *Yesterday and After* (New York: Barnes and Noble, 1967), p. 11.

2. The much beloved Helene ("Lenchen") Demuth. See Franz Mehring, *Karl Marx: The Story of His Life*, trans. Edward Fitzgerald (1935; reprint, New York: Humanities, 1962), p. 174.

3. H. G. Wells, *Kipps: The Story of a Simple Soul* (New York: Scribner's, 1924), p. 386.

4. To understand Wells's own social practice I propose to rely on some basic concepts of Pierre Bourdieu, who seems to me our most acute and important analyst of the sociology of culture. Three of Bourdieu's terms that I find particularly useful (in addition to the emphasis on *practice*) are: *habitus*, which accounts for how attitudes appropriate to the class of origin persist in new class situations; *distance from necessity*, a synonym in many cases for *wealth* but nuanced to allow for various kinds of wealth and various stances; and *misrecognition*, for Bourdieu the reason style has social importance, since the injustice of the social system could never seem so rational were it not that style transforms and disguises the material facts. *Misrecognition* is something like *ideology*, and it accounts for Wells's conscious and resolute rejection of class. These terms recur throughout Bourdieu's

work, but the central text for the present analysis is *Distinction: A Social Critique of the Judgment of Taste*, trans. Richard Nice (Cambridge: Harvard University Press, 1984).

5. Bernard Bergonzi, *The Early H. G. Wells* (Manchester: Manchester University Press, 1961), p. 56; Darko Suvin, *Metamorphoses of Science Fiction* (New Haven: Yale University Press, 1979), p. 240; Alex Eisenstein, "Very Early Wells: Origins of Some Major Physical Motifs in *The Time Machine* and *The War of the Worlds*," *Extrapolation* 13 (1972), 119–26.

6. See my *The Logic of Fantasy: H. G. Wells and Science Fiction* (New York: Columbia University Press, 1982), p. 44.

7. Anthony West, *H. G. Wells: Aspects of a Life* (New York: Random House, 1984), pp. 226–27. West's meditation on Uppark is complex and includes Wells's anger at his mother's acceptance of servitude and her willingness to commit Wells himself to such a life along with a more general critique of the serene injustice implicit in the architecture of the house.

8. Bergonzi, p. 56. Bergonzi remarks that Wells "had disliked and feared the working class in a way wholly appropriate to the son of a small tradesman." A sign of how such social dynamics can be misunderstood later is that in Harry Geduld's introduction to *The Definitive Time Machine*, this passage is twice misquoted and the fear and dislike are said to be "wholly *in*appropriate" (*The Definitive Time Machine*, ed. Harry M. Geduld [Bloomington: Indiana University Press, 1987], pp. 3, 21).

9. H. G. Wells, *Experiment in Autobiography* (New York: Macmillan, 1934), pp. 143, 207, 215, 626.

10. This letter is often quoted. See Bernard Loing, *H. G. Wells à l'oeuvre: Les débuts d'un écrivain 1894–1900* (Paris: Didier, 1984), pp. 416–17; Bergonzi, p. 40; Geduld, p. 7.

11. Bourdieu himself is very concerned with the problem of vulgarity. At the very beginning of *Distinction*, he addresses the way the accusation of vulgarity is commonly used to deny the importance of sociological insights. And he concludes *Distinction* with an essay entitled "A Vulgar Critique of Pure Critiques," in which he argues that philosophizing itself (his main examples are Kant and Derrida) is a social strategy.

12. Bergonzi, pp. 49–50.

13. It is important that this novel was conceived immediately after the success of *The Time Machine*. Loing suggests *The Wheels of Chance* was begun August 14, 1895 (the date mentioned by the narrator at the beginning of the story) and finished by the end of the year. It was serialized from May to September 1896 and published in book form by Dent in September (Loing, pp. 387, 389).

14. H. G. Wells, *The Wheels of Chance* (London: Dent, 1984), p. 5.

15. Ibid., p. 116.

16. "'Lizabethan Dramatists,' it was; but it seemed a little high-flown, you know" (Wells, *The Wheels of Chance*, p. 170).

17. "Clearly there was only one course open to a gentleman under the circumstances. 'In that case,' said Mr Hoopdriver, 'if you don't mind trusting yourself to a stranger, we might continue as we are perhaps—for a day or so; until you heard.' (Suppose thirty shil-

lings a day, that gives four days, say four thirties is hun' and twenty, six quid—well, three days, say; four ten.)" (Wells, *The Wheels of Chance*, p. 118).

18. Ibid., p. 162.

19. Ibid., p. 32.

20. [H. G. Wells], *Boon, The Mind of the Race, The Wild Asses of the Devil, and The Last Trump*, prepared for publication by Reginald Bliss (New York: Doran, 1915), p. 107.

21. See Janet Gabler-Hover, "H. G. Wells's and Henry James's Two Ladies," in *The Critical Response to H. G. Wells*, ed. William J. Scheick (Westport: Greenwood, 1995), pp. 145–64, for a fine discussion of the differences in sexuality that divided Wells and James. The class analysis I am proposing seems to me entirely complimentary to Gabler-Hover's sexual one.

22. It may be this self mockery that led him to think that James would not be devastated by *Boon*. It may also be that he could not resist sending the book to James because he knew that James would appreciate—in the sense of see—the stylistic accomplishment better than any other reader.

23. Wells, *Boon*, p. 60.

24. Raymond Williams, *The English Novel from Dickens to Lawrence* (London: Paladin, 1974), p. 105.

25. Wells, *Boon*, p. 171.

26. Ibid., p. 193.

27. Wells, *Kipps*, p. 397.

28. Bergonzi, p. 35, first noted the Frankensteinian aspects of Nebogipfel and the importance of the ugly duckling story.

29. Geduld, p. 148.

30. Here the year is 12,203, a good deal earlier than the final version's 802,701. Loing, p. 91, suggests that at this point Wells had not thought of the final interpretation and that is why the *National Observer* version is "slightly different" ("en des termes légèrement différents").

31. Geduld, *The Definitive Time Machine*, p. 171. Wells's socialism was never egalitarian. While in his social comedies he can show how class conditions sensibility, he is also attracted to a theory of psychological types (two here in the *National Observer* version of *The Time Machine*, four in *A Modern Utopia*), which will account for humanity's different motives and ambitions. In this early version of *The Time Machine*, the unequal distribution of wealth and toil does not seem to bother him. I would argue, however, that this vision is not entirely un-Bourdievian, since the future toiler, though less wealthy, is nevertheless secure—"life and property must have reached almost absolute safety"—and therefore, in Wells's vision, at an equal distance from necessity.

32. Ibid., p. 173. As the previously mentioned passage in Anthony West's *H. G. Wells: Aspects of a Life* makes clear, Wells's rebellious insight into his mother's pride in her office at Uppark may be responsible for this description of the dynamics of servitude.

33. Bourdieu argues (especially in Pierre Bourdieu and Jean-Claude Passeron's *Repro-*

duction in Education, Society, and Culture, trans. Richard Nice [London: Sage, 1990], pp. 107–38) that the scientific fields are the choice of lower class students because they do not depend on the preliminary education into subtleties of allusion and style that are available only to students from privileged educations and family backgrounds.

34. Loing, p. 55.

35. Theodor W. Adorno, "Cultural Criticism and Society," in *Prisms*, trans. Samuel and Sherry Weber (Letchworth: Neville Spearman, 1967), pp. 19–34.

36. The narrator's comment in *Kipps*: "Our world to-day is a meanly conceived one— it is only an added meanness to conceal that fact" (p. 397).

From Rome to Richmond

Wells, Universal History, and Prophetic Time

PATRICK PARRINDER

When H. G. Wells published his *Short History of the World* in 1922, some readers might have reflected that he had made his literary début twenty-seven years earlier as the author of an even shorter, yet much more comprehensive, essay in world history. The 1922 *Short History* ends by affirming that the story of the human past forms "but the prelude to the things that man has to do."[1] *The Time Machine* had concluded with the narrator's speculations about "man's culminating time," the high point of human civilization, which could only be found in one of the "nearer ages" (E, 91), all too quickly bypassed on the Time Traveller's journey to the end of the earth.

The Time Machine narrates a journey in prophetic time—that is, into an imagined real future, described by a traveller who claims to have directly participated in it—as opposed to a journey in metaphorical or hypothetical time. This means that future history is the continuation of past history in *The Time Machine*, just as it had been for the Christian historiography that Wells's post-Darwinian narratives set out to replace. Archbishop Ussher had set the Creation at 4004 B.C., and in 1779, as Wells would later record, a group of London booksellers had published the forty-two volume *Universal History*, which begins by discussing whether the precise date of the first day of Creation was March 21 or September 21, 4004 B.C.[2] The Last Judgment, too, would no doubt be precisely datable in due course. Wells's romance is like the pronouncements of Christian prophets and pseudoprophets in claiming to set a term to humanity's tenure of the Earth.

In *The Time Machine* we perceive that historical past and revealed future are connected both literally, as a consequence of time travel, and symbolically, as a result of the existence in the future of creatures who are our descendants and of monuments such as the White Sphinx and the Palace of Green Porcelain. The Sphinx—encountered by the Time Traveller in the first moments of his arrival in

the future—bears witness to the continuity of universal history, but it also suggests that the riddle of the future may be unanswerable or, perhaps, that the answer is too horrible to contemplate. The existence of the Palace of Green Porcelain, however, implies that the history of the future can be positively known and
that the Time Traveller's voyage of discovery has not been in vain.

Nineteenth-century travellers confronting a sphinx did not necessarily expect
to solve its mysteries. We shall never know exactly which items from the rich
literary and pictorial iconography of sphinxes may have influenced Wells; all we
can say is that the presence of a sphinx in *The Time Machine* would have been
unlikely had there not been so many contemporary and near-contemporary pre-
cedents for it. One passage that throws a little light on Wells's Sphinx, whether
or not Wells recollected it, occurs in Alexander Kinglake's vastly popular oriental travelogue, *Eothen* (1844). Kinglake visits the Great Sphinx of Egypt and observes that it "bears awful semblance of Deity—unchangefulness in the midst of
change." Starting with Herodotus, the first great historian, he recalls earlier travellers who had come under the Sphinx's gaze:

> And we, we shall die, and Islam will wither away, and the Englishman straining far
> over to hold his loved India will plant a firm foot on the banks of the Nile and sit in
> the seats of the Faithful, and still that sleepless rock will lie watching and watching
> the works of the busy new race, with those same sad earnest eyes, and the same
> tranquil mien everlasting. You dare not mock at the Sphynx.[3]

In fact, as Wells and his Time Traveller would have known, the Sphinx mocks
Kinglake and his imperialist agenda. In his petrified, trancelike state before the
White Sphinx, Wells's Traveller begins to realize that the future will be different
from anything the nineteenth century has yet known or imagined. This prophecy takes on substance as the story unfolds and as the Time Traveller's curiosity
necessarily takes him from the White Sphinx to the Palace of Green Porcelain.
Here, under one crumbling roof, is a confirmation that future history is not entirely alien to us. Before the age of the Eloi and Morlocks when history split into
two, there was a time, perhaps a very brief time, when—to parody the title of
Wells's later pamphlet on the need for a universal history—history was still one.[4]
For the Traveller, the great future museum is remarkably familiar territory, a kind
of millennial home from home.

But the Palace of Green Porcelain (like the White Sphinx) is also a quint-
essentially nineteenth-century symbol that plainly dates Wells's story. A novelist
of our own time, writing in the age of television, cinema, and the computer, would
hardly choose a great cavernous building full of faded objects in dusty glass cases

to represent a future civilization's idea of historical memory. In several ways, this ultimate imaginary museum speaks of humanity's failure to progress beyond the nineteenth-century level of civilization. It is a conscious or unconscious repetition of nineteenth-century museology and museum architecture, and its contents fail to disclose any qualitative advancement of technology beyond that of the age of steam. There are "huge bulks of big machines" (8, 66) made of corroded metal, one with a projecting lever "not unlike those in a signal-box" (8, 67); there are dummy dynamite cartridges and a model of a tin mine; and many of the exhibits are lit in the nineteenth-century manner by "white globes" hanging from the ceiling (8, 66) and displayed in the "old familiar glass cases of our own time" (8, 65). The Traveller does not recognize all the exhibits—he spends some time in the "academic examination of machinery" (8, 67), able to make only "the vaguest guesses at what they were for" (8, 66)—but one thing he clearly would have recognized, had there been one in the museum, is a model of his own primitive time machine. It seems that his invention has remained unique, and so has largely been in vain. Not only does the time machine stand outside the history of machinery as seen in the museum, but the Traveller, on his subsequent voyage, seems not to have imparted the secret of time travelling to his descendants. And none of this should surprise us, since a society that had time machines would no longer need museums.

The Palace of Green Porcelain has two local, late-nineteenth-century models: the Crystal Palace in Sydenham, and, more specifically, the group of museums on Exhibition Road, then collectively known as the South Kensington Museum. (This is why the Traveller describes the Palace as "some latter-day South Kensington" [8, 65].) Like many of the topographical details that contribute decisively to the vividness of Wells's narrative, the Palace first appears in the *New Review* text, the third serial version of *The Time Machine*. This version is also the first to locate the Time Traveller's home and the scene of his subsequent adventures in the southwest London suburb of Richmond. Moreover, it changes the date of the future world that the Traveller explores from A.D. 12,203 in the *National Observer* version to A.D. 802,701. Neither the topographical nor the chronological setting of the final text have been satisfactorily explained by previous commentators on the story.

Richmond is named in the opening paragraph of the *New Review* version in a very revealing sentence (this whole passage was later deleted, perhaps because it said rather too much about the story's ambitious young author): "Several ingenious and one or two profitable patents were his [the Time Traveller's] [. . .] very profitable they were, these last, as his handsome house at Richmond testified."[5] A "handsome house" at Richmond would probably be located either on or close to the riverfront or on the Hill. Wells's choice for the Time Traveller's house is presumably indicated by a discarded manuscript passage, apparently written in August 1894, which refers to his "house at Richmond Hill."[6] Until August of the previous year, Wells and his first wife had been living in a terrace house at 28 Haldon Road, Wandsworth, a much more plebeian address in southwest London close to the railway line to Richmond and to the start of the Upper Richmond Road. If Wells at this time ever dreamed of upward mobility, of a move to a more expensive and more salubrious neighborhood such as his doctors would certainly have recommended (and who can doubt that he did so dream?), Richmond must inevitably have beckoned. He and his wife must have made the odd excursion to Richmond Park and Kew Gardens—though to my knowledge the only evidence for this is in the landscapes of *The Time Machine*. There is, too, a more poetic reason for associating Richmond with affluence and wealth. The name itself can easily be understood as *riche monde* or rich world: a rich world such as the Time Traveller initially assumes he has found in the land of the Eloi. I now want to turn to the date of this new world, 802,701, before returning to the place of wealth and prosperity in the Wellsian vision of universal history.

The Time Machine is set not just in the future, but extraordinarily far in the future. In the *National Observer* version, the Philosophical Inventor gets no further than the year 12,203, and in "The Chronic Argonauts," the two explorers only reached the years 17,901–902—perhaps a more significant date. For to reach 17,901, the Argonauts have to traverse 16,000 years from the beginning of the twentieth century, 1901. In each version the point of arrival is at the beginning of a new century, but only in "The Chronic Argonauts" is the date of departure— 1887, or, strictly speaking, fourteen years before the turn of the twentieth century—specified.[7]

Since "The Chronic Argonauts" was written and published in 1887–88, the events as revealed to the outer narrator are set in a very recent but little-known past. The same kind of temporal setting is the rule in Jules Verne's science fiction. Dr Nebogipfel's secret scientific invention is thus, as Marie-Hélène Huet has argued, a kind of "missing link" connecting the past to the prophetic future time revealed in the story.[8] The fact that Nebogipfel's laboratory is located in a remote Welsh village is an obvious device to make the secrecy surrounding his invention more plausible. (We may recall that the events of *The Island of Doctor Moreau* take place on a mysterious Pacific island in the same year, 1887.) But in revising what was to become *The Time Machine*, Wells made a significant change. The Time Traveller was now a minor London celebrity, whose disappearance at least was no longer a secret. According to the *New Review* version, "The man who made the Time Machine—the man I shall call the Time Traveller—was well known in scientific circles a few years since, and the fact of his disappearance is also well known. He was a mathematician of peculiar subtlety, and one of our most conspicuous investigators in molecular physics."[9] The final version deletes this passage, adding a touch more ambiguity to the narrator's final statement: "The Time Traveller vanished three years ago. And, as everybody knows now, he has never returned" (12, 90).

Here the narrator's "everybody" could simply be confined to those who have read to the end of the story—but it seems advisable to treat that shade of meaning as a Wellsian joke at the narrator's expense, comparable to the *double entendre* in the full title of the first edition, *The Time Machine: An Invention.* In other words, the narrator's "now" belongs either to a fictitious alternative present, in which the Traveller's disappearance is already the subject of public speculation, or to a prophetic near future. Both possibilities remain open, though we should reflect that, if the story is being written down in what we might call an alternative 1895, then the future that it reveals must also be fictitious. What is missing from *The Time Machine* is the openly prophetic narrative rhetoric later exemplified in *The War of the Worlds*, where (in a story published in 1898) we are given, without benefit of a time machine, an eyewitness narrative of events occurring "early in the twentieth century."[10] It may be argued that in the earlier story, the presence of a time machine made it unnecessary to specify a near-future baseline for the narrative. Nevertheless, if we think of the date of the Time Traveller's invention as 1901 (so that the time of composition of the story is 1904), the numerology involved in his trip to the future becomes very much simpler and more elegant.

As we have already seen, 802,701 is the first year of a new century. Subtract 1901 from 802,701 and you have a time voyage of 800,800 years. This figure contrasts significantly with the 16,000 years or so (actually 16,014 years) of "The Chronic Argonauts," and it is also strangely reminiscent of Archbishop Ussher's dating the beginning of the world to 4004 B.C. Moreover, the number 800,800 splits neatly into two parts; and I believe that we can understand *The Time Machine* better by seeing both an "800,000-year" and an "800-year" timescale at work in it. The 800,000-year future turns out to correspond to the alien world overseen by the Sphinx, and the 800-year future to the more familiar world represented by the Palace of Green Porcelain. The world of the Eloi and Morlocks is then revealed as a brilliantly executed palimpsest, in which the two different timescales are superimposed.

The 800,000-year future is the timescale of biological evolution—a timescale to be understood in relation to contemporary estimates of the evolution of species by natural selection, of the age of the human species, and of the possible dates of the hypothetical "missing link" between humanity and the apes.[11] The Sphinx's association with biological evolution is confirmed when, looking up at the "crouching white shape," the Traveller instantly interprets both himself and the new world in bestial terms, as if a species difference is necessarily involved: "What if in this interval the race had lost its manliness, [. . .] I might seem some old-world savage animal, only the more dreadful and disgusting for our common likeness—a foul creature to be incontinently slain" (3, 22). But the need for his hero to travel through 800,000 years creates several difficulties for Wells. First of all, there is the difficulty of measuring such a journey, and the later journey of twenty-nine million years, on a time machine with dials calibrated, we are told, in "days, [. . .] thousands of days, [. . .] millions of days, and [. . .] thousands of millions" (11, 80).[12] Even though you can just about read off days and years on the same dial, the pointer of the smallest dial must have been under enormous physical strain from the speed with which it had to revolve, and the whole concept imposes considerable imaginative strain on the reader. In any case, the units of time measurement themselves are not constant. The Traveller reports that the terrestrial day eventually slowed down under the influence of "tidal drag" to the point where it "seemed to stretch through centuries" (11, 81), leaving us to wonder whether the dials can possibly measure time objectively, and how they can cope with its relativity.

A second difficulty is the sheer speed with which the machine is moving. To make the Traveller's experiences plausible, the average speed of his machine through time must have been around ten times the fastest speed that he actually mentions. During his first voyage, he speaks of travelling at over a year a minute— but at that rate it would take him nearly eighteen months to reach 802,701! Later, approaching the "Further Vision," apparently at full throttle, he tells us that "the thousands hand was sweeping round as fast as the seconds hand of a watch— into futurity" (11, 81). If one complete revolution of the thousands dial equaled a million days, he would then be travelling at a million days per minute, or roughly fifty years per second. But with this as his average speed, it would still take four and a half hours to reach 802,701 and about a week to reach the "Further Vision." It follows from this that a plausible average speed on each of his voyages would be closer to five hundred years per second, but this, too, stretches credulity. Wells must have been very determined indeed to force his Traveller to go so very far into the future.

But in other respects, our narrator does not seem to have travelled very far at all. During his first voyage, he sees the architecture of successive civilizations rising and falling, but this would take place much more quickly than the astronomical and climatic changes he also witnesses. Moreover, the ruined buildings of the age of the Eloi and Morlocks are, however implausibly, culturally continuous with our own civilization. The landscape is full of classical motifs: cupolas, obelisks, fauns, and griffins' heads, as well as the Sphinx, which—in the light of the existence of the Palace of Green Porcelain—could be seen as little more than an item in a sculpture garden or a dilapidated outdoor museum piece. The Eloi, clad in "[s]andals or buskins" (3, 23) and purple tunics, match this archaic ruined landscape. We have to conclude that if the 800,000-year timescale seemed necessary to allow for the degenerative biological development of the Eloi and Morlocks, the cultural and architectural transition from our world to theirs suggests, in some respects, a much shorter timescale, one of historical rather than biological time. Eight hundred years, providing as it were the total of 800,800 necessary for the resultant date of A.D. 802,701, would certainly suffice.

In terms of European history, a span of eight hundred years may take on a particular significance, since A.D. 800 was the date of the coronation of Charlemagne in St. Peter's, Rome.[13] Charlemagne was crowned by the Pope, who "hailed him Caesar and Augustus."[14] Since the Roman Empire had reached its zenith in the first century A.D., the interval of eight hundred years represents not only the time elapsing between two major civilizations, but the beginning of the decline of the later civilization. In the Holy Roman Empire, this took place under Charlemagne's successors, the Carlovingians, who are the subject of a puzzling and apparently gratuitous allusion on the Time Traveller's part: "The Eloi, like the Carlovingian kings, had decayed to a mere beautiful futility" (7, 58).[15] The Traveller's association of the Eloi with the Carlovingians is thus a further clue to the presence of a historical as well as a biological timescale in the story.

The two timescales come into conflict when the Traveller arrives at the Palace of Green Porcelain, a combined museum of human and natural history that clearly testifies to the historiographical understanding and taxonomic methods of the future civilization that now lies in ruins. The builders of the Palace must have been not merely scientists, but scientists working in the cognitive tradition of nineteenth-century positivism. Since he finds its logic and layout instantly comprehensible, the Time Traveller might expect to have some difficulty in convincing his hearers that the Palace (whenever it was built) still survives in 802,701. To anticipate their likely objections, he draws attention to the chronological incongruities of this episode by trying to explain the miraculous preservation of matches and camphor in the "familiar glass cases":

Now, I still think that for this box of matches to have escaped the wear of time for immemorial years was a most strange, as for me it was a most fortunate, thing. Yet, oddly enough, I found a far unlikelier substance, and that was camphor. [...] In the universal decay this volatile substance had chanced to survive, perhaps through many thousands of centuries. It reminded me of a sepia painting I had once seen done from the ink of a fossil Belemnite that must have perished and become fossilised millions of years ago. (8, 68–69)

This passage shows Wells's storytelling at its most audacious, reducing the chronological difficulties of his story to a kind of scientific "believe it or not" exercise. The analogy with the fossil Belemnite is ingenious but (needless to say) false. Camphor is a naturally volatile substance just as fossils are naturally stable. If the builders of the Palace of Green Porcelain had intervened to "fix" the camphor in its crystalline state, then it is extremely unlikely that the Traveller would have been able to set fire to it so easily. The matches, too, are the familiar contemporary safety matches (they need to be struck on the side of the box, as the Traveller later discovers), not the products of some hypothetical future stage of chemical engineering.

Wells's biological timescale broadly reverses the contemporary evolutionary model of human development. His historical timescale follows identifiable historiographical models without, in this case, needing to reverse them, since degeneration is already a recognized historical process.[16] Twenty-five years later, when he came to write *The Outline of History*, Wells identified a process of imitation-with-degeneration as a fundamental, and essentially retrograde, force in human history. Charlemagne's coronation as the new Caesar, he argued, had initiated eleven centuries of "imitation Caesars," which led the world inevitably to the bloody apocalypse of 1914–18:

> Europe drifted towards a dreary imitation and revival of the misconceived failures of the past. For eleven centuries from Charlemagne onwards, "Emperors" and "Caesars" of this line and that come and go in the history of Europe like fancies in a disordered mind. We shall have to tell of a great process of mental growth in Europe, of enlarged horizons and accumulating power, but it was a process that went on independently of, and in spite of, the political forms of the time, until at last it shattered those forms altogether.[17]

Should we see *The Time Machine* as foreshadowing the existence of a future high civilization that was itself decadent (or, we might now say, postmodern), with its imitation classical landscapes and imitation Sphinx? Wells's later image of two historical processes taking place independently of one another, until finally they come together in a shattering collision, is to some extent anticipated by the Time Traveller's hypotheses about the development of the Eloi and the Morlocks.

Wells the historian, as the above quotation shows, used the afterlife of the Roman Empire as one of his principal models for understanding European and world history. Throughout his life, Wells's historiographical imagination was profoundly influenced by a single work, Edward Gibbon's *Decline and Fall of the Roman Empire*, in which the afterlife of ancient Rome was traced as far as the Renaissance.[18] (To the extent that it identifies further "imitation Caesars," ending of course with Tsar Nicholas II and Kaiser Wilhelm, *The Outline of History* may be said to bring Gibbon's story down to the twentieth century.) In *The Time Machine*, the Traveller's reference to the Carlovingian kings may be an allusion to Gibbon, though this cannot be established with any certainty.[19]

Gibbon first conceived of *The Decline and Fall of the Roman Empire* when he saw the ruins of the Capitol in Rome and observed that the "largest portion of the seven hills [was] overspread with vineyards and ruins."[20] He charts the causes of the decay that leaves a rich and powerful civilization in ruins. To the extent that, like Wells's later universal histories, *The Time Machine* may be understood as a rewriting of Gibbon, it transfers the "most awful scene in the history of mankind" from Rome to Richmond.[21] The Eloi from this standpoint become the degenerate successors of the once wealthy Romans, while the Morlocks are resourceful and energetic Barbarians. To understand how such an apparently far-fetched analogy can hold, we need to take account of certain correspondences between Gibbonian historiography and nineteenth-century degeneration theory.

In his recent book, *Degeneration, Culture, and the Novel*, William Greenslade remarks on the similarities between Wells's vision in *The Time Machine* and E. Ray Lankester's *Degeneration: A Chapter in Darwinism* (1880). (Wells and Lankester later became friends, though not until some years after the publication of *The Time Machine*.) In Lankester's view of the laws of evolution, species are constantly threatened by degeneration. He cites anthropologists who regard certain primitive tribes as degenerate and linguists who use the degeneration hypothesis to explain the decay of languages (a point surely relevant to the Time Traveller's perception of the Eloi's language). Among the causes of degeneration are a reduction in size—the Eloi are a little people "perhaps four feet high" (3, 23)—and the ready availability of food.[22] For Lankester, indeed, the basic cause of degeneration is, quite simply, security and prosperity. Almost inevitably, he uses Ancient Rome as one of his examples:

> Any new set of conditions occurring to an animal which render its food and safety very easily attained, seem to lead as a rule to Degeneration; just as an active healthy man sometimes degenerates when he becomes suddenly possessed of a fortune; or as Rome degenerated when possessed of the riches of the ancient world.[23]

The degeneration of Rome is reduced here to little more than a late-Victorian commonplace—which to some extent is a reflection of the proverbial status of Gibbon's historical epic. *The Decline and Fall of the Roman Empire* begins in the second century A.D., the period of world history during which, Gibbon writes, the condition of the human race was at its happiest and most prosperous. The subsequent ruin of Rome and its empire was, however, "simple and obvious," the "natural and inevitable effect of immoderate greatness." Rome was destroyed by its own complacency, by the extinction of the "fire of genius" and the evaporation of the military spirit. "Prosperity ripened the principle of decay; the causes of destruction multiplied with the extent of conquest; and as soon as time or accident had removed the artificial supports, the stupendous fabric yielded to the pressure of its own weight."[24] The architectural metaphor here closely resembles one that the Time Traveller was accustomed to use, as we learn in the epilogue to *The Time Machine*: he "saw in the growing pile of civilisation only a foolish heaping that must inevitably fall back upon and destroy its makers in the end" (E, 91).

That Gibbon's reasoning anticipates *The Time Machine* in other respects will be seen from the following quotations from the Time Traveller's speculations about the fall of the Eloi:

> Strength is the outcome of need; security sets a premium on feebleness. [. . .] One triumph of a united humanity over Nature had followed another. [. . .] And the harvest was what I saw! (4, 31)

> the balanced civilisation that was at last attained must have long since passed its zenith, and was now far fallen into decay. The too-perfect security of the Upper-worlders had led them to a slow movement of degeneration, to a general dwindling in size, strength, and intelligence. (5, 50)

These passages, typical of what is (rightly) seen as Wells's Darwinian analysis of social and species degeneration, can also be aligned with an earlier historiographical view of the impermanence of the "rich worlds" of social power and prosperity. In this way, *The Time Machine* supplements its combination of biological and historical timescales with a compound of biological and historical reasoning.

In conclusion, Wells's rewriting of the *Decline and Fall of the Roman Empire* in *The Time Machine* gains extra salience from Gibbon's famously complacent analysis of the state of modern Europe, on which Wells would comment at length in *The Outline of History*. Gibbon's conclusion to the *Decline and Fall* affirmed that not only was modern Europe secure against barbarian invasions, but the gradual ascent of the human species would prove irreversible, and the wealth of the West would continue to increase.[25] This optimistic forecast (which was true enough, of course, in the short term) reverses the thrust of Gibbon's grand historical narrative, just as Darwin's rosy view of human prospects comes incongruously at the end of *The Origin of Species*. Wells, much more unambiguously in *The Time Machine* than in his later writings such as the 1922 *Short History*, draws from the *Decline and Fall* the bleak lesson that its author had refused to draw. In his greatest scientific romance, it is not the ruin of Rome but the ruin of Richmond, the "rich world" on the outskirts of London made possible by nineteenth-century industrialism, that spells the doom of humanity. The Time Traveller's invention, revealing prophetic time to us as the forward projection of universal history, is (as the narrator implies) a doubtful blessing. In the words of one of Wells's favorite poets summing up the "history of mankind" in a landscape of ruins, "Look on my works, ye mighty, and despair!"

Notes

1. H. G. Wells, *A Short History of the World*, in *The Works of H. G. Wells*, Atlantic Edition, vol. 27 (London: Unwin, 1927), p. 458.

2. H. G. Wells, *The Outline of History: Being a Plain History of Life and Mankind* (London: Cassell, 1920), p. 521.

3. A. W. Kinglake, *Eothen* (London: Nelson, n.d.), pp. 223–24.

4. H. G. Wells, "History Is One," in *The Works of H. G. Wells*, Atlantic Edition, vol. 27, pp. 1–16.

5. Harry M. Geduld, ed., *The Definitive Time Machine: A Critical Edition of H. G. Wells's Scientific Romance* (Bloomington and Indianapolis: Indiana University Press, 1987), p. 175.

6. Ms. Wells Collection, University of Illinois, reproduced in Bernard Loing, *H. G. Wells à l'oeuvre: Les débuts d'un écrivain 1894–1900* (Paris: Didier, 1984), p. 477. The dating of the manuscript is Loing's. I am grateful to John Hammond for drawing this to my attention.

7. This is a point unfortunately overlooked in the discussion of this question in my *Shadows of the Future: H. G. Wells, Science Fiction and Prophecy* (Liverpool: Liverpool University Press, 1995), p. 42.

8. Marie-Hélène Huet, "Anticipating the Past: The Time Riddle in Science Fiction," in *Storm Warnings: Science Fiction Confronts the Future*, ed. George E. Slusser, Colin Greenland, and Eric S. Rabkin (Carbondale and Edwardsville: Southern Illinois University Press, 1987), pp. 38–41.

9. Geduld, *The Definitive Time Machine*, p. 175.

10. H. G. Wells, *The War of the Worlds* (London: Heinemann, 1898), p. 2.

11. In *The Outline of History*, Wells was to date the earliest human ancestor, the subhuman *pithecanthropus erectus*, at around 600,000 B.C. The dating of the Paleolithic has been greatly extended, and has become much more precise, since the advent of radiocarbon analysis. Very recent discoveries suggest that the prehistory of humanity stretches over four million years or more. (Wells, *The Outline of History*, p. 28.)

12. In Stephen Baxter's "sequel" to *The Time Machine*, *The Time Ships*, (London: HarperCollins, 1995), p. 18, this difficulty is dealt with by allowing the Traveller to perform prodigies of mental arithmetic. He even remembers to allow for leap years.

13. I am grateful to Edward James for drawing my attention to this point.

14. Wells, *The Outline of History*, p. 346.

15. The reading in the first (Heinemann) edition is "Carlovignan"; this was corrected to "Carlovingian" in later editions.

16. Wells's modeling of the future is drawn to some extent from Morris and other nineteenth-century utopian and socialist writers, though none of these, I think, looks as far forward as the twenty-eighth century.

17. Wells, *The Outline of History*, p. 344.

18. See Parrinder, *Shadows of the Future*, pp. 65–79.

19. The reference to the Carlovingian kings may equally, of course, be linked to some proverbial or as yet undiscovered nineteenth-century source. Charles Darwin's family claimed to be descendants of the Carlovingian kings.

20. Edward Gibbon, *The Decline and Fall of the Roman Empire*, ed. Dero A. Saunders (London: Penguin, 1985), p. 689.

21. Ibid., p. 690.

22. E. Ray Lankester, *Degeneration: A Chapter in Darwinism* (London: Macmillan, 1880), pp. 50–51.

23. Ibid., p. 33

24. Gibbon, *Decline and Fall of the Roman Empire*, pp. 81, 107, 621.

25. Ibid., p. 628.

Change in the City

The Time Traveller's London and the "Baseless Fabric" of His Vision

CARLO PAGETTI

The English fin de siècle was, like so many epochs of transition, a time of loss of historical memories, in which the past and its values (tradition, continuity, familiar roots) tended to become a blurred, distorted Babel of events impinging on the present and heralding the future. The triumph of Darwinian thought and positivism implicitly looked forward to the future as a potentially much more relevant area of human interest and commitment. In 1893, in a review of the *Sketches of Modern London from Life* first published in 1834 by the German author Otto von Rosenburg, S. Baring-Gould acknowledged how difficult it was for the common reader to hold a clear remembrance of the past: "We hardly realise the changes that take place under our eyes, the revolution in social life, unless we go back to old books or diaries that belong to the period when we began to look out in the world."[1]

Four years later, another article in the same popular monthly, *Cassell's Family Magazine*, expressed a very similar sense of urban metamorphosis, involving not only the ordinary people, but the main civic authorities in London: "And it is with difficulty that the Lord Mayor of 1837 would recognize his City could he see it now. Even for such a short distance as from Charing Cross to the Cathedral of St. Paul the changes are so great that barely anything save Wren's churches would remind him of the street he knew."[2]

London was indeed a strange place, the abode of terrifying creatures of the night, such as those who haunted the pages of Bram Stoker's *Dracula* and Arthur Machen's *The Great God Pan*. The popular lower-middle-class magazines (whose sales burgeoned in the 1890s), though theoretically bound to a more benevolent, "advanced" view of the present times, made a contribution to the decadent sensibility. With the introduction of new printing techniques—photographs superseded illustrations during the 1890s—and the exploitation of an improved circulating network, they helped their readers explore the marvelous but alarming wonderland of the imperial metropolis, so large as to be compared to an entire continent. This potentially dangerous journey could, after all, be accomplished by the simple act of reading. In the same way, the Wellsian Time Traveller's skeptical but intrigued audience had only to listen to the incredible tale of their (g)host in order to see the future. More unknown than the far-off regions conquered by British Imperialism, fin de siècle London—a "wildest Africa," in the words of that militant crusader, General William Booth, who suggested compulsory emigration from its corrupted body—is a map to be redefined and reshaped not by detached *flâneurs* visiting the intricate maze of its streets, but by daring explorers moving in space-time.

General William Booth had built his *In Darkest England and the Way Out*, published by the Salvation Army in October 1890 and republished four times in 1890–91, on the worldwide fame of Henry Morton Stanley's *Through the Dark Continent* (1878) in order to suggest an "African parallel" involving the very heart of the British Empire, London: "While brooding over the awful presentation of life as it exists in the vast African forest, it seemed to me only too vivid a picture of many parts of our own land."[3] In retrospect, some of the sketches of African life depicted by Stanley and exploited by Booth seem to imply an intriguing racial duality not totally different from the Eloi-Morlock pattern of the future in *The Time Machine*. One wonders whether Wells might have taken into account the description of the "two kinds" of pygmies, which had struck Booth as symbolic of the London scene:

> one a very degraded specimen with ferretlike eyes, close-set nose, more nearly approaching the baboon than was supposed to be possible, but very human [*the Morlocks?*]; the other very handsome, with frank open innocent features, very prepossessing. They are quick and intelligent, capable of deep affection and gratitude, showing remarkable industry and patience [*the Eloi*].[4]

General Booth's book, offering a utopian scheme based on the widespread emigration of the urban working classes and the foundation of new colonies, was rudely attacked by an eminent personality well-known to Wells, Professor T. H. Huxley, and the resulting quarrel, raging in the pages of newspapers and magazines, constituted one of the main cultural debates of the early 1890s at a time when the boundaries between utopian romances and utopian "rational" planning were easily blurred.[5]

The utopian romance seemed to suggest both the need for a powerful dream of coherence and harmony in the reborn London of the future (William Morris's

News from Nowhere [1891]) and the awareness of the transient nature of the urban experience itself (Richard Jefferies's *After London* [1885] and W. H. Hudson's *A Crystal Age* [1887]). Although in *The Time Machine* Wells basically adheres to the latter point of view, he holds a more dynamic attitude in his early scientific romances, namely the idea that *change* is the great theme of contemporary life and literature. This change, at the very heart of the domestic household, at the center of the urban organism, can occur under the eyes of anyone who cares to open them wide in the expectation not of a leap toward a longed-for ideal epoch of the past (after all, both Jefferies and Morris superimposed their personal interpretations of the Middle Ages on their texts), but toward "the dim elusive world that raced and fluctuated before my eyes! I saw great and splendid architecture rising about me, more massive than any buildings of our own time, and yet, as it seemed, built of glimmer and mist" (3, 20).

One of the great achievements of Wells's first scientific romance is that it denies the static frame of nineteenth-century utopian fiction, where the vision of the future is clarified through a double perspective. If the narrators are usually truthful though highly emotional eyewitnesses, they are allowed to compare their experiences with the explanations of another character, an inhabitant of the future world endowed with firsthand knowledge of its social and historical background. For the Time Traveller things are different: "It may be as wrong an explanation as mortal wit could invent. It is how the thing shaped itself to me, and as that I give it to you" (10, 79). If, instead of the cryptic *thing*, we utter a familiar name—Lord Jim, for instance—we realize that the same technique would soon be developed by Joseph Conrad through his creation of Marlow, the narrator-traveller who is also a character involved in the plot: "He existed for me, and after all it is only through me that he exists for you."[6] In *The Time Machine* the Wellsian Traveller challenges his own interpretation of the future in a sort of revisionist attitude that makes his audience even more skeptical. He asks his respectable guests to believe in the reality of time travel and his subjective impressions, not in the correctness of his ideological positions.

The relativity of time, the unending operation of change and transmutation—this is the one solid truth emerging from the tale of the Wellsian hero, although he pretends to visit worlds without change. When he tries to have a second chance in order to capture the objective, physical features of the future, rather comically he equips himself with "a small camera" and a "knapsack," posing as a pedantic tourist or, maybe, as an overzealous, trendy journalist of the 1890s, eager to declare to his most sympathetic listener, the first narrator, that "If you'll stop for lunch I'll prove you this time travelling up to the hilt, specimens and all" (12, 89).

In the meantime, his guest can wait and spend *his* time reading "some magazines." Thus, the Time Traveller disappears for good, like an awkward magician; maybe he stops for lunch himself, "not where he eats"—Prince Hamlet would say—"but where a' is eaten." We do not see his future any longer, we do not see his strange vehicle, nor do we see him except as a "phantasm," a voice—again reminiscent of Conrad's darkly romantic adventurers—to be interpreted exactly as that voice had tried to interpret the unsubstantial pageant of a millennial London. The best comment comes from the first narrator: "The story was so fantastic and incredible, the telling so credible and sober" (12, 89), a good definition of science fiction itself and of its fictional devices. After all, the Time Traveller melts into thin air as a ghost or one of the ghostlike characters of his tale. The future world has the ambiguous quality of the island in Shakespeare's *Tempest*, revisited through a popular decadent imagination and ready to materialize for a second time as the hideous laboratory of a certain Doctor Moreau.

The dream of an earthly Paradise inhabited by graceful Ariel-like creatures is conjured up, only to be destroyed by a horde of grotesque Calibans reclaiming their inheritance. In this sense the Time Traveller is a Prospero of the Darwinian age, and his wand is the lever of his machine, giving birth to a not-so-marvelous brave new world, where he adopts Weena as an incestuous Miranda, a daughter-wife, deprived of memory and desire. His self-styled "occidental" resourcefulness, his intellectual superiority based on Darwin, Carlyle, Marx, and other masters of nineteenth-century thought, and his heroic stand against the creatures of darkness, are the bones he throws at an audience well-fed with imperial pride and daring deeds. He makes a valiant attempt at self-dramatization, concealing his failure as a scientist to decipher the London of the Eloi and the Morlocks, or, for that matter, all the other Londons he visits: his role is more that of a succulent piece of flesh than a Victorian *savant*.

The Time Traveller does not fully understand his own visions. The "human" future he explores lacks any satisfactory means of verbal communication. The Eloi's speech is so simple that the reader is reminded of the description of the childish prattle of very primitive people—the Fuegians, the Australian aborigines—as reported by Victorian anthropologists. The Morlocks "[whisper] odd sounds to each other" (6, 56), or this is the way in which the Time Traveller perceives their voices, submerged by the "throb and hum of machinery" underground (6, 54). In the forest, near the Palace of Green Porcelain, "The wood behind seemed full of the stir and murmur of a great company!" (9, 73). Inside the White Sphinx, the Time Traveller hears the Morlocks' "murmuring laughter," mirroring the inner feelings of the Wellsian hero himself, who had suppressed "a strong inclination to laugh" (10, 79–80) after realizing their plans. In any case, laughter is indeed the one emotional reaction the two races of the future share with the Time Traveller and with his skeptical audience, represented in this case by Filby, who "contented himself with laughter" (1, 7).

But this universal emotion will not suffice to interpret the future history of humankind, whose written languages confound the Time Traveller: some of the inscriptions he discovers are destroyed, while the books in the library of the Palace of Green Porcelain are totally ruined. No future *Sketches of Modern London from Life* are available. The one surviving text is the Time Traveller's own tale of failure and inadequacy. He does not manage to save his beloved Weena, he is unable to take her back to an improbable Victorian respectability, and he possesses no material proof of his journey except for two strange flowers accidentally left in his pocket. Above all, he fails to utter the words of consciousness thanks to which, at the end of *The Tempest*, Prospero accepts Caliban as his own historical responsibility—"this thing of darkness / I acknowledge mine" (V.1.278–299). We can believe his sincerity when he heaps insults on the Morlocks: apelike creatures, gray creatures of half-light, ghosts, human spiders, rats, lemurs. . . . But such a negative attitude implies the fearful recognition of a deep similarity, the one—to recall another source of *The Time Machine*—inexorably connecting Gulliver to the hateful Yahoos in Swift's *Gulliver's Travels*. Nevertheless, a quaint and rather racist observation pushes the Time Traveller a step closer to a kind of hidden truth:

> Conceive the tale of London which a negro, fresh from Central Africa, would take to his tribe! What would he know of railway companies, of social movements, of telephone and telegraph wires, of the Parcels Delivery Company, and postal orders and the like? Yet we, at least, should be willing enough to explain these things to him! And even of what he knew, how much could he make his untravelled friend either apprehend or believe? Then, think how narrow the gap between a negro and a white man of our own times, and how wide the interval between myself and these of the Golden Age! (5, 41)

The brutal comparison between the sophisticated British scientist and an African savage implicates the audience as well, whose readers *see* through the eye of a civilized Yahoo, or maybe a renegade Morlock, identifying with the Eloi. And it works also from another point of view, because the strange tale is really about London, the hyperactive London of the popular press, of the penny novels and of *In Darkest England*, the London of a new style of barbarians, to whom journalists and magazine editors were addressing their writings.

Two of the guests listening to the Time Traveller look like migrants from the pages of George Gissing's *New Grub Street* (1891). They are, of course, the Journalist and the Editor "of a well-known daily paper" (2, 13). The first narrator treats them a bit ironically: "They were both the new kind of journalist—very joyous, irreverent young men" (2, 15). The Journalist makes a joke about "Our Special Correspondent in the Day after To-morrow," and the Editor suggests the most effective headlines: "Remarkable Behaviour of an Eminent Scientist" (2, 15). The Editor is the one who urgently requires a story from the hungry Time Traveller, although in the end he is quite disappointed: "What a pity it is you're not a writer of stories!" (12, 87), a statement meaning either that the Time Traveller should stick to mere fiction without any pretension to truth, or that he is a failure as a storyteller. The Editor and his journalists would pride themselves on publishing better and more believable stories of change in the city. What they would find unacceptable is a chronicle of a real London dissolving into nothingness and chaos.

In the popular magazines of the 1890s, London achieves new visual dimensions as its multifaceted map is observed from the air or explored underground. In an 1891 article entitled "London from Aloft," the description of a spectacular trip over London in a balloon belonging to Mr. Percival Spencer, a well-known aeronaut, stresses the overwhelming silence of the atmosphere:

> There is nothing—absolutely nothing—for minutes altogether. One talks in order to make some sound and put an end to the odd feeling of soundlessness and the voice makes the surrounding stillness the more intense, [. . .] a picture which neither camera nor pen may do justice to, for London is all below, lying away for miles in every direction. From Richmond to the docks, from the Crystal Palace to the Northern hills, the eye may sweep by the mere turn of the head; and still we rise and rise.[7]

The balloon moves above the clouds, toward the Essex countryside, where the frame of the huge metropolis disappears altogether with an effect of spatial—but also temporal—alienation.

Seen from the skies, London is still a dense spot, a great web of buildings clustered on the earth, but on its surface, the urban reporter experiences different and distant regions, sometimes endowed with a hellish Morlock-like bleakness. This is illustrated, for instance, in an 1894 article, "How London Gets Its Gas: A Visit to North Woolwich." In a desolate area, on the border of eastern London, "the ground is frequently black and heaps of strange-coloured dirt and slag lie about, while busy little engines, drawing long trains of coal and coke, are hurry-

ing hither and thither in all directions—even overhead, on an iron-built railway."
And yet such an infernal landscape is on the verge of a new magical metamorphosis, as the careful narrator reveals to his readers: "I suppose gas will soon go
out before electricity."[8]

The urban organism is so delicate and perishable that the power of fire seems
to hover over its fragile texture. The only continuity between past and present is
paradoxically marked by the occasional eruption of devouring flames, as in the
great fire of Cotton's Wharf in June 1861, vividly recollected by Sidney Greenwood in the *Strand Magazine*: "From the bridge was to be seen a spectacle rarely
to be witnessed: the river appeared turned to blood, the neighbouring houses
and churches lit up as if at a great pyrotechnic display."[9]

What is even more fascinating for the fin de siècle journalists and their readers
is the realization that the underworld is teeming with activity, because down there
any energy source required by the hungry city is conveyed through a complex
system of pipes and wires. The construction of the subway lines adds a new dimension to this literal netherworld. In 1890, for the *Cassell's Family Magazine*
reporter Henry Frith, going underground is not only potentially dangerous (as
he discovers when made nearly deaf by the workings of the machine injecting
compressed air into the subway tunnel) but also requires a kind of social degradation: "Certainly a tall hat, town clothes, an umbrella and a parcel of books were
not the best things with which to descend into a railway subway." At the end of
his adventure, with his nose bleeding pitifully, Frith emerges "into the higher
road—half deaf, very muddy," an urban savage longing for daylight and the security of his social class.[10]

Eight years later, in 1898, a *Strand* reporter eulogizes the clean soil of London, fertilized by industry and technology, where thousands of law-abiding citi-
zens descend to catch the subway trains that had been running since the beginning of the decade. All is well down there, and there is no danger whatsoever.
But there is another underground, full of "noxious fumes," waiting to be discovered by the *Strand* reporter. When they go there, he and the Superintendent of
Waters have to put on heavy clothes like the skins worn by prehistoric cavemen:
"Curiously looking objects we were when fully dressed." They let themselves
down "the shaft" by employing "a primitive sort of ladder," and reach the crude,
carefully concealed organic matter of the sewers, a netherworld of filth and sti-
fling air, which the Superintendent tries to describe as a decent place, whose smell
"is no worse than that you often encounter in the open street." He could indeed
be right. In the meantime, the reporter-traveller glances at a mysterious shadow
lurking in the gloom, experiences the fear of utter darkness, and has the unpleas-

ant—although maybe mistaken—feeling that "though never a rat made his appearance when, with candles lit, we stood on the look-out, they simply came out in shoals and rioted about our feet when we were journeying slowly and painfully in the dark."[11] In order to celebrate the Descent into Hell, a photograph is aptly reproduced in the pages of the *Strand* with the following caption: "Group of Commissioners and Author, in the Old Fleet Sewer." Or, rather, we could say, "Group of overdressed Morlocks, pretending to be Time Travellers."

Obviously, no camera can give the idea of a world of change, or of the coming future. Only a magical instrument created by an oriental wizard—a last reincarnation of Prospero—could reveal something of the doom awaiting civilized fin de siècle humankind. This is what happens in "The Tragedies of a Camera," a whimsical little *Strand* story of 1898 illustrated by naively distorted and grotesque photographs. An "amateur photographer," armed with this exotic machine, walks through London and captures the images of children, cyclists, roads, magnificent buildings: the "cloud-capped towers, the gorgeous palaces, the solemn temples," compared by Prospero with the ephemeral spirits summoned by his wand. When the amateur photographer develops the plates, he realizes that each image is utterly deformed, because "the camera fiend was no respecter of sex or age." The same thing happens with such well-known places as the General Post Office: "that dreadful fiend crumpled up those stately columns as if they were so many pieces of wire, and slit open the massive Grecian arch of that noble pile in a gaping yawn"; New Oxford Street: "The ponderous piles were heaped up in one long mass of common ruin, flanked by a row of falling chimneys and shivering window-panes"; and the Imperial Institute: "that noble embodiment of Britain's wide domain, that glorious testimony of her high destiny, was struck down by celestial fire, in the photograph, of course." Even "that ark of British Liberty—the Houses of Parliament" is not spared. The anguished artist of the camera is tormented by an atrocious question: "What if this camera fiend was no fiend at all, but a sudden convulsion of Nature or a gradual subsidence of the earth? This, indeed, was the day of desolation." When the magical or scientific explanations are no longer sufficient, the Book of Revelation is introduced in the story and the readers witness a sort of mock Apocalypse:

> Azrael has come from the East, and from a gap in the clouds blows a trumpet-blast against the pedestal of Nelson's statue, and hurls down this noble hero from his high eminence. The wave of destruction passes swiftly from east to west, and even now shakes the stout pillars of the National Gallery—then on and on to its relentless destiny. The stricken people below sway hither and thither under the surging wave in drunken fear, ere they lie crushed beneath the falling ruins. Above the scene

of desolation, the veil of the sky is rent asunder and is falling to the earth. Verily, the world in ashes lies in waste.

A popular product of the scientific age, the camera, has brought more chaos to the most powerful of cities than an army of Wells's Martians. No need to worry, however, because the trick is disclosed at the end of the story and the audience assured that it was simply a clever hoax:

> Gentle reader, we have played long upon your feelings. Dry your tears and weep no more. Shut the floodgates of your eyes. The British Empire yet stands where it ever stood. The "total destruction of London" has yet to be encompassed. It *may* be, after all, that the mystic camera was no prophet, but merely that something went wrong with the plates.[12]

Such a cheerful declaration is possibly what would have pleased the Editor at the end of the Time Traveller's story and what could make his tale acceptable to the fin de siècle reading public and their leaders. But the Time Traveller wants us to acknowledge the literal/literary truth of his experience and plans to take photographs as proof. He is bound to vanish, torn between a faith in his progressive age and the dark forebodings of his vision.

The "fascination of the primitive" was a common attitude of the late-Victorian period, and it was related both to the "inferior" races of the African wilderness and to the "lower classes" of the urban underworld. The ambiguity of such a fascination will help us understand the Time Traveller's moral and psychological reaction to the Morlocks. George Gissing, Wells's friend and a writer whom he appreciated, had expressed such a powerful ambivalence in *The Nether World*, completed in 1888 and published in 1889. In this naturalistic novel of urban destitution and descent into a Darwinian Hell, Gissing's impersonal narrator, apparently unconcerned with the suffering and the brutality of his debased creatures, nevertheless follows them to the Crystal Palace, described as "the Paliss—the great ugly building," during the August Bank Holiday.[13] There he becomes a bitter, but also clearly fascinated, eyewitness. This would-be "scientific" observer mingles with the crowd, to whom he belongs; he is clearly excited by the bestial behavior of his men and women and, on the way home at the end of the long day, becomes one of them, with a sort of physical, even sexual, euphoria:

> A rush, a tumble, curses, blows, laughter, screams of pain—and we are in a carriage [—] off we go! It is a long third-class coach, and already five or six musical instruments have struck up. We smoke and sing at the same time; we quarrel and make

love—the latter in somewhat primitive fashion; we roll about with the rolling of the train; we nod into hoggish sleep.[14]

The same kind of recognition binds the Time Traveller to the Morlocks. He is no ancestor of the gentle, ineffectual Eloi. Instead, he is a man of scientific training and practical actions, addicted to machinery as the Morlocks are, who buries himself at home in his laboratory as the Morlocks squat in their dark and secluded place, and he comes back from his journey "starving for a bit of meat" (2, 14). "Save me some of that mutton," he cries, and then, "Where's my mutton?" (2, 14–16)—which, as Peter Kemp has pointed out,[15] sounds a bit funny for someone horrified by the sight of a "red Joint" in the obscurity of another dining room. We are reminded of the appearance of Caliban in the first act of *The Tempest* and of his straightforward statement, "I must eat my dinner." The Time Traveller can also understand the Morlocks' curiosity about his mechanical invention and the working of their apparently clever minds when they try to trap him inside the White Sphinx, maybe in hopes of being taught by him how to start the time machine, so that they—instead of Weena—might be able to travel to the middle-class house in Richmond where everything begins and ends. If you'll stop to lunch I'll come back with one of those pallid creatures. You could even like the vermin, gentle reader, *mon semblable, mon frère.*

Wells's archetypal hero—a fin de siècle Prospero contaminated by Morlockian instincts—is both a creator and a destroyer. He does create the time machine and the beautiful, frightening, bitter tale that the time machine spins out of the abyss from another dimension, but he cannot rid himself of his aggressive nature. In fact, he is immediately aroused by the loss of his precious property, which he is unwilling to share with anybody, especially with another, uglier self. Living in a Lilliputian world (he is the biggest and strongest individual), he despises the Eloi and hates the Morlocks. He sadistically likes kicking the brutes, crushing their skulls, burning their bodies. His violence does not spare the Palace of Green Porcelain, where he unsuccessfully experiments with dynamite, and later on he manages to set the virgin forest on fire. He brings havoc and destruction into the stagnant world of the future. As the interpreter of that process of degeneration he foresees in the year 802,701, he is, in a sense, a perfect hero of the 1890s, a popular character embodying the sense of alienation of his own age, unaware that he is himself a vital force in its impending decay. He dreams of being one of the Eloi, or rather, the patriarchal master of the Eloi, and is akin to the Morlocks he refuses to accept as sons and brothers. What he learns is that the throbbing heart of the future city lies in the shafts, in the darkened rooms, and in the pits where the Morlocks live as the preservers of the last remnants of human knowledge. Rather than a heart, however, we should speak about the bowels of the earth, where we can detect "the system of subterranean ventilation," the unmentionable "sanitary apparatus" (5, 41) not so much of the Eloi, but of reality as a whole—the *anus mundi*.

The underground tunnels are not only the missing clue in explaining the degenerative processes destroying rational humankind, but also the umbilical cord stretching between the experience in and out of present-day London and the ever-changing future of our inheritors. The Time Traveller has to descend into this bottomless hole in order to *illuminate* the connections between his scientific vision and the subterranean race of his own creation. There he is forced to look for his technological apparatus and to fight with Calibans for a piece of knowledge that makes them human brothers, builders of machines. The cruel irony of the false Eden the Time Traveller visits does not lie in the unavoidable defeat of the Eloi, but in the Morlocks' reversion to bestiality; not in the Time Traveller's inability to save the Eloi from their destiny as "fatted cattle," but in his inability to communicate with the Morlocks. A patient "schoolmaster amidst children" (4, 27) in his dealings with the lovely race of the Eloi, he becomes a ruthless enemy to the Morlocks. Outside and inside realities clash and collapse into the nightmare of a Darwinian struggle for survival, while the "Golden Age" has to be perceived by the fin de siècle explorer in terms of radical oppositions, racial conflicts, and cultural fragmentation.

Such an ambiguity of perspectives is reflected in the deceptive polarity enacted by the closed place of the Time Traveller's house at Richmond, which is basically reduced to three rooms—the dining room, the smoking room, and the laboratory—visited by the indifferent and anonymous male bourgeois guests, as greedy as the Morlocks and as chatty as a bunch of Eloi, and by the invisible landscape of a historical suburban area. London is everywhere and nowhere. When we see it through the eyes of the Time Traveller, the scenery embraces the Thames Valley, with its overgrown vegetation, the great decaying buildings and monuments, and the expanded estuary of the river, a liquid extension reverting to the primeval sea of the later episodes of the book. In one case, we have the seemingly comfortable present—a room without a view—in the other, the open visionary future, or, rather, a "cosmic age" linking *The Time Machine* to the tradition of Victorian utopian novels, where the triumph of mighty cities, the cradle of industry and empire, has been wiped out by a new Universal Flood, the great event of pre-Darwinian geology. But, of course, we have no replica of Jefferies' *After London*. The Eloi are not warlike knights, nor are the Morlocks wild nomadic tribes dwelling in the Great Forest. One of the most remarkable aspects of *The Time Machine* is the complete lack of any preindustrial fantasy of redemption.

If the Thames Valley, with its wealth of wood and waters, reminds the reader of an antediluvian scene, it is also the stage where the popular imagination of the fin de siècle located the inevitable doom awaiting civilization not in the far future, but in the present, as a consequence of the gigantic forces unleashed by technological progress in the daily life of the metropolis: electric power, underground tunneling, gasworks, dams, and so on. "Wells's *The Time Machine*," as Patrick Parrinder has pinpointed, "portrays the end of civilization, and the imminent end of all life on earth, in a Thames Valley setting radiating out from the site of the Time Traveller's former house at Richmond."[16] Two years after publication of *The Time Machine*, Grant Allen, in his story "The Thames Valley Catastrophe," imagined a "barrier of red-hot lava," a "sea of molten gold" swallowing villages and towns, and moving inexorably towards London: "As yet it did not occur to me that the catastrophe was anything more than a local flood. My imagination could hardly conceive that London itself was threatened. In those days one could not grasp the idea of the destruction of London."[17]

What we have in *The Time Machine* is the perception of an everlasting change happening both outside and inside the mind of an individual character, the Wellsian Traveller. We see him shifting in time in search of a dramatic role, displaced and yet doomed to remain in the same place, now and forever London, the misshapen focus of his visions. Leaving aside the easy irony of editors, journalists, and amateur photographers juggling with the public credulity, we can only pity the Traveller who is destined to see the Valley of the Thames transformed into a Valley of Shadows. We may, too, acknowledge as our own his reaction when confronted with Weena's tears: "They were the only tears, except my own, I ever saw in the Golden Age." (5, 51)

Notes

1. S. Baring-Gould, "London Sixty Years Ago," *Cassell's Family Magazine* 19 (1892–93), 758.

2. Theodore A. Cook, "After Sixty Years," *Cassell's Family Magazine* 24 (1897), 291.

3. William Booth, *In Darkest England and the Way Out* [1890] (London: Charles Knight, 1970), p.11.

4. Ibid., p. 11. The sense of urban displacement and bewilderment is a distinctive mark of Victorian fiction from Gaskell and Dickens to Gissing and George Moore. It also plays

a very effective role in Herman Melville's *Redburn* (1849), where the young American sailor discovers that the guidebook of Liverpool, inherited from his dead father, is utterly useless in the architectural chaos of the waterfront and the surrounding slums.

5. On 30 January 1891 Huxley wrote to Hooker: "I trust I have done with Booth & Co, at last. What an ass a man is to try to prevent his fellow-creatures from being humbugged! Surely I am old enough to know better. I have not been so well abused for an age. It's quite like old times." (Quoted in T. H. Huxley, *Life and Letters*, ed. Leonard Huxley, [London: Macmillan, 1903], 3: 180.) Among the "abusers" of Huxley, we can number the anonymous reviewer (that is, Alexander Allardyce) of *In Darkest England*, in "The Problem of the Slums," *Blackwood's Magazine* 149 (January 1891), 123–36.

6. *Lord Jim*, chapter 21.

7. "London from Aloft," *Strand Magazine* 2 (1891), 679.

8. F. M. Holmes, "How London Gets Its Gas: A Visit to North Woolwich," *Cassell's Family Magazine* 20 (1893–94), 488.

9. Sidney Greenwood, "Great London Fires," *Strand Magazine* 6 (1893), 488.

10. Henry Frith, "In an Air-Lock: An Underground Experience," *Cassell's Family Magazine* 16 (1889–90), 159.

11. "Underground London," *Strand Magazine* 16 (1898), 146–47.

12. "The Tragedies of a Camera," *Strand Magazine* 16 (1898), 545–52.

13. George Gissing, *The Nether World* (London: Dent, 1973), chapter 12, "To Saturnalia."

14. Ibid., p. 112.

15. Peter Kemp, *H. G. Wells and the Culminating Ape: Biological Themes and Imaginative Obsessions* (London: Macmillan, 1982), pp. 14–15.

16. Patrick Parrinder, "From Mary Shelley to *The War of the Worlds*: The Thames Valley Catastrophe," in *Anticipations*, ed. David Seed (Liverpool: Liverpool University Press, 1995), p. 58.

17. Grant Allen, "The Thames Valley Catastrophe," *Strand Magazine* 14 (1897), 493.

PART 3

The Rewriting

The Time Machine in the
Twentieth Century and Beyond

Time at the End of Its Tether

H. G. Wells and the Subversion of Master Narrative

LARRY W. CALDWELL

Centenary celebrations inevitably seem to suggest an equation of "century" with "epoch," and thus to confer upon scholars an attendant privilege of deriving from chronological construct some ideological cogency. The arbitrariness of such an exercise would no doubt have amused H. G. Wells, given the final irrelevance of both chronology and ideology in his earliest, most celebrated, and now centenarian novel, *The Time Machine*. For though Wells the historian could apprehend, as well as deploy, the imposed epochal structurations of, say, geology, biology, and sociology, Wells the romancer and student of narratives remorselessly interrogated epochal logic, and with it the self-congratulatory subtexts of linear causation and progressive developmentalism. Indeed, despite Wells's frequent relegation, by authors as diverse as Forster, Woolf, and Orwell, to the slag heap of Victorian smugness,[1] the elemental contradiction at the heart of his work has always been his intuition that epochal logic and narratology—depictions of progress and depictions of storytelling—are incongruent. As a consequence, his reliance upon progressive evolution for a narrative strategy in such works as *The Outline of History*, *The Science of Life*, and *The Work, Wealth and Happiness of Mankind*—and hence his apparent advocacy of the preeminent master narratives of Victorian science—is antagonized by the instability and overt experimentalism of his fiction.

Of course, modern scholarship on narrative aesthetics seldom treats Wells even as a minor contributor, preferring instead the more formal manifestoes of Wells's mentor, Henry James, and of the latter's modernist heirs. Yet it was quite specifically against these that Wells—often with great clarity and force—exalted the protean potentialities of the English novel: the art of fiction was "anarchic," not to be contorted by the predictable programs and forms of psychological realism or the interiorized "lucubrations" of a Virginia Woolf.[2] Rather than straining against dignity to grasp a pea,[3] fiction must "grapple with ideas new and difficult [...] for the reader," must sometimes caricature rather than characterize, must in any case concern itself with more than adherence to inherited formulae or magisterial conceptions of "the Novel as an art form": must, in short, confront its own conservatism, its rootedness in "social fixity." By contrast, both Jamesian realism and modernist experimentation simply *missed the point*, consigning to the titillation of Bloomsbury snobs narrative projects, which in their precise scrutinizing of individual motivation and constraint, of discourse and memory, ought to have interrogated and unsettled the bourgeois order forever—and failed utterly to do so.[4]

Mark Schorer's thorough misreading of *Tono-Bungay* in 1948 is the literary-critical manifestation of that same failure. Arguing that Wells's rejection of "technique" obstructs his "discovery" of meaning, Schorer calumniates *Tono-Bungay* as a mere collage of Dickens, Shaw, Conrad, and Verne. Its final vision reflects not the authoritative point of view or singularity of insight that meticulous scrutiny of perspective and attention to technique are presumed to produce, but a "rhapsody" of the future altogether at odds with "everything [Wells] meant to represent." The author's obligation, Schorer insists, is through rigorous formalism—the precise "manipulation" of subject and medium—actually to *tell* readers "what he meant." Wells's conscious "flight" from the aestheticism of James and the modernists into "journalism" signals, therefore, his "disappear[ance ...] into the annals of an era," a lapse from art into "social history."[5]

Schorer's tendentiousness here—his assertion that in repudiating rigorous technical skill Wells simultaneously failed to tell us what he meant and failed to mean what Schorer always *thought* he meant—discloses a kind of dogmatism in the modernist aesthetic.[6] For in his preoccupation with technique, Schorer finally refuses to *apprehend* meaning. Arguing that the protagonist George Ponderevo's discovery of his life's purpose in "science, [...] power and knowledge," and the emblematizing of that purpose in the naval destroyer "x2," "defeats" Wells's critique of "social waste" throughout *Tono-Bungay*, Schorer contends that the "Jules Verne" rhapsody at the end is a mere "hypothesis," a "nihilistic vision." He concludes, "As far as one can tell, Wells intends no irony, although he may have come upon the major irony in modern history."[7]

Schorer's compulsion to ignore his own insight, to subordinate attentive reading to established critical theory, obliges him to suppress the textual illumination he comes so near to achieving in his evaluation of *Tono-Bungay*: "As far as one can tell, Wells *intends* no irony," but has only by accident, as it were, "*come upon* the major irony in modern history" (my emphasis). Such a reading occludes not only the simple fact that Wells, in deploying his "technique" (however modest), has, by "discovering" the ironies of the destroyer, "x2," satisfied Schorer's principal aesthetic criterion; it ignores as well the degree to which the relentless mechanisms of futurity embodied in that destroyer prefigure the ideological tensions of modernism itself.[8] It is far from clear, indeed, that Wells "intends no irony," and any scrutiny of the closing chapter of *Tono-Bungay* must account for, rather than dismiss, the distressful nature of its vision(s), the dissonance of its tone(s). George Ponderevo aboard his ship, slicing through the "oily waters" of the North Sea, discovers in movement, in velocity, in the throb of engines a remorseless alien logic that exhibits no interest whatever in the problem of "social waste," which has preoccupied him throughout the novel.[9] For embedded in the machine is the assertion that "science, power, and knowledge," like their analogue aesthetic technique, may seduce as readily as they compel.

Wells's narrative signature is here unmistakable. In closing *Tono-Bungay,* he attempts to commingle irreconcilable narrative compulsions: the inherited realist compulsion toward authoritative closure and the organic fusion of moral with narrative voice; and the modernist compulsion to interrogate the implicit order of that fusion, juxtaposing it with technical experimentation and the search for new forms. The external, "scientific" narrative and the subjective interiority of George Ponderevo's ponderings are thus displayed as antagonistic, and both forms are interrogated without any presumption of disclosing "truth" or creating a novel order. Indeed, each is denuded as a "master narrative" with attendant ideological freight: Ponderevo's musings, for all their summative structure, extract no "answer," no conclusion from the almost purely sensual representation of science, power, and knowledge; both are "hypothetical," just as Schorer perceives but does not grasp; and Wells abandons his readers in precisely the timeless, non-narrative space where he had left them fourteen years earlier at the end of *The Time Machine.*[10]

Wells's critical affiliation, therefore, is with the *post*-modern.[11] His radical skepticism about narrative reflects that of his near-contemporary Nietzsche and anticipates stances taken, for example, by writers like Barthes, Derrida, and Foucault. And while it is probable that he would have had even less patience with their theoretical lucubrations than he had with those of James or the Bloomsbury set, his intellectual allegiance is clearly given to the mind that embraces "hypotheses" together with the narrative subversions they entail. The fractures and interstitial vacancies toward which postmodernism directs its eye are all familiar in Wells's narrative practice, from his indiscriminate blending of "high" and "low" genres,[12] through his ultimate refusal to distinguish fiction from history,[13] to his repeated ploy of the dinner-party dialogue that concludes confoundedly.[14] *The*

Time Machine's embrace of both epochal logic (the master narrative of science, causation, "realism") and dialogical dissonance (the narrator's "theories," the irresolution of the dinner guests, the frame narrator's musings) discloses that text as subversive of narrative ends.

Wells's ambition in *The Time Machine*, then, is to foreground the artificiality and arbitrariness of storytelling. Yet his orientation is not that of the puritan fundamentalist who confuses fiction with "lie," nor yet that of the Philosopher to whom *poiesis* is frivolous. Rather, Wells insists upon the provisional character of perception and representation, making his Time Traveller, for example, "too clever to be believed" (2, 12) and the Time Traveller's seemingly empirical demonstration of the model time machine subliminal. The time machine itself, as has often been noted, is characterized even by the Time Traveller as insubstantial, as a work of fantasy, or more properly, as a solid object whose insubstantiality is unaccountable.

That these features serve as analogues of narrative seems likely, given the dissonances and formal contortions to which *The Time Machine* as a whole is prone. The novel is, for example, constructed with a frame, as a story-within-a-story, a genre that typically insists upon rhetorical interplay among narrators. The nameless interlocutor of Marlow in Conrad's *Heart of Darkness*—to cite only the most familiar modern case—interposes himself between the "real" story and the audience, mediating the latter's experience of events. The critical distance he establishes ironizes his intimacy with Marlow, converting Marlow's narrative into parable and Marlow himself into an inscrutable Buddha. The frame narrator of *The Time Machine* serves a similar function, emphasizing likewise his long acquaintance with the Time Traveller, the familiarity and intimacy of the surroundings, and the seemingly incommensurate nature of the tale told within those surroundings.

Yet where Wells distinguishes himself from his friend Conrad is precisely in the nature of that tale and its *relationship* to the frame. Marlow's audience aboard the *Nellie* hears an orderly reminiscence, chronological and linear despite its meditative tone; and the irony of Marlow's encounter with Kurtz emerges from the structural rationality of its representation, the apparent certainty of its causative sequences, and the assonance it establishes between England and the Congo. The closural passage, in which the Thames "seem[s] to lead into the heart of an impenetrable darkness," insists with authoritative finality upon that assonance.[15] The Time Traveller's audience, by contrast, hears a tale that foregrounds chronology and linearity and interrogates both without mercy. The Time Traveller's revision of the laws of dimensionality in the opening frame is not, therefore, merely some bit of "hocus-pocus," as early reviewers charged;[16] it is a radical and deliberate disorientation that annuls traditional emplotment and prepares both for the Traveller's final experiences in the dead world "thirty million years hence" and for the closural equivocations uttered by the frame narrator.

The difficulties of a "time-travel" narrative are likewise not simply matters of physics or the paradoxes of, say, meeting or extinguishing oneself, as the literal minded have always maintained. They are difficulties of narrative per se. How *does* one represent the passage of time? How does one reconstruct past time? How, to take another Wellsian example, does one characterize the vision of "Davidson's eyes," with their gift for spatiotemporal apprehensions beyond our ken? By casting his central narrator into the future and obliging him to recount his experiences there—then?—as a narrative of events that are still to happen yet *already have happened*, Wells discloses for us the rank artificiality, the arbitrariness, the dirty secret of all our storytelling: narratives are constructs that work against themselves, denuding our predisposition to order yet confounding our impulse to comprehend.

Further, in assigning to the Time Traveller a compulsion, while he is in the future, to reconstruct a past whose every element is, for his audience, likewise the future, Wells deconstructs the very notion of linear-narrative representation, its obligatory "sense of an ending," its implicit determinism, and hence its utter fatality.[17] To "know" that Victorian social relations must produce Eloi-Morlock relations is to enact yet another master plot, that of nineteenth-century socialism, the inevitable triumph of the proletariat. The ghoulish consequence of this triumph—the literal parasitizing of the children of men by the children of men— foregrounds the artifice of socialism and its corollary master plots, progressivism and liberalism, insisting that narratives so constructed are infinitely, indeed ironically, deflectable, and their closural strategies merely contrived. There is, in short, no narrative logic of causation that produces the world of 802,701 that does not also entail a multitude of alternative outcomes.

Hence, even the master narratives of evolution and cosmic process, so critical to the Time Traveller's account, are revealed as constructs, as plots deriving from human beings' unacknowledged predispositions, and are thus inherently unstable. From the frame narrator we learn that, despite the Time Traveller's confidence in his own physical strength, initiative, resourcefulness, and analytical skill, he has long "thought but cheerlessly of the Advancement of Mankind" (E, 91) and in some sense, therefore, merely discovers in Eloi-Morlock degeneracy the narrative outcome he has always anticipated. The apparent consistency of that outcome with the final stages of his tale—his journey to entropic cessation "more

than thirty million years hence"—is undercut altogether by failures of orienta-
tional detail. For though the Time Traveller apprehends structural parallels between the Eloi-Morlock world and the later phases—the continued bifurcation
of dominant life-forms (giant butterflies versus crustaceans); the tentative tick-
ling of these latter, so like that of the Eloi and Morlocks both; the final blending
of light and dark—his "position" in space and time has become indeterminate
and narratively intolerable. The instrumentation of his machine, which recorded
the *year* 802,701 with such precision, now appears to consist of dials recording
days, hundreds of days, thousands of days, and so on, in mockery of that precision. The "flapping of [the] black wing" (3, 19), which signals the rapid passage
of days while the Traveller is in motion, settles into a perpetual twilight, mocking
in turn the very concept of "day" and undoing the notion of recordable, hence
narratable, time. His spatial directions, too, become irrelevant, the sun merely
rising and setting in the west and coming to rest at the end—unaccountably—in
the southeast (11, 81-2).

The frame narrator's closing equivocations complicate rather than resolve this
disorientation. For not only does he seek to locate the Time Traveller in familiar
epochal logic, speculating in reverse order (and asymmetrically) on his possible
experiences in the Palaeolithic, Cretaceous, Jurassic, and Triassic periods, he also
undercuts his own speculations with a self-conscious aside about his use of the
adverb "now" (E, 91), highlighting not, as Donald Williams has asserted, *Wells's*
"uneasiness about the consistency of time travel," but the frame narrator's uneasiness about time.[18] If, subsequent to the Time Traveller's narrative, "now" must
signify a moment three years after his final disappearance as well as a moment *at
any time*, past, present, or future, then the term has ceased to be meaningful, has
indeed ceased to orient the speaker in any sort of dependable sequence or space.
Yet the frame narrator seems to overlook the importance of having disarticulated
the concept of narrative time, for, ironically, his repudiation of the Time Traveller's
determinism is made to appear grounded in the earnest sanguinity of the Victorian meliorist: his final pronouncements are contaminated by sentimentality about
the survival of "gratitude and a mutual tenderness [. . .] in the heart of man" (E,
91). In this matter he contrives to forget that the heart of man in 802,701 is irre-
trievably bifurcated, while Weena's "now [. . .] brown [. . .] and brittle flowers"
(E, 91) were presented to the Time Traveller as a gesture in a typically vapid Eloi
game. The frame narrator's hope is thus disclosed (like Mark Schorer's misap-
prehension) as the product of a structured misreading.

Consequently, Wells is able to demonstrate at the end of *The Time Machine*
that while time and therefore narrative are human constructs with few if any em-

pirical referents, human beings are resolved to ignore this fact and indeed to persist in the familiar configurations of chronometry and storytelling, together with the forms of essentially consolatory order they provide. That this demonstration anticipates Wells's own bafflement in middle age and helps to account for his periodic recourse to hectoring is, perhaps, self-evident. Certainly the recurrence in his fiction of such devices as the dream, the vision, and the hallucination, to say nothing of the distressfully gratifying closural tensions already cited from *Tono-Bungay*, suggest a lifelong concern for educating his not always educable readers to the artifice of their epistemes.

I say "lifelong" because Wells, for all the apparent ideological permutations he underwent in his long career—Lovat Dickson's paradigm is only a sketch[19]—remained postmodern to the end. In his final book-length work, *Mind at the End of Its Tether* (1945), Wells condensed and rearticulated the narratives of *The Time Machine*, subjecting his readership to a somewhat more expository but no less disruptive experience. Despite reviewers' dismissal of the text as a terminal incoherence and despite its marginalization (even by sympathetic scholars) as Wells's despairing last will and testament,[20] the voice that speaks in *Mind*—or rather, the voices that speak—are not those of a deranged geriatric on his deathbed; and while Wells acknowledged unequivocally that this would be his *last* work, he had already done that—prematurely, he notes with chagrin—in his memoir, *'42 to '44*. There is, in any case, a suspect "tidiness," as Dickson implies,[21] in the scholars' and biographers' rush to take him at his word and impose upon *Mind* the same kind of closural drama they rush to impose upon George Orwell's *Nineteen Eighty-Four*. That they should in this fashion embed *Mind at the End of Its Tether* within the constraints of a generic convention, the familiar narrative that entails its own expedient terminus and attributes to "last writings" a privileged mortal clairvoyance, proves how easily, after all, we tumble into well-worn tracks.

To read *Mind at the End of Its Tether* in this way—even if, like Dickson, Norman and Jeanne Mackenzie, and numerous others, we link it with *The Time Machine* as one of the two brackets of Wells's literary life—is to risk obscuring the work's virtues in order that we may bring our own fable about Wells, not Wells's fable, to a close. It obscures, in particular, the relationship between the brackets themselves. For *Mind at the End of Its Tether* is essentially "Time at the End of Its Tether," an unrepentant reworking of the narrative concerns that are central to *The Time Machine*. Three aspects of the opening chapter, "The End Closes in upon Mind," illustrate this with great clarity. While the title of the chapter appears, with its finality, to forestall demurral and thus to enact Wells's most authoritarian intellectual mode, the text itself is far more playful than promised—

and rather more recognizable. One may indeed imagine Wells's eyes twinkling as he expounds the following recondite matter:

> The writer finds very considerable reason for believing that, within a period to be estimated by weeks and months rather than aeons, there has been a fundamental change in the conditions under which life, not simply human life but all self-conscious existence, has been going on since its beginning.[22]

The very audacity of this passage, its rhetorical cheek, disdains the fecklessness of simple assent; and indeed, Wells continues:

> This is a very startling persuasion to find establishing itself in one's mind, and [the author] puts forward his conclusions in the certainty that they will be entirely inacceptable [sic] to the ordinary rational man.... [Yet] [i]f his thinking has been sound, then this world is at the end of its tether. The end of everything we call life is close at hand and cannot be evaded. He is telling you the conclusions to which reality has driven his own mind, and he thinks you may be interested enough to consider them, but he is not attempting to impose them upon you. He will do his best to indicate why he has succumbed to so stupendous a proposition. His exposition will have to be done bit by bit, and it demands close reading. He is not attempting to win acquiescence in what he has to say.[23]

Compare this to the Time Traveller's words to his dinner guests at the opening of *The Time Machine*:

> You must follow me carefully. I shall have to controvert one or two ideas that are almost universally accepted. The geometry, for instance, they taught you at school is founded on a misconception. [...] [Yet] I do not mean to ask you to accept anything without reasonable ground for it. (1, 3)

He proceeds, of course, to characterize the fourth dimension of geometry as time and to "demonstrate" the possibility of controlled movement within it as within the other planes. Structurally, the significant parallels between the passages are the admonition to "follow [...] carefully" and read closely; the controverting of accepted ideas and their replacement by "startling persuasions;" and the prohibition against simple "acquiescence" or "acceptance."

To put the matter concisely, then: from the very beginning of *Mind at the End of Its Tether,* readers are once more invited into the drawing room of the Time Traveller, that resolute illusionist who knows himself too clever to be believed but whose peculiar gift is to unsettle even the most cherished epistemes, those of time and space and narrative representation. The orderly and hierarchical "story" of evolution, for example, implicit throughout *The Time Machine*, appears explicitly in *Mind*, but in both cases its consolatory prefiguration—to adapt Hayden

White's term—as the epic triumph of the "hominidae" is denuded by the counternarrative of regression and devolution. In a similar way, the grandeur of the narrative of cosmic process, of the dissipation of heat and the cessation of movement, discloses in its rush to closure both the totalizing impulse and the stark fatalism inherent in all storytelling: narrative *is* entropy.

In this respect, *Mind at the End of Its Tether* is even more radical than *The Time Machine*. For Wells begins with finality, with closure as an inescapable condition, and derives from it the proposition that any "convergence" whatever between the ordering principles of "Mind" and the external universe has been fortuitous. As a consequence, he now sees that master narratives are not merely arbitrary, or even hypothetical, as *The Time Machine* reveals them to be; they are irrelevant. Narrative as a category is shown to be dispersed, a mere "jumbled movie," and all explanatory fictions are inadequate to sustain even the illusion of explicability. The corollary—that the closural compulsions once held to empower the anticipatory or predictive aspects of narrative must likewise be dispersed—eliminates completely any lingering temptation to valorize narrative as moral didact, as significant, in other words, for future conduct. "After all," Wells writes, he "has no compelling argument to convince the reader that he should not be cruel or mean or cowardly. [. . .] [T]his is a matter of individual predilection."[24]

Mind at the End of Its Tether thus seems to approach far nearer to nihilism than *The Time Machine*, or indeed any of Wells's other works; and this accounts in some measure for *Mind*'s enduring reputation. Yet the unmistakable "undertone of glee" with which Wells sets out to erase all familiar forms of cognition has analogues throughout his corpus. It is partly, as David Lodge has observed, the old "game" of scandalizing the bourgeoisie.[25] There is also, however, a distinct courage and even ferocity in Wells's rearticulation, in 1945, of so Nietzschean a set of principles as the arbitrariness of intellectual constructs and the relativity of moral judgments. Fully half of *Mind at the End of Its Tether* is devoted to demonstrating the irreconcilability of impersonal cosmic process with redemptive biological adaptation and to proving, therefore, that though man, as Nietzsche maintained, is something to be superseded, there is virtually no likelihood that his supersession will matter.

It is precisely here that the Time Traveller's equivocating friend, the frame narrator, reappears with an even more convoluted closural passage than that which puts *finis* to *The Time Machine*:

> [M]y own temperament makes it unavoidable for me to doubt [. . .] that there will not be [some] small minority [of newly adaptive humans] which will succeed in seeing life out to its inevitable end.[26]

The triple-negative syntax and the commingling of Spencerian evolution with its own annulment resonate with the discords of Wells's earliest successful narrative. Insisting with ironic calm upon the integrity of an incommensurable vision, he anticipates and refutes John Middleton Murry's characterization of *Mind* as "curiously incoherent," a token of the failure of Wells's "mental grip."[27] To the contrary, Wells asserts, he has "simply been working out and elaborating, with [. . .] a certain ebb of intensity, the forms of thought into which [he had] shaped [his] convictions" as a youth.[28] George Orwell, not always a generous critic of Wells but certainly Wellsian in his criticism, saw more clearly than Murry that, despite the apparent "disjointed[ness]" of the text, *Mind at the End of Its Tether* recalls explicitly the terminal images of *The Time Machine*: "that world of cooling stars and battling dinosaurs which Mr Wells has made so peculiarly his own."[29]

The project to debunk the consolations of narrative—recurrence, pattern, predictability—that Wells inaugurated with *The Time Machine* he concludes with *Mind at the End of Its Tether*. "Events no longer recur," there is no pattern, and prediction is impossible.[30] Without these elements, narrative—at least narrative as we know it—fails, and its most elusive promise, the closural revelation of "reason" or "purpose," the *telos* that impels but is never spoken,[31] disintegrates: evolution and cosmic process must, like all such constructs, forfeit their claim to comprehensive validity. There is "no reason whatever" in any of them, they merely "happened so." In the "hitherto incredible chaos" thus denuded, even these master narratives of science appear epigonic, feckless, effete, while the frame narrator's "now" surfaces once again as a gesture of epistemic evasion, "this ever contracting NOW of our daily lives," upon which we impress an elaborate and futile structuration we know to be "faked."[32]

No tidy closural summation, therefore, permits us to complement J. R. Hammond's apt characterization of *The Time Machine* as a "young man's book, . . . a brave book"[33] with an equally apt characterization of *Mind at the End of Its Tether* as "an old man's book, a cowardly book." Wells's last work is demonstrably of a piece with his first. "It has the power that Mr Wells's writings have always had," Orwell observed, "the power of arresting the reader's attention and forcing him to think and argue," and its thesis "has a sort of grandeur."[34] The repudiation of the later realists' as well as the modernists' "social fixity"; the consequent assault upon narrative; the distressful commingling of two or more master plots, each claiming ultimacy; the epistemological outrages against time and space, and indeed against epistemology itself; the refusal to acquiesce in any conspiracy of consolation; and above all, the persistent, denuding, ironic gaze that foregrounds the artifice even of Wells's own plots, especially his reliance on the shock of "apocalypse," of "revelation," of seeming inevitability—all of these features betoken an intellectual critic as unrepentant at seventy-nine as he had been irreverent half a century before.

Notes

1. Wells's "rehabilitation" from the penumbra cast over his literary reputation by the modernists has been a persistent theme since the 1986 symposium hosted by the Wells Society in London. See, for example, essays by Robert Crossley, J. R. Hammond, Bonnie Kime Scott, and Warren Wagar, among others, in *H. G. Wells Under Revision: Proceedings of the International H. G. Wells Symposium, London, July 1986*, ed. Patrick Parrinder and Christopher Rolfe (Selinsgrove: Susquehanna UP, 1990).

2. H. G. Wells, *Experiment in Autobiography: Discoveries and Conclusions of a Very Ordinary Brain (Since 1866)* (New York: Macmillan, 1934), p. 388.

3. [H. G. Wells], "Of Art, of Literature, of Mr. Henry James," in *Boon, The Mind of the Race, The Wild Asses of the Devil, and The Last Trump* (London: Unwin, 1915). Reprinted in *Henry James and H. G. Wells: A Record of Their Friendship, Their Debate on the Art of Fiction, and Their Quarrel*, ed. Leon Edel and Gordon N. Ray (Westport, Conn.: Greenwood Press, 1958), p. 249.

4. *Experiment in Autobiography*, pp. 416, 419, 421–22.

5. Mark Schorer, "Technique as Discovery," *Hudson Review* 1 (Spring 1948), n.p. Partially reprinted in *Critical Essays on H. G. Wells*, ed. John Huntington (Boston: Hall, 1991), pp. 34–35. I am indebted to John Huntington for providing me with a copy of his book, and to Brian Murray for his brief but insightful discussion of these issues in *H. G. Wells* (New York: Continuum, 1990), pp. 146–58.

6. For a thorough discussion of the doxological imperatives of modernism see Bruce Robbins, "Modernism in History, Modernism in Power," in *Modernism Reconsidered*, ed. Robert Kiely and John Hildebidle, Harvard Studies in English 11 (Cambridge, Mass.: Harvard University Press, 1983), pp. 229–45.

7. "Technique as Discovery," p. 35.

8. Cf. Romolo Runcini, "H. G. Wells and Futurity as the Only Creative Space in a Programmed Society," trans. Fernando Porta, in *H. G. Wells Under Revision*, pp. 153–61. Runcini's insight is that Wells, from *The Time Machine* onward, can be seen as an avant-gardist, hence modernist and antirealist. My point, however, is that Wells outpaces even modernism in the radical nature of his vision and technique.

9. H. G. Wells, *Tono-Bungay* (New York: Grosset & Dunlap, 1908), pp. 457–58.

10. See Runcini, "Futurity," for discussion of the "hypothetical" in Wells's plots.

11. The theoretical background for the argument that follows is derived primarily from Peter Brooks, *Reading for the Plot: Design and Intention in Narrative* (New York: Knopf, 1984) and Hayden White, *The Content of the Form: Narrative Discourse and Historical Representation* (Baltimore and London: Johns Hopkins University Press, 1987),

Metahistory: The Historical Imagination in Nineteenth-Century Europe (Baltimore and London: Johns Hopkins University Press, 1973), and *Tropics of Discourse: Essays in Cultural Criticism* (Baltimore and London: Johns Hopkins University, 1978). I have also consulted Harold Bloom, *Deconstruction and Criticism* (New York: Continuum, 1985); Robert Con Davis, ed., *Contemporary Literary Criticism: Modernism Through Structuralism* (New York and London: Longman, 1986); Linda Hutcheon, *The Politics of Postmodernism* (London and New York: Routledge, 1989); Vincent B. Leitch, *Deconstructive Criticism: An Advanced Introduction* (New York: Columbia University Press, 1983); K. M. Newton, ed., *Twentieth-Century Literary Theory* (London: Macmillan, 1988); Christopher Norris, *Deconstruction: Theory and Practice* (London and New York: Methuen, 1982) and *What's Wrong with Postmodernism: Critical Theory and the Ends of Philosophy* (Baltimore: Johns Hopkins University Press, 1990); and Paul Rabinow, ed., *The Foucault Reader* (New York: Pantheon, 1984).

12. Cf. Marianne DeKoven's discussion of the appearance of this attribute in *recent* utopian fiction: "Utopia Limited: Post-Sixties and Postmodern American Fiction," *Modern Fiction Studies* 41 (Spring 1995), 75–97. I am grateful to Phyllis Toy for bringing this essay to my attention.

13. For example, in *The Shape of Things to Come* (1933) and *The Holy Terror* (1939). The narrative subversiveness of these two late works, composed in the climactic decade of High Modernism, is grossly underappreciated. For a discussion of the renewed collision between history and fiction in contemporary theory see White, *Tropics of Discourse*, pp. 81–100 and 230–82, and Hutcheon, *The Politics of Postmodernism*, pp. 31–92.

14. This feature, like others noted by Romolo Runcini, derives in utopian tradition directly from Thomas More, but it has interesting affiliations with the postmodern "Bakhtinian" embrace of dialogue as adapted by, for example, Julia Kristeva.

15. Joseph Conrad, *Heart of Darkness*, ed. Robert Kimbrough (New York and London: Norton, 1971), pp. 5, 79.

16. R. H. Hutton, review of *The Time Machine*, *Spectator* (13 July 1895), 41–43, reprinted in *H. G. Wells: The Critical Heritage*, ed. Patrick Parrinder (London and Boston: Routledge, 1972), pp. 34–37.

17. See Peter Brooks, *Reading for the Plot*, esp. pp. 94–111.

18. Harry M. Geduld, ed., *The Definitive Time Machine: A Critical Edition of H. G. Wells's Scientific Romance* (Bloomington and Indianapolis: Indiana University Press, 1987), p. 120n.

19. Lovat Dickson, *H. G. Wells: His Turbulent Life and Times* (London: Macmillan, 1971), pp. 320–22.

20. See G. P. Wells's introduction to his edition of *Mind at the End of Its Tether* in *The Last Books of H. G. Wells* (London: H. G. Wells Society, 1968), pp. 7–17. Unfortunately, though mitigating the almost universal critical opinion of the text as "despairing," the younger Wells attempts to clarify his father's stance by disarticulating his text. The net

effect is to provide a useful historical reminder of how *Mind* was composed, but less insight into its significance.

21. Dickson, *H. G. Wells*, p. 309. For a remarkable enactment of this tidiness, see Antonina Vallentin, *H. G. Wells: Prophet of Our Day*, trans. Daphne Woodward (New York: John Day, 1950), pp. 325–26.

22. H. G. Wells, *Mind at the End of Its Tether* (London: Heinemann, 1945), p. 1.

23. Ibid., pp. 1–2.

24. Ibid., pp. 3–9, 14–15, 18.

25. David Lodge, *The Novelist at the Crossroads* (Ithaca: Cornell University Press, 1971), p. 208.

26. *Mind at the End of Its Tether*, p. 34.

27. John Middleton Murry, obituary essay, *Adelphi* (October–December 1946), 1–5, reprinted in *H. G. Wells: The Critical Heritage*, pp. 324–29.

28. *Mind at the End of Its Tether*, p. 28.

29. George Orwell, "Are We Really Done For?," review of *Mind at the End of Its Tether*, *Manchester Evening News* (8 November 1945), 2. Microfiche at the Orwell Archive, University College, London. I am most grateful to the staff of the Archive for their patient assistance.

30. *Mind at the End of Its Tether*, pp. 5–6.

31. Brooks, *Reading for the Plot*, p. 61.

32. *Mind at the End of Its Tether*, pp. 6, 7, 14, 27.

33. J. R. Hammond, "*The Time Machine* as a First Novel: Myth and Allegory in Wells's Romance," in this volume.

34. Orwell, "Are We Really Done For?," 2.

The Legacy of H. G. Wells's *The Time Machine*

Destabilization and Observation

JOSHUA STEIN

There were numerous observers in imaginary voyages before H. G. Wells's *The Time Machine*, but in none of these previous works do we have the importance of the observer's presence as the catalyst for change. Without the Traveller's presence, the future he describes would not exist. Before *The Time Machine*, seeing the future was a matter of going, seeing, and returning with a report. Wells's Traveller creates a particular future by going there; his presence moves the abstract into a very distinct, concrete reality. He does not just report what he sees but literally creates it. And what is created is entirely contingent upon the society that has created him. I want to deal with the implication of this idea in two very different versions of *The Time Machine*: Wells's 1895 text and George Pal's 1960 film. I hope to make clearer the similarities and differences between the two versions, including how the presence of the Traveller influences his descriptions and what his actions portend for the futures he visits, as well as the legacy that Wells's text has left for Speculative Fiction, particularly within the United States and the United Kingdom.

Wells's Traveller is a seeker of utopia who, having perfected the technologies—the "wonderful advances upon [his] rudimentary civilisation" (3, 20)—that allowed him to build his machine in his time, looks for a flawless world. This goes to the heart of all that the Traveller embodies in Wells's text. What he discovers upon entering the future is not by any means perfection—at least not perfection as he and his society define it. The Traveller is a representative late-nineteenth-century imperialist who has no intention of trying to be objective in his evaluations. Upon his arrival in the future, he voices the assumptions he holds dear, asking, "What if cruelty had grown into a common passion? What if in this interval the race had lost its manliness, and had developed into something inhuman, unsympathetic, and overwhelmingly powerful?" (3, 22). From the outset we know that his definition of "civilisation" is the exact opposite of what he expects to find. While what he seeks is a world where, in his own words, "there were no signs of struggle, neither social nor economical struggle" (4, 32), he knows, even before looking, that his expectations will not be fulfilled. And more to the point, these assumptions about what he will find bring about their opposites. Considering the legacy of imperialism, it is not difficult to assume that anything the Traveller encounters that is not exactly the same as his society, or his version of an extension thereof, will be seen by him as barbaric. By prejudging, the Traveller creates a reason for travelling that is exactly the opposite of his original reason for travelling.

What the Traveller observes is two mutually dystopian societies that are kept in place by violence and submission. But would these societies be seen as such without his presence as observer? By entering into a time that is not his own, that has a context and a set of preconditions drafted hundreds of thousands of years previously by his society, the Traveller creates this dystopia between Eloi and Morlock. As far as the two tribes of humans are concerned, if they are concerned at all, their symbiotic relationship is natural and normal. The Eloi have a perfectly, in their own terms (if they have any), peaceful way of life and in fact do not realize that this naturalized power relationship, to summarize the Traveller's point of view, is anything but natural. Both societies do not know anything different and have not even the language to envision any further form of existence. It is the Traveller who has the alternative point of view, and whose possession of such allows him to place himself in a position of superiority to the natives of the future. Upon first sight of the Eloi, he remarks that he has "suddenly regained confidence" (3, 23). This "confidence" allows him to enter this new world and to classify what he finds, to make the Eloi into his "grateful children" and the Morlocks into "human spider[s]" that are "bleached, obscene, nocturnal Thing[s]" (5, 47). His paternal attitude toward the Eloi and objectification of the Morlocks emphasize his perception of power relations between himself and these future peoples, as well as between Eloi and Morlock. What the Traveller never realizes is that it is his own physical presence that destabilizes the mutually entwined societies into mutually dystopic races.

Wells's Traveller is the prototypical scientist, the archetypal observer of his culture reporting back what he has witnessed. He deals in Newtonian and Darwinian absolutes, as when describing what has caused human society to split: a change of conditions that causes a reaction in the evolutionary process. The Traveller is well aware of the major problems of his era, particularly the socioeconomic pressures of Victorian England, which he alludes to by postulating the separation between Eloi and Morlock as that between capital and labor taken to the extreme. The anxiety of 1895 is evolutionarily reversed in the Traveller's description of the Eloi-Morlock relationship, with the ultimate manifestation of the split between worker and owner becoming the literal consumption of the consumer. Having realized, but only on his own terms, what the future of humanity will be, and having become disenchanted with all of society in any modern age, the Traveller goes even further into the future to witness the eventual end of all life and the resulting hopelessness of believing in progress. From there he returns to his own time to have his observations validated by his own people. This hopelessness that he feels and then gives to his contemporaries illustrates the problem with the Traveller's, and hence Wells's, culture's ideology. Ultimately, Wells's text is a subversive gesture—subversive because of the destabilization of cultural authority—and can be seen as a forerunner of much later poststructural attacks on science and its cultural ideologies.

If the original version of *The Time Machine* is in some sense subversive, then George Pal's film is anything but. Pal's observer is very different from Wells's, although the plot of the film, at least on the surface, remains relatively faithful to the plot of the book. Where Wells's Traveller is content to go to the future, make a few haphazard changes, and return, Pal's "George" takes a far more active, purposeful, and participatory role. Once again, though, this time in the film, we have an observer whose observations are culturally bound. And while the culture of America in 1960 as seen in Pal's film is not altogether different from Wells's late-Victorian England, there are some major distinctions. Rather than searching for utopia, George is concerned with free will, asking early on, "Can man control his destiny?" Instead of the Traveller's notions of Darwinian evolution, George presents a Lamarckian alternative, motivating and coordinating the Eloi's actions for all future time. This sets the stage for what becomes a very American, technocratic, Horatio Alger–influenced manifesto for seizing all future days—a manifesto that reinscribes the American ideology of manifest destiny. Also, rather than illustrating the book's "queer friendship" (5, 43) with Weena, Pal has George fall for the blonde-haired, blue-eyed, very statuesque Yvette Mimieux and leave the Morlock attack not to continue onward as does the Traveller, but to return to his own time to pick up a few things and hurry back. While he is also guilty of being the locus of destabilization of the future, his goal is to return and make it new. Continuing in the American mythic tradition of a new Edenic start, George is not content to view the Eloi as the book's "indolent" and "easily fatigued" "children" (4, 28). Rather, he becomes their savior, inciting them to rebel against their unnatural masters and thereby causing the utter destruction of the Morlocks' inner world. The film is not concerned with the book's "Haves" and "Have-nots" (5, 50). From his first moments in the future, George cares very little for a passive observatory role. He is the American man of action, bringing the pioneer spirit back to his long-lost cousins, and looking, remarkably, with his dungarees and vest, as if he had just stepped out of a black-and-white "Wild West" movie from the Golden Age of Hollywood.

The main plot differences between the two versions are a direct result of the distinction between cultures, but that is not the only reason for difference. A temporal distinction exists as well. Wells's observer heads straight for the far future in a millennial impulse to know what the eventual product of his day will be. Pal's film stops periodically throughout the twentieth century to let us know that the future we are seeing is our past. We see the world wars and the nuclear age, and the reason for the existence of the mutual dystopias shifts. Rather than Wells's capital/labor split, we see the result of nuclear annihilation as accelerated evolution and species specification and fragmentation. Pal does Wells's social Darwinism one better, changing the latter's social evolution as a precipitator into literal landscape degradation and radioactive fallout as the instigators of ever-increasing change. The constant reminder of this difference is most notable in the representation of the Morlocks' air tubes, through which George gains entry into their lair as well as facilitates their destruction: they look remarkably like ICBM launch tubes. One conclusion that can be drawn about the film is that the Morlocks, rather than representing labor, are the remains of the missile defense networks, still protecting their charges but taking a very literal fee for their services. Another conclusion concerns the ideology of the nuclear age: all risks taken can be redeemed given the right man in the right place at the right time. A final conclusion is connected to this last point and involves the waves of technology displayed for us during George's start-and-stop time travelling. While Wells's Traveller sees nothing of his "local" future and goes onward to the Earth's entropy-laden conclusion, Pal's George stops again and again, and by doing so brings this technical knowledge into the future with him, suggesting a redemption of technology not at all present in the original text. Here, too, the presence of high technology unused by the Eloi, the "rings that talk" and their direct connections to historical chronicles, does not produce the same sense of isolation and seclusion that fills the novel. Arriving not for exploration alone, George has made it to the future to give back to the Eloi "their" history. Because the rings use "modern" English, and the Eloi speak the same language, George doesn't need to learn the natives' language as the Traveller does. Once again, via technology, there is a sense of promise brought to fruition, of a destiny waiting to be made.

I turn now to a discussion of the implication of the travellers' actions in the book and film. To be forthright, Wells's Traveller's very existence in a future that has no memory of his machine means that he is not in his future. His tour of the Palace of Green Porcelain gives an overview of the meaningful inventions of humanity, yet his own machine is not included among these objects. Causality has started to fracture because of his presence in the future. I reiterate: the Traveller is visiting and consequently drawing conclusions for his own time based upon a future that is not his or his society's. Adding to the fragmentation is the presence of the flowers he brings back from the future. When the Traveller leaves for the second time, he goes, if he does indeed go forward, not into the same future from which the flowers came, but to a different future entirely. The presence of the flowers, this future-anachronism, suggests one reason he never returns—he has been looking for the right future, or conversely the right past, to return to. Taken to logical extremes, the Traveller could be even now planting and removing objects from different pasts and futures, seeking to reopen the one-way door of his personal history, and, in actuality, creating even more fragmentation by his actions; creating and recreating a Möbius strip of possibilities that never repeats—a labyrinth of time that never ends nor reverses itself.

The Traveller's haphazard playing around with causality occurs in both the past and future and is a direct result of his perceived superiority and right of authority. In the past, or rather the Traveller's present, is the presence of the flowers, brought back to his time because he has forgotten they are in his pocket. In the future is Weena's rescue from drowning and the crumbling of books in the Palace of Green Porcelain, both spur of the moment occurrences, neither of whose outcomes are considered by the Traveller before he acts. Instead of the later grandfather paradox in which presence in any form or an accident upsets the balance of causality, the Traveller's bumbling about is a direct result of his cultural norms. He saves Weena because he values particular forms of life, yet he destroys the history of the ages because his desires have been thwarted by time. Completing the sense of subversion mentioned above is what the Traveller's actions mean for himself. The fragmentation of reality he has caused in the past and future begins to affect him as well. He states near the end of the text, after having given full disclosure of his activities: "This room and you and the atmosphere of every day is too much for my memory. Did I ever make a Time Machine, or a model of a Time Machine? Or is it all only a dream? They say life is a dream, a precious poor dream at times—but I can't stand another that won't fit. It's madness. And where did the dream come from?" (12, 88). Rather than change the linear future, as, for example, stepping on a butterfly does in Ray Bradbury's "A Sound of

Thunder," the Traveller changes himself. The fragmentation of causality becomes embodied within him as the "sickness and confusion that comes with time travelling" (11, 80). Because he is the agent of change, his mental state becomes a series of disruptions. The Traveller becomes entirely disconnected from time, and therefore never returns. Adding insult to injury is the attempt by the narrator, the observer's observer, to recoup this final fragmentation. He has in his possession the wilted remains of the flowers and notes that they bear "witness that even when mind and strength had gone, gratitude and a mutual tenderness still lived on in the heart of man" (E, 91). Once again we see just how subjective these observations are. The definitions of "gratitude" and "mutual tenderness" are valid only within their own contexts and, additionally, are dependent upon an imperialistic sense of those definitions. If anything, the legacy of the Traveller is one of only increasing fragmentation and destabilization—the result of the paradigm of observation. If we are present and do nothing, things will deteriorate; if we do do something, we make things even worse. In other words, we cannot help but change the relationships we find—and change them we shall by our very presence. Moreover, because these sentiments come at the very end of the text they bring us full circle, pointing out that what the Traveller sought all along was in the one place he did not look: his own time. In terms of imperialism, this illustrates Wells's subversive take on power inequality: why go, when what you really want you can find back at home?

The film only partially solves the above paradoxical notions of causality with the replacement of nuclear holocaust as the reason for the split between Eloi and Morlocks. George may very well be in his own future, given that systematic destruction would include any remnants of his previous existence and work, yet he too brings the flowers back and then leaves again. There is no postscript as in the novel, which leaves the presumption, given the difference in tone, that he goes back to the same future he left, or that due to what he brings with him, he will find his way to his destination. George's actions differ greatly from the Traveller's, most notably in how far he is willing to go to control his own destiny. Rather than retreating, particularly because he goes no further than the year 802,701, Pal's George sees the future as something to be overcome and made right.[1] His visitations to the twentieth century, where we see progress in fashion, architecture, warfare, and knowledge, provide the basis for continuing to push forward, and when he finds that growth has become retarded, he has no compunctions about making the changes he sees as necessary to bring humanity back to its full glory—westward expansion becomes literal four-dimensional forward movement. His example of post-Apocalypse survival is very much influenced by the Cold

War—with the right knowledge, and the right woman, society can be rebuilt and made better than before. A section from the book finds its full articulation in the film: "What, unless biological science is a mass of errors, is the cause of human intelligence and vigour? Hardship and freedom: conditions under which the active, strong, and subtle survive and the weaker go to the wall; conditions that put a premium upon the loyal alliance of capable men" (4, 32). George finds men, but they are not yet capable. He never doubts his ability to make the Eloi into "capable men" and brings them back from the brink of human chattel-hood. Part of controlling your own destiny, George's actions show, is through the acceptance of doing things the hard way if you want your freedom. This puts Pal's observer and his film smack in the middle of American libertarianism. To carry this last point even further, the film refuses the book's ending. Rather than leaving the book's questions unanswered, including the problems of the Traveller's ever returning, and whether he went backward or forward on his second voyage, Pal's film leaves only one question unanswered: which three books did George take with him to found his new society? The film ends with a final rhetorical flourish that merges perfectly with the American pioneering tradition: which three books would we, the audience, take with us to found our own societies? This completes the chain of signification that the film creates. Not only can the future be changed, not only can it be made better, but anyone can do it given the proper resources and mental attitude: the future is promise, not stagnation.

To summarize, part of the legacy of *The Time Machine*, in both versions, is that the presence of the observer is the actual cause of destabilization. What continues to make it a seminal classic is not so much what Wells detailed but what he left unsaid. He created a space for exploration in which any future traveller can revisit the terrain, and in doing so make it into his or her culture's self-envisioned future. The greatness of Wells's book lies in its recognition that things only get worse the more we strive to change them—and change them we must—by our very presence. Pal's film proves that within different cultural contexts, the Traveller makes different changes for different reasons, thus causing different results to ensue. Wells has made use of the observer as the literal producer of change, yet leaves enough unsaid so that anyone can return to his or her ideas and make use of them for their purposes and within their own contexts. Following this idea, I wish to turn briefly to how this legacy has been used in one particular later text. The crux of Wells's legacy tends to rest upon the observer's presence as destabilizer, and there are countless examples of this within the genre of SF, but one particular instance based on that presence has been seldom examined. Consider the moment when the Traveller finds himself without culture, seemingly a

Robinson Crusoe without natives to make into a Friday, a colonizer without his ship. The Traveller's thoughts at this point are not to destroy the Morlocks or rescue the Eloi—instead, he seeks only to get his machine back and leave the situation at all costs. Pal's film differs the most at this point. George finds not one Friday, but a whole (presumably) breeding population of them. "Crusoe" becomes "Christian" in an American *Pilgrim's Progress*. If he can just put the pieces together again properly, George will reach his just rewards. This moment of isolation, which for the Traveller is utter disaster, is opportunity for George. Again, in reference to the discussion above, cultural difference plays a major role in the comparison. In addition, taking a chronological approach to this dilemma reveals, once again, the usurpation of Wells's ideas. Pal's George sees his "exile" as the perfect opportunity to remake the world in which he finds himself and promptly carries out his revolution.

In comparison, D. G. Compton's *Farewell, Earth's Bliss* presents a Coventry-like prison society on Mars. The novel recounts the first year in the life of a group of subversives shipped into exile on the planet and goes into great detail to display the hardships endured by the newcomers and the society as a whole within their existence of almost complete dissolution. The story mirrors Wells's text in that the characters' subsequent efforts at survival do not bifurcate toward concerns with free will as Pal's film does, but instead come full circle back to Wells's "Haves and Have-nots": those who have survived the ninety-plus percent mortality rate and who therefore know what to do to survive, and those who are fresh from Earth, with no notions about survival, still drugged from the trip to Mars and at the mercy of their soon-to-be contemporaries. The text proceeds from the sandstorm that greets the exiles' crash landing, which kills everyone but seven transportees, to their incorporation into the demarcated society that has sprung up through generations of deportees, ending finally with the landing of the next group and the artificial sand storm "our" group helps create to kill off as many of the people on the ships as possible. We are given, in a sense, a version of accelerated Lamarckian evolution: Eloi are made into Morlocks; and the innocent become the cannibals in this future-anachronistic society.

Aside from the concurrence of ideas, how does Compton's novel fit in with this discussion of Wells's legacy? *Farewell, Earth's Bliss* confronts an issue that we never see George face, an issue he seems entirely unaware of: if the Morlocks are the ones who provide sustenance, and they have been destroyed along with all of their technology, how will a stranded George (or one who never returns) find food? Compton's answer to this hypothetical question is that he would not. That people stranded on a Mars just as, if not more, desolate than the "Eden" of

Pal's film would face constant starvation and would in fact revert to oligarchic, pitiless rule. Unthinking, ideologically fanatic George might save Weena, but in Compton's world he would let her, and as many others as possible, die before stepping in to try to sustain some form of culture among the survivors. A George-like character might have books, but that would not be enough. A zero-sum game would take place, and without the threat of mutated nature that George faces in Pal's sequel (and one that ignores completely the above problem), the inevitable result would be the relearning of artifice and deceit. George's Eloi would bifurcate into two societies once again. This observer/participator would become, because of his knowledge, some type of king, ruling over his serf-Eloi in the same naturalized predator/prey relationship he had deposed. Wells's subversion becomes reversed in Pal's American context, but Compton provides the never-considered question (and at least one answer) to Pal's reactionism. In the same way that Pal's film rhetorically involves his viewers, Compton's text uses his readers: it is not until the very last page of the text that a fairly disheartening dystopia is turned into complete horror at what the deportees are willing regularly to do to ensure their own survival. It is our reactions that cause this, though. *We*, the readers, become the observers of this situation. It is *our* presence that reacts this way to the creation of the artificial storm that locks the transportees, newly liberated from their ship-board food, into a month and a half of slow starvation. The people causing the storm have been disciplined by "society" and its notions of survival into no longer seeing this occurrence as anything but natural and normal. Only we, via Compton's use of Pal's methods, know that this is a naturalized power relationship. Compton completely reverses the arc of Pal's version of Wells's story. Progress only produces atavism. This chain of intertextuality is a revitalization of Wells's subversive ideas—the future is not progressive, it is either barbaric or uncaring.

In conclusion, Wells's legacy, the importance of the observer as the cause and/ or catalyst for change, works differently depending on the cultural context. Both British texts disavow an emancipatory role for technology, as well as the possibility of a human observer who does not do damage by being present in that role. This is an archetypal theme for SF of the United Kingdom. The observer and his or her technology is only liberating for British authors in two ways: either as an alien presence, as in Arthur C. Clarke's *Childhood's End*, or as something so evolved from current humanity it's unrecognizable as human, as in the work of Olaf Stapledon, most particularly his *Last and First Men*. The ideological co-option that occurs in Pal's film is symptomatic of the difference in themes for the SF of the United States, in which the role of individuals is consistently vital, and without which "satisfactory" conclusions do not occur, as in the collected works of both American grand masters, Robert A. Heinlein and Isaac Asimov. The aesthetic of paradigmatic American SF must have prosperity via individuals. The observer must be present, because without that presence success can neither be guaranteed nor valued as success. Both trends result from the larger cultural concerns that seminal Speculative Fiction cannot help but incorporate within itself.

Notes

My gratitude to George Slusser for discussion and brainstorming, without which this paper would appear in much altered form.

1. Of interest along this line of thought is Pal's sequel to his film, the novel he cowrote with Joe Morhaim, *The Time Machine II*, in which George does indeed return to Weena and the same future to combat the marauding mutant organisms of nature. This continues the manifest destiny of the film: once the natives are killed off (using a different tribe of natives!) or converted, nature is the next target to be beaten into submission by any means necessary. My gratitude to Gary Westfahl for bringing this text to my attention.

Wells and the Sequency-Simultaneity Paradox

Heinlein's Rewriting of *The Time Machine* in "By His Bootstraps"

DANIÈLE CHATELAIN AND GEORGE SLUSSER

 At first glance, Robert A. Heinlein's story "By His Bootstraps" seems radically different from Wells's *The Time Machine*.[1] In terms of scope no two works, it seems, could be farther apart. For where Wells's Time Traveller traverses all of human and geological time, the movements of Heinlein's protagonist turn around a single "stuck" instant in his initial space-time line.

In a sense, one could say that *The Time Machine* is a common ancestor to all time-travel narratives. Its 1927 publication by Hugo Gernsback in *Amazing Stories* inspired a long series of such stories. Indeed, Heinlein himself, rarely one to render homage, credits Wells's influence: "Mark Twain invented the time travel story, six years later Wells perfected it and *revealed its paradoxes*" (our emphasis).[2]

Given the cryptic nature of these remarks, we can only speculate. They suggest, however, that for Heinlein, Wells's work was important less for its famous machine than for the paradoxes the use of such a machine posed. Heinlein saw the Traveller's journey less as a meaningful or prophetic adventure than as an exercise in space-time geometry. *The Time Machine* is a work that demands to be rethought, and rethought again. To rethink *The Time Machine* is, for Heinlein as for other SF writers, to *rewrite* the Traveller's trajectory in terms of new and ever changing views of the nature of space-time. Heinlein's "By His Bootstraps" stands, in intertextual fashion, as analytical analogue to Wells's text. To analyze it is to discover, through Heinlein's eyes, certain essential but otherwise overlooked aspects of Wells's narrative. To approach one work in light of the other, in fact, provides mutual illumination on both.

Heinlein, we imagine, as post-Einsteinian reader, was above all interested in one problem: how the Traveller, once he departed from his initial space-time continuum, could claim to return to that continuum at (or even around) the instant of his departure. The crux of Heinlein's reading seems to be the Mrs Watchett episode. Here, the Traveller's housekeeper, in relation to his "exit velocity," is seen to fly across his workshop in one direction, only to retrace her trajectory in the *exactly opposite* sense upon his return. The detail is troubling. For the Traveller makes no use of this precise benchmark to measure the exact time of his arrival. Moreover, given this fixed point, the reader cannot account for the physical marks of time spent during the journey to the Eloi and beyond. The Traveller's beard and torn clothes do not mesh with the conclusion the Watchett measurement forces on the reader: that the time of departure and time of return are the same, that no time has passed at all. Read on this level, Wells's narrative poses a paradox—that of simultaneity-sequency. At the same time, the Mrs Watchett episode may have suggested to Heinlein the possibility of generating a narrative structure around the paradox itself. Reading Wells, Heinlein discovers paradox buried deep in Wells's temporal lapses. Rewriting Wells, he brilliantly reengineers these lapses. What in Wells remains a disparity between temporal geometry and narrated experience leads, in Heinlein, to a dazzling experiment in narrative.

Heinlein's "By His Bootstraps"

Heinlein's story makes ingenious use of conventional narrative forms in order to do what might seem impossible within narrative's traditional allegiance to linear time—to *tell* the paradox of sequency-simultaneity. "By His Bootstraps" is constructed as three successive loops, each of increasingly wider amplitude, yet each turning upon a same and unique instant on the protagonist's initial timeline. The narrative opens with Bob Wilson, a graduate student, at his desk writing a dissertation on problems of time in metaphysics. Selfish and cynical, Bob begins a reluctant argument against the material feasibility of time travel when, as if in response to some secret need, the keys on his typewriter stick. At the same instant a "Time Gate" opens in the wall of his room, through which first one, then a second individual appears. The first wants Bob to go through the gate, the second seeks to prevent this. A fight ensues between the two, and when Bob intervenes, he is knocked through the Gate. He awakens in what appears to be another space-time world—a distant future, peopled by decadent humans yet ruled by an older man who calls himself "Diktor." Diktor explains to Bob that the "Time Gate" is actually a machine and shows him how to control it. He promises Bob "a great future" if he will return to his space-time and bring back a list of things Diktor needs to secure his hold on this world of Norkaal. The suggestion is of a far-future "Northern California," analogous to Bob's unnamed space-time locus in the way that the Eloi's Thames Valley is to the Time Traveller's Richmond.

Bob passes the Gate to find himself in his room, behind a person who is typing. When another person follows him through the Gate, he realizes he is experiencing the same scene as before but from a different point of view, that of the first person to enter the room the time before, the one who sought to persuade him to enter the Gate. When the third person appears, he engages in the same scuffle, and as before the unwitting punch knocks the thesis writer through the Gate. What he now experiences is what went on *simultaneously* with his *earlier* self's encounter with Diktor. The other person tells Bob that Diktor, whom the first self is just now meeting, has *already* played both for fools. Not heeding this, Bob passes the Gate to get an explanation from Diktor. Not satisfied, he goes back to the room, now in the position of the third person, the one determined to stop anyone from passing the Gate.

It now becomes clear to Bob that space-time is twisting like a pretzel. He has repeated the same restricted loop again, but from a third space-time position, like a Möbius strip with figures that appear successively on one side or another of the same band. Yet in this looping, Bob becomes increasingly aware of the passage of his own biological time as well: the time it takes him to awake on the other side of the Gate, to talk to Diktor, to return to find his earlier self at the typewriter, and so on. A number of Bobs may be simultaneously in the same room, but the narrator, *at the same time*, can only follow one Bob, the one whose consciousness successively unfolds, through these various positions, to arrive at an understanding of his predicament in space-time. Once this occurs, Bob becomes aware of a larger amplitude of time—time he can measure with *his* watch—in which the seemingly simultaneous encounters in his room around the instant of the stuck keys took place.

After Bob in the first role and Bob in the second role go through the Gate, Bob (who is now in the third position) is left alone in the room. At this point, a new set of events occurs, tracing a wider loop that, at one and the same time, circumscribes, and inscribes itself into, the room and knot of his three "selves." This loop is bound by the hat that the second figure, in the earlier segment, tossed through the Gate to demonstrate time travel. Bob sits down to his thesis again but is interrupted by (what is for him "another") call from his girlfriend, Genevieve. He rudely dismisses her. She threatens legal action; he, moving along the line of his unfolding consciousness, has no idea why. Some time goes by, and he hears footsteps in the hall. Thinking it is Genevieve, he goes through the Gate. He finds himself alone in the control room but sees the hat on the floor and Diktor's list. Picking up both, he manipulates the Gate and displaces to a time that (he will later learn) is slightly *before* the time frame just experienced. He gets Diktor's items and returns to find the Gate gone. Glancing at his watch, which reads 2:30, he realizes the Gate is in his room and will remain there until 4:30, when he himself had moved it. He now relives this segment, going to Genevieve's room, seducing her, and leaving behind the hat she "later" returns to its point of departure in Bob's room. In the narrative, which follows Bob's adventure from his point of view, all this occurs later than the opening scene, when the hat is in Bob's closet. But if we heed Genevieve's phone call in that scene, where she claims to have the hat, then the hat is in two places at once, and the moment of its return is simultaneously later and *earlier* than the scene in the room. For how did it get there in the first place?

Bob now uses the Time Gate to inscribe a third loop of even wider amplitude around the same initial space-time point. Returning to the empty room, close to the moment of his earlier departure, he crosses the Gate as it disappears, within a hair's breadth of meeting himself. He goes back ten years in time, carrying the items on Diktor's list, and sets himself up as ruler of Norkaal. He lives ten years of biological time, up to the day when, while making adjustments on this time machine, he sweeps the original scene in the room. All at once, a person tumbles through the gate. He realizes this is the same scene he has already lived, but as the youngest Bob meeting Diktor. Suddenly, he sees he *is* Diktor. Bob's biological drama, which has played out in opposition to Diktor, now enfolds into Diktor; the person he has replaced (he realizes) is himself, just as another self waits, in an endless loop, to replace him in turn. The far points of his space-time curve meet to fix forever the "now" moment that broke from the continuum when Bob's keys stuck. In one sense, Bob's life is inscribed by this meeting as the minimal distance from one side of the Gate to the other. The "space" here is from Diktor's initial promise of "a great future" to Bob's final iteration of these exact same words. This is, as with the Watchett instant, the point where going out and coming back meet exactly, where linear time seems curved into itself to form here (as Heinlein extrapolates it) an ever repeating loop. Yet at the same time (as with Wells's Traveller, who, despite the Watchett instant, *knows* his travel was a unique experience in time, repeatable only in the retelling), the Bob whose journey was narrated must realize that he has *both* a great future and no future at all. As in *The Time Machine*, the "distance" between these two mirroring statements is Bob's biological timeline, a segment of which is this story's narrative.

Heinlein and Wells's Desktop Model

We remember, in Wells's novel, that the Traveller's narrative is preceded by the first narrator's telling of his demonstration of a model time machine. What is learned from this demonstration, as the miniature machine on the table "suddenly swung round, became indistinct, was seen for a ghost of a second [. . .] as an eddy of faintly glittering brass and ivory" (1, 10) and then vanished, is that the object travelling in time is simultaneously present in space. It is both "vanished," and still present. An attempt to explain this paradox is made by the Traveller: we are experiencing "diluted presentation," "presentation below the threshold." The Psychologist concurs:

> "We cannot see it, nor can we appreciate this machine, any more than we can the spoke of a wheel spinning, or a bullet flying through he air. If it is travelling through time fifty times [. . .] faster than we are, if it gets through a minute while we get through a second, the impression it creates will of course be only one-fiftieth [. . .] of what it would make if it were not travelling in time." [. . .] He passed his hand through the space in which the machine had been. (1, 11)

He is only reiterating the Traveller's earlier definition of time as a fourth dimension: "*There is no difference between Time and any of the three dimensions of Space except that our consciousness moves along it*" (1, 4). When the Traveller, however, mounts the real machine and goes from his laboratory into the future, what moves along this dimension is more than mind. For the Traveller not only tells of time lived in the far distant future, but his biological body bears marks of this experience. And yet, like the model that is simultaneously absent and present, Wells's protagonist, it seems, has and has not travelled. For, by his measurements, he returns both to the same place and the same time of his departure. Spatial location, as with the temporal coordinates provided by Mrs Watchett, are also precisely matched. Before this happens, however, there is a bit of drama, the possibility of an *almost* exact match, that shakes him from the tempting idea that "the whole thing [might] have been a dream," dreamt in a flash as he dozed off: "The thing had started from the south-east corner of the laboratory. It had come to rest again in the north-west." This discrepancy he immediately restores to exactitude: "That gives you the exact distance from my little lawn to the pedestal of the White Sphinx, into which the Morlocks had carried my machine" (12, 86).

For the Morlocks did move the machine, causing him to return to a slightly displaced spatial location. And Mrs Watchett's exact reversal of trajectory, which should make point of departure and return the same, proves (when the Traveller seeks to clock that return) slightly displaced as well. Whatever Wells intended, the ambiguity surrounding the measurement of the Traveller's time and place of return proves most fortunate for the future of time travel. The results might be called the pseudorelativity of the near miss. It is this that allows the post-Einsteinian Heinlein to generate Bob Wilson's loops as an unbroken timeline, which this narrative of a life follows (in the steps in fact of the Traveller's trajectory) from its beginning to end. Thinking perhaps of Wells's desktop model, Heinlein, in "By His Bootstraps," effects a miniaturization of the classical travel narrative. His construction of Bob's first set of loops, confined to a single room where he is at once fixed and moving in space-time, suggests an analogy with the Traveller's parlor and parlor game.

Mrs Watchett and the Geometry of the Loop

A close look at the clocks and temporal measurements of *The Time Machine* reveals discrepancies and uncertainties that imply at least a subliminal awareness on Wells's part of time as a relative phenomenon. It may seem strange then that Wells insists, in Newtonian fashion, on the fixed spatiotemporal locus inscribed by Mrs Watchett. For through the reversal of her trajectory in space-time, she would have to encounter the *exact* moment that she stepped into the laboratory. With this point established, Wells's Traveller begins to reintegrate his initial temporal frame. He will exactly do so at 10 A.M., the instant of his departure. As he puts it, "It was at ten o'clock today that the first of all Time Machines began its career" (3, 18). But can the reader be sure this departure was *exactly* at 10 A.M.? Here is the Traveller's next comment in his narrative:

> I took the starting lever in one hand and the stopping one in the other, pressed the first, and almost immediately the second. I seemed to reel; I felt a nightmare sensation of falling; and looking round, I saw the laboratory exactly as before. Had anything happened? For a moment I suspected that my intellect had tricked me. Then I noted the clock. A moment before [. . .] *it had stood at a minute or so past ten*; now it was nearly half-past three! (3, 18; emphasis added)

The Traveller is given, throughout his narrative, to using vague adverbs of time, such as "presently" or "nearly." Indeed, one can understand that his time sense—as consciousness moving along this fourth dimension—could easily be "tricked" by the astonishing nature of the experience. Yet Wells's stroke of genius, it seems, was to establish Mrs Watchett as insignificant absolute, as *sole* fixed point amid a timescape of temporal uncertainty, where if clocks still tell the time, the act of telling becomes increasingly fuzzy. In this passage, the slight discrepancy between the absolute precision of the Watchett measurement and the Traveller's vaguer sense of arrival time raises the possibility of two very close, yet different, times of return for a same person, placing him in two locations at once. In what seems a collision of two systems of temporality—one absolute, the other "relativistic"— Wells hits upon something akin to the later formulated sequence-simultaneity paradox. The relation of Mrs Watchett to the Traveller's story may have led Heinlein to reflect on the narrative possibilities of sequency-simultaneity—a situation no one had even proposed to *tell* until Wells.

From his post-Einsteinian viewpoint, Heinlein would notice certain, more obvious temporal discrepancies in Wells's narrative and discount them as quaint. *The Time Machine* takes no account of what later will be called The Twins Paradox. Indeed, why should it, as it involves physics Wells's age did not possess? Wells offers, however, an interesting "clock" problem in this domain. If the Traveller moves away from Mrs Watchett at a relative velocity increasingly greater than that of his initial space-time frame, the clock on his machine continues to measure days and years as if it were still located in the initial frame. As velocity increases, this clock should of course slow down in relation to clocks in the initial frame. The Traveller, looking out from his frame to that frame, sees the sun "hopping swiftly across the sky, leaping it every minute, and every minute marking a day" (3, 19). But the clock on the machine should only measure his time—the seven or so days of his experiences in the world of the Eloi and beyond.

Given this disparity—eight days on his timeline, 800,806 in the initial frame (802,701 A.D., his "arrival time," minus 1895 years, assuming that is the date of his departure, the date of the Heinemann edition of *The Time Machine*)—the Traveller would not need to go home. Were he able to do so, the world he would encounter would be precisely the one he describes—unless the very fact of his building a time machine and going to the future would have in turn deflected the timeline of the past. But then, the world he witnesses would never come into being, and we do notice that the Traveller does not find a model of a time machine among the exhibits at the Palace of Green Porcelain.

Other SF writers have shown interest in this aspect of Wells's narrative but generally only to "correct" it. Poul Anderson for example, in "Flight to Forever" (1952), revisits *The Time Machine* through the eyes of the "Einsteinian concept of light as limiting velocity." Given this barrier, the Traveller's puny machine could never have enough fuel to begin to get home:

> As you approach the speed of light, the energy needed to accelerate increases ever more rapidly. You'd need infinite energy to get beyond the speed of light—which is just a fancy way of saying you can't do it.[3]

Gregory Benford, in *Timescape* (1980), has his protagonist ask: "How do you get onto a spaceship moving by you faster than light? The idea's nonsense."[4] Wells's Traveller would have to travel faster than light to return to 1895. And even if he could (Benford posits faster-than-light particles or "tachyons" that, at most, may allow us to communicate with the past), where might that past be located?

> Aim for *what*? Where *is* 1963? Quite far away, as it works out. Since 1963, the earth's been going around the sun, while the sun itself is revolving around the hub of the galaxy, and so on. Add that up and you find 1963 is pretty distant.[5]

Benford's protagonist is speaking of the "distance" between 1963 and his time, 1999. Imagine the calculation required to find 1895 from the year 802,701!

The Twins Paradox addresses space-time travel, and it is to that domain that Heinlein relegated it, notably in the novel *Time for the Stars* (1953). But Wells specifically offers (however "erroneous") strictly *time* travel. His "invention" is a narrative form. And for it he insists that a time traveller can, indeed must, return to the point of departure. But must he return to the *exact* point, as the Watchett measurement seems to imply? Or rather, does or *can* he? Temporal discrepancies exist in Wells's narrative, but they all occur in a very tight radius around the simultaneity of departure and arrival suggested by Mrs Watchett. The disparities arise from the fact that, around this point, *some* time does seem to pass. Whatever the means of measurement—clock time or the biology of the Traveller—because time's arrow has moved ever so little the same problem Benford notes of *finding* the precise moment of departure is still present, all the more acutely perhaps because of the near miss, the promise of an elusive simultaneity. Rather than the broad space-time vistas of *The Time Machine* that later attracted Anderson, Heinlein focused on the narrow amplitude. His tribute to this focus is "By His Bootstraps."

Heinlein must have noticed how notoriously imprecise the temporal measurements around Mrs Watchett are. The Traveller tells that, touching the lever on his machine at 10:00 A.M. on the same Thursday morning as his return, he nudged forward in time so that when he glanced up after an instant, he read 3:30 P.M. on the clock. Now pulling the lever in earnest, he notices Mrs Watchett entering the laboratory: "I suppose it took her a minute or so to traverse the place, but to me she seemed to shoot across the room like a rocket" (3, 18). The "suppose" of the departure is matched by like vagueness in the description of Mrs Watchett on the return, where her motions only "appeared" to be the "exact inversion of her previous ones" (12, 86). The word "previous" indicates as well that, despite the measurement just taken, the Traveller still perceives in terms of sequential time.

It is significant that the Traveller is confident he can recalibrate spatial discrepancies but not temporal ones. When he notices his machine has come to rest in the northwest corner of the lab, not the southeast corner from which he departed, he says that the distance separating the two is the *exact* distance the Morlocks dragged it to bring it into the Sphinx. Whether or not he was in any state to make exact measurements when in terror of the Morlocks is not the point here. It is his manner of speech that is significant. For when he seeks to establish the same confluence in time, his language becomes much more vague. Upon returning, he tells the following: "For a time my brain went stagnant. Presently I got up and came through the passage here limping. [. . .] I found the date was indeed to-day, and looking at the timepiece, saw the hour was almost eight o'clock" (12, 86). The adverb "presently" covers a possible span of time from the "around 10am" of the initial departure, to the "almost 8pm" of his entrance into the dinner circle. The Traveller gives his audience the option of taking his narrative as the conventional dream—no time passes but that of a brief nodding off—or as artistic "lie," where there is no physical travel and the only time involved is the time it takes to tell the story. There is, however, as fact, a measurable span of time, of small amplitude in relation to the cosmic vistas narrated, but a real span nonetheless. The *terminus ante quem* is the departure on Thursday at 10 A.M. The Watchett measurement says the Traveller returned at exactly that time. Yet it seems unlikely, given the swiftness with which he calculates the relative spatial position of the machine, that the period his brain "went stagnant" lasted anything near ten hours. Say he returned instead at 2:30 P.M. There is time to be dazed, then go tell the story, see the guests off, and prepare for his new departure at 2 P.M. on the narrator's clock the next day. All in all, Wells is able to fit a vast time loop into a slice of the Traveller's timeline that hovers, with tantalizing imprecision, around the twenty-four hours called for by the classical unity of time. It remained for Heinlein to tighten this "window of opportunity," and by removing all suggestion of the dream or lie, to make the paradoxical complexities of this loop rigorously physical in nature.

An interesting exercise is to read *The Time Machine* in light of Heinlein's rigorous geometrizing of time in "By His Bootstraps." Through "Heinlein's eyes," otherwise unseen patterns in Wells's narrative appear, and the problems they pose may give a clue to how Heinlein, responding to them, came to shape the dynamics of his story. The first point is Bob Wilson's multiple loopings through a same space-time segment. In Wells's text, there are, if we look closely, three distinct loops contained within the larger loop, which is the departure–return–telling of the story–new departure.

The first loop is the scene in the parlor with the model, in which the instant of the miniature machine's departure, as it exists "below the threshold," is so close to that of its physical presence that it can be considered to be both there and not there at once. This may have inspired Heinlein's first scene in the room, where Bob, oscillating back and forth through the Time Gate in rapid succession, encounters other near instants of his own timeline, creating an effect of being present and yet absent in almost-simultaneous fashion.

In the second loop, the Traveller's exploration of the world of the Eloi and Morlocks inscribes a circuit that moves from a bench to a return "to the same seat of yellow metal from which I had viewed the world upon the evening of my arrival" (10, 77). This loop is in turn circumscribed by one generated from the seat of the time machine itself. Thrown from this saddle upon arrival, the Traveller "scrambles" back on it at the end of his stay under attack from the Morlocks. As we know, however, the emplacement of this seat is not exactly the same, as the machine has been dragged from its initial place of impact to inside the Sphinx. This may correspond with Bob's second loop—the hat circuit—in which he brackets a segment of larger amplitude around the initial instant of the Gate's appearance. Bob now is no longer a thing experimented on, a "model" knocked back and forth through time. Here he directs the process of time travel; in turn however, like Wells's Traveller, the extent of his travel, its amplitude, is simultaneously controlled by the geometry of the loop.

The third, overarching loop in Wells's story is that of the Traveller's fling into futurity and its return, controlled as we have seen by the Mrs Watchett instant. Once again, the fixity of a spatiotemporal instant offers a slight, but very significant, possibility of variance—the minimal displacement of the machine from one corner of the lab to the other, the inability to make a precise (or absolute) Watchett measurement. The sweep of this third loop is apparently that of all of human history, indeed, that of the life and death of the earth itself. It corresponds, on our schema, to the loop whereby Bob, taking control of the world of Norkaal, becomes Diktor, only to discover that the "distance" between this future world and his present one is still only that of slightest interval between Time Gate and student room, as the Bob he once was, and always will be, tumbles through to meet him, just as he had met Diktor in the beginning. Heinlein, sacrificing historical scope for logical rigor, chooses to condense Wells's macrocosm not just to a single destiny (the unnamed Traveller, too, is an everyman of sorts), but (following the Watchett logic to its inevitable conclusion) to a *single instant in that single destiny*. Somewhere between the absolute fixity of Wells's Universe Rigid— the Traveller moving forward, and backward, along a fixed row of numbers on a single timeline—and the law of special relativity that bars *this* traveller from ever returning to an exact point of departure, the Watchett episode opens a space of play, of pseudosimultaneity, in which Heinlein, it seems, generates his entire narrative. Indeed, given the Watchett measurement, Heinlein may have concluded that the only way to retain the sanctity of the original timeline is to imagine, in relation to the instant of departure and return, two or multiple Time Travellers in the form of the time doubles that plague Bob's existence. Heinlein might ask whether Traveller 1, the one that by Mrs Watchett's clock returns around 10 A.M., is actually older or younger than Traveller 2, whose return is "presently" before 8 P.M. As both are now in the same frame of reference, will not Traveller 1 have to live ten more hours before he can enter the dining room, while his double need only live five or six hours? The Traveller who first appeared to lose *no time*, returning to the exact space-time location from which he left, may in fact be the *older* of the two, having to live more time to catch up with his counterpart.

Differences may seem more significant than these similarities. For instance, the trajectory of Wells's Traveller to the end of human and even geological time seems to present an incomparably vaster sweep than Bob's solipsistic adventure. Yet, if we think in terms of loops, the Traveller's tale in fact enfolds its terminal future as the *past* of his narrative in the temporal continuum of Mrs Watchett and the primary narrator and dinner guests. The first narrator goes directly from the model demonstration to the dinner the following Thursday evening, into which the Traveller bursts. From this point in space-time, with only his own biological clock ticking as he progresses with the story, the Traveller returns in his tale to 10:00 A.M. that morning, then tells of travelling to the far reaches of time, to return via Mrs Watchett to "catch up" with the present moment. The scope of this analepsis (as with Odysseus at the Phaeacians) is at one and the same time vast and tiny. In the latter sense, as with Bob and the Gate, the distance between beginning and end of this space-time odyssey is measured in terms of the listeners' incredulity. As with Bob in his room, the Traveller both went to the end of time and never left his present location.

The largest amplitude in Wells's story is that of the birth and death of life on Earth, indeed of the thermodynamic process itself. This, however, is not physically experienced by the Traveller, but rather poetically rendered. At the farthest reaches of silence and darkness, the Traveller utters a recessional, in which he spells out (in direct analogy with the movement of Mrs Watchett in the physical realm) step by step the *exact* reversal of the process of entropy. He names a devolution from mankind's highest form of organized life back down through less-organized species to end on the primal shore from which these life forms first emerged: "All the sounds of man, the bleating of sheep, the cries of birds, the hum of insects, the stir that makes the background of our lives—all that was over"

(11, 84–85). The entire sweep of this process turns upon the Traveller's "now," enfolded in the observer's sole self, who in this mininarrative (another "model" of the time machine) can erase the forward thrust of time itself, making forward and backward, creation and end, coincide just as the two trajectories of Mrs Watchett seem to erase the temporal experience of the Traveller. Yet however condensed this "story," there remains the time of its telling, however brief. In Heinlein, this is the "time" that separates each successive copying of Diktor's notebook, each one coinciding with and erasing the other, yet each time leaving the slightest residue of linear time.

Heinlein in fact uses a direct bow to *The Time Machine* to present this same coincidence of farthest and nearest instants of the "historical" loop of his narrative. The "future" realm of Norkaal is peopled by degenerate (female) humans who resemble the Eloi. As Diktor explains, the High Ones "ruled more than twenty thousand years, and completely obliterated human culture as you knew it."[6] And yet, as with Wells's Traveller and his end-of-the-world narrative, the circumference of this future is clearly the sole life of Bob, and its amplitude no more than that of this life's two most distant temporal points—Bob and Diktor, as the person Bob has become meets the person he once was. Heinlein has tightened the loop; there is no longer, as with the Traveller's second voyage, any possibility of not returning to the point of departure. Diktor may tell Bob, in the beginning of the story as at the end, that more than 30,000 years separates their worlds. Simultaneously, however, that separation can never be greater than these two most distant stages of a seemingly ever-renewable life.

Confronting his own predicament caused by time displacement, Bob first responds in a way that reminds one of Wells's Traveller in his "Universe Rigid":

> Experienced as he was with the phenomena exhibited by the Time Gate, it nevertheless required a strong and subtle intellectual effort to think other than in durational terms, to take an *eternal* viewpoint.[7]

Bob, however, soon clearly sees (just as the Traveller learns how unfeasible it is to divide spatial and temporal dimensions along lines of physical location and "consciousness") that intellectual process cannot be separated from physical process. His term is "perpetual motion fur farm," and in it the dream of conservation of energy—the loop of self-perpetuation—is returned to time in the form of entropy. Not only must Bob ask: where did the energy come from? But more importantly: where does it go? Every Diktor has to copy the notebook containing the language of Norkaal. And though Bob's mind sees that "there never had been two notebooks" ("they were simply different segments of a same physical process"), his body, which has copied the new notebook, cannot explain where the old one goes. Where does each Diktor go after meeting with the new Bob who will replace him? If the system is renewed, it is winding down at the same time. The simultaneity of Bob/Diktor allows conservation. But given the lost notebooks and Diktors, even simultaneity cannot ultimately prevent the system itself from slowly winding down. The Time Traveller saw heat death and returned to inform his present of its inescapable future. At this final crux of paradox, Heinlein creates a story where a man is damned to relive endlessly the words of Wells's narrator—to live "as if it were not so" (E, 91). The "great future" promised Bob by time travel turns out to be not just a bad future, but no future at all. Trapped in the loop that promises him perpetual life, Bob can only "provide for his past," turn all his actions to shoring up the loop of paradox that sustains him.

Through the Needle's Eye: Sequence and Narrative

The problem Heinlein engages, at this Watchett moment or fixed point in the otherwise fluid space-time of time travel, is simultaneity. If Bob can establish the fact that he is in two places at once—both in the room and in the "future," both Diktor and Bob—then he can anchor the loop of his existence and shape his life as perpetual motion, in a constant if restricted present as past and future cancel each other in an endless "now." In a later story, Robert Silverberg describes time travellers like Bob (in thoroughly Einsteinian terms) as a "drifting bubble of now time ripped loose from the matrix of the continuum."[8] The continuum here is not only Wells's historical-evolutionary line but any world line relative to that of the time traveller—the line for instance in which Bob's keys stick. This bifurcation results, at one and the same time, in total freedom and total restriction. Silverberg describes this paradoxical state: "You can travel [in time travel stories] anywhere in *the* future, but there is no way at all to get into *your* future or *your* past."[9] Inscribed in the simultaneity loop then, because anchored in the single instant of departure from this "matrix," is that ineluctable sequence of events that constitutes the biological lifeline of the individual traveller.

Toward the end of the story, Bob Wilson becomes intellectually aware of this divided condition:

> When he had doubled back on himself, the difference had become apparent, for the separation was now in space rather than in time, and he happened to be so equipped as to be able to *see* a space length, whereas he could only remember a time difference. Thinking back he could remember a great many different Bob

Wilsons ... They were all different ... The only thing that bound them together into a feeling of identity was continuity of memory. And that was the same thing that bound together the three—no, four, Bob Wilsons on a certain crowded afternoon.[10]

This awareness is the product of a sequence. And the medium in which this unidirectional flow of biology and memory occurs, in continuous fashion, is the narrative itself. Bob does not tell his own story, but the narrator closely follows, from beginning to end, the point of view of the single consciousness whose fingers first stick on the keys, who then passes through a series of encounters, leading to the discovery that he has not just displaced a Diktor figure in space, but has physically become Diktor in time, has acquired gray hair and lines on his face.

In like manner, Wells's Traveller bears marks of the passage of biological time on his person, marks that cannot be explained in terms of the spacelike loops around the simultaneous departure and arrival of Mrs Watchett. Wells's Traveller too can go anywhere he wants in *the* future. But he can move into his own future only by telling his story, by telling what happened to him, in whatever time frame, in the order he perceived the events. The story of Heinlein's Bob would be much less troubling if there were only solipsistic space-time, a floating bubble of now time, to contend with. But there is the narrative of Bob as well. As it is in Wells, so in Heinlein the sense of sequency derives not from the *story* of future travel, but from the Traveller's narrative of his ongoing exploration of a world of physical data, an exploration that comprises the growth of a *consciousness*, a mind increasingly aware of the meaning of its environment. It is not far-fetched to say that a particularly striking aspect of Wells's Traveller may have given Heinlein the means of reintroducing sequency at the center of his implacable geometry of the loop. This aspect is the Traveller's markedly open-ended manner of perceiving his world. For it is Bob's similar ability to perceive and conceive—all along, from beginning to end, as unbroken process—that lets Heinlein, now on the level of narrative function, restore sequency to a world otherwise frozen in time.

The activity of Wells's Traveller, while travelling in time, is that of the modern perceiver-in-duration. He picks up information, forms tentative hypotheses, encounters further information that leads to altered or new ideas, and so on, all in a ceaseless and unbroken process of exploring his strange environment, becoming familiar with it in hopes of understanding it.[11] For Wells's Traveller, unlike voyagers of earlier travel fiction, conception is never the end product of perception, a statement fixed and finished, abstracted from duration. Here instead, the difference between these stages has become one of degree, not of kind. As the Traveller moves through the world of the Eloi, he first registers vague generalizations, then picks up more precise details, and finally formulates a hypothesis that is in turn modified or abandoned as new data is acquired. In terms of his expectations, the process may prove regressive (he hopes to find a highly advanced civilization but gradually discovers a retrograde one). The important thing, however, is that the process is never broken or completed. The geometry of the loop is formed of this unbroken band of experience, which will change, age, but never reverse direction nor end until perception is occluded, or until the perceiver vanishes or dies. In the land of the Eloi and the Morlocks, the Traveller's activity ends only as his last match is extinguished, and he climbs on his machine in the dark. Or in his final "fling" into time, past or future, from which he never returns.

Bob Wilson may be caught in a fatal loop. But as he moves through this loop, *during the space-time of the narrative,* he functions as an active consciousness in the manner of Wells's Traveller. From the story alone, its fatal geometry, we imagine Bob, beyond the limits of the narrative, continuing to inscribe a figure that passes through the same set of space-time locations, over and over forever. Within the duration of the narrative, however, Bob *as individual consciousness* passes each of these locations only once, moving in an unbroken stream of pickup of information and conceptualization. In terms of the story—that of a man doomed to loop through a single space-time instant, endlessly meeting near-alike "versions" of himself—there can be no first or last Bob. In terms of the narrative, however, the reader begins with one Bob and follows his single consciousness as he perceives and conceives what is (however solipsistic) his entire environment. Each of his entries into what he soon perceives as the same room and situation is made from a different, yet new and continuous, point of view. New data are picked up and processed each time, new conclusions are drawn, refuted, adjusted, until finally Bob, in the Oedipal manner of the Traveller (whose world is explicitly presided over by the White Sphinx of time), figures out his predicament and realizes he is trapped in the toils of his own logic—that he is the mystery he set out to solve.

Heinlein, then, uses the traditional form of narrative itself, as the process of perceiving and telling in duration, to restore sequency within the elegant yet dehumanizing geometry of space-time curves generated by temporal paradox. Rather than simply construct the paradox of sequency-simultaneity, he succeeds in *telling* it. Admittedly, the conclusion to this essay must remain highly speculative, for there is no concrete "evidence," other than the parallels suggested, that Heinlein reduced the riches of *The Time Machine* to a sequency-simultaneity problem. Or, more significant, that he developed (in stunningly original fashion) the narrative possibilities of this paradox and the means of resolving it by combining what otherwise might appear contradictory elements in Wells's novel. There is, on the one hand, Mrs Watchett and the geometry of simultaneity her presence suggests. On the other, the following the loop in unbroken manner, there is the sequential activity of the Traveller: his biological timeline, and more importantly, the growth of his mind as reflected in the duration of his narrative. In the end, however, whether and to what degree Wells "influenced" Heinlein is less important than the insights gained into the deep structure of *The Time Machine*—the less-than-evident and troubling aspects that underlie its expression of the paradox of time travel—when reread through the hypothetical eyes of Heinlein, in light of his brilliant restructuring.

Notes

1. Robert A. Heinlein, "By His Bootstraps," in *The Menace from Earth* (New York: Signet, 1959).

2. Cited in Robert P. Mills, *The Worlds of Science Fiction* (New York: Paperback Library, 1970), p. 102.

3. Poul Anderson, "Flight to Forever," *Super Science Stories* (January 1952), 18.

4. Gregory Benford, *Timescape* (New York: Pocket Books, 1980), p. 33.

5. Ibid., p. 9.

6. "By His Bootstraps," p. 47. The comparison here is with Diktor's call for "twentieth-century style go-getters" to regenerate this decadent future world, the same way George Pal, in his 1960 film version of *The Time Machine,* brought his modern time traveller into a future where he neither observed nor despaired and spoiled, but actively sought to regenerate the Eloi, to give them back the will to fight in actively "go-getter" fashion.

7. "By His Bootstraps," p. 86.

8. Robert Silverberg, *Up the Line* (New York: Ballantine, 1969), p. 34.

9. Ibid., p. 31.

10. "By His Bootstraps," p. 82.

11. See Danièle Chatelain, *Perceiving and Telling: A Study of Iterative Discourse* (San Diego: San Diego State University Press, 1998). Especially relevant is chapter 6, "Aspects," which discusses the process of narrative as one of ongoing pickup of information and conceptualization.

A Revision and a Gloss

Michael Bishop's Postmodern Interrogation of H. G. Wells's *The Time Machine*

DAVID LEON HIGDON

 With the coining of one word—*counter-book*—and the penning of a few deft sentences written in 1935, 1939, and 1940, the Argentinean author Jorge Luis Borges pinpointed the key directions both postmodernist fiction and theory would pursue during the rest of the twentieth century. The term made its appearance in his 1940 "Tlön, Uqbar, Orbis Tertius," in which he noted: "A book which does not include its opposite, or 'counter-book,' is considered incomplete."[1] If one pursues the idea of a counterbook within the text, he or she moves further and further into deconstructive theory; on the other hand, if one pursues the idea between texts, he or she moves into the realm of intertextuality. In "Pierre Menard, Author of the Quixote" (1940), Borges pursued the former; in "The Approach to Al-Mu'tasim" (1935), he sought the latter, especially when its narrator announces: "That a present-day book should derive from an ancient one is clearly honorable: especially since no one [. . .] likes to be indebted to his contemporaries."[2]

One of the most pervasive tendencies in postmodernism has been the production of such counterbooks, and one of the most unusual mannerist features within this larger category has been the creation of books that self-consciously appropriate texts and then colonize, parasitize, and actually replicate them.[3] I am not speaking of those novels such as Jean Rhys's *Wide Sargasso Sea* (1966), B. S. Johnson's *Albert Angelo* (1964), John Fowles's *The French Lieutenant's Woman* (1969), or Stephen Baxter's *The Time Ships* (1995), which explore and fill in gaps, aporia, and interstices in older texts, but rather to works such as George Macdonald Fraser's *Royal Flash* (1971), Brian W. Aldiss's *Frankenstein Unbound* (1973), and even William Golding's *Lord of the Flies* (1954), which quite literally dismantle the original work and then reconstruct it along radically new lines of thought or attitude. *Royal Flash*, for example, purports to unveil the historicity freely fantasized in Anthony Hope Hawkins's *The Prisoner of Zenda* (1894). Behind the fictions of Ruritania, Rudolf Rassendyll, Princess Flavia, and the sinister Duke Michael, Fraser asks us to see the historical realities of the Schleswig-Holstein affair, Dano-German political tensions during the 1840s, Otto von Bismarck's machinations in the interest of a larger German state, Lola Montez's escapades, and the 1848 revolutions that tore Europe apart. Both Flashman and his "editor" insist that their reality impeaches, displaces, and deconstructs the romantic fictions of Hope: "Only once did I tell the tale," Flashman recalls, "and that was privately some years ago to young Hawkins, the lawyer—I must have been well foxed, or he was damned persuasive—and he has used it for the stuff of one of his romances, which sells very well, I'm told," while the editor notes, "Whether Flashman's real-life experiences in Germany provided Anthony Hope with the basis of his famous romance, *The Prisoner of Zenda*, is a matter which readers must decide for themselves."[4] Aldiss's *Frankenstein Unbound* even more boldly, audaciously, some would say, appropriates the structure, the characters, the themes, even the closing sentence of Mary Shelley's *Frankenstein* (1818) in order to foreground the relevance of the novel's themes to twentieth-century society, creating what Aldiss has called "an exegetical novel" that is "pastiche and something more."[5]

Theory and history concur: whether it is Northrop Frye, in 1957, stating the neo-classical viewpoint that books are made of other books,[6] or Julia Kristeva, who is generally credited with coining the term "intertextuality," commenting in 1966: "any text is constructed as a mosaic of quotations; any text is the absorption and transformation of another,"[7] or—even more succinctly—"texts smell of other texts. [. . .] Every text is from the outset under the jurisdiction of other discourses, which impose a universe on it."[8]

In America in 1983, Michael Bishop's *No Enemy but Time* (1982) received one of science fiction's highest awards, the Nebula Prize, and was praised for "its depth of characterization" and its "believable and poignant" depiction of the "dilemma of a person caught out of time."[9] "Brilliant and memorable, written with great conviction," the standard science fiction encyclopedia, *Anatomy of Wonder*, describes it.[10] Bishop's fellow authors praised him as "one of the most inventive writers in the current science fiction field," recommending him "without reservation."[11] *Science Fiction and Fantasy Book Review* went so far as to declare his novel "required reading for those who take science fiction seriously."[12] Surprisingly, no one remarked its many ties with and to H. G. Wells's *The Time Machine*, although Bishop's novel is indeed explicitly a Borgesian counterbook to Wells's novel—a counterbook that appropriates, replies, supplements, and "wraps." I have found Fredric Jameson's discussion of the Frank Gehry house and his appropriation of the architectural term "wrapping" most useful in describing the relationship between these two texts—as well as others. Jameson comments: "one text is simply being wrapped in another, with the paradoxical effect that the first [...] becomes affirmed as autonomous and as a kind of unity in its own right. [...] The next discourse works hard to assimilate the 'primary text' [...] into its own substance, transcoding its elements, foregrounding all the echoes and analogies, sometimes even borrowing the stylistic features of the illustration in order to forge the neologisms, that is to say, the official terminology of the theoretical wrapper from them."[13] Gehry himself commented quite relevantly: "I wanted to explore the relationship between the two. I got fascinated with the idea that the old house should appear to remain totally intact from the outside, and that you could look through the new house, and see the old house as though it was not packaged in this new skin."[14]

As one reads *No Enemy but Time*, one probably need not be told that Bishop majored in English, took a master's degree in English literature (from the University of Georgia), and wrote a thesis on the poetry of Dylan Thomas, to explain the obvious literariness of his novel.[15] *No Enemy but Time* is replete with literary allusions, allusions to figures as diverse as Edgar Allan Poe, Jonathan Swift, J. R. R. Tolkien, Charles Lamb, Sir Thomas Browne, John Collier, William Butler Yeats, Stephen King, and others, but, by far, most of its allusions point directly to H. G. Wells.[16] True, one could pass over all its references to time travel, chrononauts, and time machines without necessarily thinking of intertextual ties with Wells. These, after all, are now standard in the vocabulary of science fiction. But then come the obvious, inescapable references: "The belly of the water tank glistened above them like the turret of a Martian war machine,"[17] an unmistakable allusion to *The War of the Worlds*. Bishop's protagonist happens to be working for the United States government on a secret time travel project whose code name—The White Sphinx Project—clearly points to *The Time Machine*. About three-fourths of the way through the novel, the references become tellingly explicit: "Time travel as H. G. Wells envisioned it is an utter impossibility,"[18] explains Alaistair Patrick Blair, leader of the project, and Joshua Kampa tells the Sambusai warriors who have blockaded the Zarakelian highway, thus stopping the scientific expedition on its way to the lake site, "H. G. Wells revisited. [...] It's a time machine. Only trouble is, you have to be me to use it."[19]

All of us have our favorite lines in the scientific romances. Surely "The Martians understood doors!" counts as one such line in *The War of the Worlds*.[20] My favorite line in *The Time Machine* succinctly captures the illusioned optimism,

hopes, and expectations of the Time Traveller: "so with a kind of madness growing upon me, I flung myself into futurity" (3, 20). Bishop's protagonist flings himself with an equal "kind of madness" into the distant past, thus setting up a dialogue with Wells's novel while also replicating most of its features. Indeed, in the
epilogue to Wells's novel, the young narrator ponders what fate befell the Time
Traveller, who has now been absent for three years, and, for a moment, he wonders if perhaps he was "swept back into the past," where he may have fallen
"among the blood-drinking, hairy savages of the Age of Unpolished Stone; [. . .]
or among the grotesque saurians, the huge reptilian brutes of the Jurassic times"
(E, 91). Because most of my readers probably do not know Bishop's novel well, I
wish to summarize it in some detail, remarking along the way its many connections with *The Time Machine*, before turning my attention to larger questions of
dialogics, intertextuality, and the contemporary culture's appropriation of texts
from the past.

   Bracketed by a brief prologue and a longer coda, both set in 2002, the thirty
chapters of Bishop's novel tell two stories: the odd-numbered chapters record in
reliable third person a young man's life from his birth in Seville in 1963 until the
moment he settles into a time machine in 1987, under the auspices of the White
Sphinx Project, to travel into the past of Zarakel, a fictional African country
"roughly coextensive with [the geographical dimensions] of Kenya";[21] meanwhile,
the even-numbered chapters report in first person his two years among the Homo
habilis of the Pleistocene Age, some two million years earlier. A narrative is thus
wrapped within a tale, or, according to the chapters, a dream within a tale, just as
are the Time Traveller's adventures in the exotic world of the Eloi and Morlocks
and Marlow's adventures in the Congo in Joseph Conrad's *Heart of Darkness*.

   Joshua Kampa's adventures on the Pleistocene shores of Lake Kiboko and in
the foothills of Mount Tharaka in Africa's Great Rift Valley have a familiar ring
to them, both because they fully integrate scientific knowledge of Homo habilis
earned through Bishop's "protracted research" in the writings of Louis and Mary
Leakey, Donald Johanson, Jane Goodall, and other paleoanthropologists, and
because the narrative line is so similar to that developed by Wells.[22] Of course,
writing ninety years after Wells, after the *Soyuz*, *Apollo*, *Mir*, and *Skylab* space
flights, after the even more widely probing *Mariner*, *Luna*, *Viking*, and *Voyager*
expeditions, and after the daily presence of high technology such as computers
in our lives, Bishop can be both more detailed and less detailed in many matters
than was Wells. For instance, he does not need to discuss the fourth dimension
or time travel as such or provide the self-authenticating evidence surrounding
the Time Traveller,[23] but he can be more detailed about the appearance of the

time machine apparatus, the kinds of supplies one might take on such a journey, and the kinds of preparatory training a contemporary time traveller would need to undergo.[24]

Like the Time Traveller, Joshua Kampa uses his technical superiority to impress his audience. He uses his matches; he uses his gun a number of times; he even uses his knowledge of cooking in a delightful parody of Charles Lamb's roast pig essay.[25] On the whole, though, he finds the hominids well on the way to humanity as he observes their sense of community, hears their rudimentary hymns to the dawn, experiences their intriguing death rituals, and even joins in their evolving sense of monogamous pairing. Bishop undoubtedly selected the Homo habilis because they have been regarded as the crucially intermediate hominid form between the Australopithecines and Homo sapiens since the initial discoveries of their fossils in Olduvai Gorge in 1960–64 and Koobi Fora on the eastern shore of Lake Turkana in 1969–76. (Lake Turkana is the site of the adventures of Joshua Kampa.) Bishop fully exploits the belief that the species made a variety of simple tools and had begun to use language.[26] Like the Time Traveller, Joshua is gradually inducted into the group, falls in love with a woman of the tribe, and loses virtually all while fleeing through a fire. Unlike the Time Traveller, though, Joshua experiences the beginnings rather than the endings of humanness. The Eloi find little to value in the Time Traveller, because their intellectual, even their sexual, curiosity has been extinguished; Bishop's hominids quickly come to value Joshua—his gun, his knife, his fire, even his height. Distanced, even repelled, at first by the tribe, Joshua becomes thoroughly integrated into it, finding in oneness with its members a comfort and a healing. At one point near the end of his adventures, he thinks: "[m]y total absorption into both the Minid band and their curious simulacrum of the Pleistocene altered even the texture of my subconscious mind. [...] By becoming a habiline and accepting the reality of their world I had purified my dreams."[27] Joshua does not rescue Helen from helpless drowning as the Time Traveller does Weena, nor do he and Helen indulge in any of what V. S. Pritchett once called "faint squirms of idyllic petting."[28] Instead, he finds in Helen a warrior woman capable of holding her own with the hunters, a woman who has made a significant evolutionary leap in reproductive organs; a woman who is brave, curious, inventive, and clever. The Time Traveller may not understand "until it was too late [...] what [Weena]" (5, 44) was to him, but Joshua immediately understands Helen. Helen's genes have placed her in the sexual vanguard, leaving her unable to breed with the habiline males but responsive to Joshua who introduces to his new world the face-to-face sexual position. Like Weena, she represents something very human. The Time Traveller posits that Weena may well be the last glimpse of humanity, because she still is capable of expressing love and affection; she still has the emotional capacity of a human being, whereas the other Eloi have surrendered virtually all signs of love, gratitude, benevolence, and caring—those qualities that we generally think distinguish the human from the animal. Likewise, Helen experiences these emotions to a much greater degree than the other members of the Minid tribe. She attracts Joshua because she "had uncanny self-reliance and poise."[29] Helen becomes pregnant but—not fully prepared by evolution—dies giving birth to their daughter, who is in many ways the first major step toward Homo sapiens. Literally killed by her daughter's large skull and brain, Helen dies on a brilliantly lit backdrop, complete with earthquakes, a sky ripped apart by lightning and powdered by the ash from Mount Tharaka's eruption. Joshua gathers up his newly born daughter and flees, just as the Time Traveller desperately fled from the Morlocks. The fire scene in *The Time Machine* is surely one of its most dramatic moments. Recall the Time Traveller's desperate plight: surrounded by Morlocks, wanting to rescue Weena from their jaws, using fire to protect himself. "The forest seemed full of the smell of burning wood," he tells us, "I was caught by the neck, by the hair, by the arms, and pulled down. It was indescribably horrible in the darkness to feel all these soft creatures heaped upon me. I felt as if I was in a monstrous spider's web. I was overpowered, and went down. I felt little teeth nipping at my neck. I rolled over, and as I did so my hand came against my iron lever. It gave me strength" (9, 74). There are no Morlocks in Joshua's world, but there are equally dangerous leopards, lions, and hyenas of several varieties, and he has the misfortune to blunder into a pack of hyenas as he flees with Grub, his immediate name for his newborn daughter. He describes the scene thus: "Running past me—away from the brand that I tried to plunge into its face—the hyena twisted its body about and took my leg into its jaws. By bracing its feet and forcibly tugging, it upended me. This, I remembered, was virtually the same tactic the hyenas at the water hole had used to drag down the rhino calf. As I fell, I tossed aside my torch and tried to shift my weight so that the Grub would receive none of the inevitable impact. [. . .] Despite my preparations, these sudden jolts sent the Grub tumbling through a powdery coverlet of ash. Stunned, I lay where I had fallen unable to go after my daughter or to resist the hateful savagery of the hyena."[30] At this moment, Bishop inscribes a *deus ex machina* of which even Wells would have been proud. These scenes in which the protagonists attempt to negotiate a return to the historic present achieve mythic status as precisely the kinds of threshold struggles with the "transcendental powers [that] must remain behind" that Joseph Campbell delineated in *The Hero with a Thousand Faces*.[31]

At one point in his narrative, Joshua thinks, "Our entire world was a negative steeping in the chemicals of a photographic developing solution,"[32] and this metaphor can usefully be extended to exploring the relationship between Bishop's and Wells's novels. The one is a negative from which the positive of the second is eventually developed. Together they bracket human history, stretching as they do from protohuman stirrings to posthuman silences. To use that dreadful word our generation has coined: Bishop's novel is a *prequel* to Wells' novel, but it is also much, much more.[33]

The "enclosing narrative" Bishop wraps around the "embedded narrative" is much fuller, more technically and thematically complex, and more engaging than the one in *The Time Machine*, largely because Bishop's protagonist has more history, more personalized past, and more contextualization. The racially and physically marginalized son of Encarnación Consuela Ocampo, a tiny, mute, black-market dealer of Morisco heritage, long considered a *bruja* (witch) by her neighbors in Seville, and "Lucky" James Bledsoe, teenage son of an African American air force officer stationed in Spain, Joshua Kampa is "on the verge of being a feral child"[34] before his mother, for all the right reasons, abandons him in June 1963 in the Santa Clara housing addition next to the air force base where he becomes the adopted son of Hugo and Jeanette Monegal. His life becomes that of the typical air force "brat," as his parents move from Spain to Kansas then Wyoming then New York before he runs away from home at sixteen and settles in Florida, experiences drawn from Bishop's own life as "an airforce brat" who once studied in Spain.[35] No expert in physical optics as is the Time Traveller, Joshua is a day laborer, working for Gulf Coast Coating sandblasting and repainting water towers when he imparts his knowledge of Homo habilis onto Alaistair Patrick Blair, Woody Kaprow, and the White Sphinx Project.

Much as his mixed racial and cultural heritage and physical appearance set him apart from the other air force children, and also from the children in the various small towns where the Monegals live, Joshua's dreaming further marginalizes him. He is as unusual, as marginalized, as the throwback Neanderthal in Doris Lessing's *The Fifth Child* (1988);[36] however, he is no throwback. Rather he is a bridge between the worlds of past and present, capable of living in both. From infancy, he has been a prodigious time traveller. We are told that he "had an especially vivid dream life," that he experienced "recurring thalamic jaunts into the Pleistocene," and that he can virtually dream himself into the past.[37] He has kept a dream diary since he was nine but recalls that his peculiar dreams began even earlier: "All my dreams were a kind of [. . .] well, I called it spirit-traveling. My spirit-traveling always took me to the same goddamn place. I'd had these special sorts of dream ever since I was a baby, but it wasn't until I was seven or eight that I began to realize not only *where* I was going but *when*." This emphasis on dreams immediately questions the reality of time travel in the novel. Does Joshua actually enter the Pleistocene past during the adventures in the even-numbered, first-person chapters, or do these record an especially vivid and lengthy dream? This challenge is posed in the novel's very first sentence: "I time-traveled in spirit long before I did so in bodily fact."[38]

The enclosing narrative avoids the linear construction of Kampa's tale and plays freely with chronology, moving from a chapter in 1969 to one in 1964, following a July 1985 action with one in 1981, and so on. This is fully to be expected, because in the 2002 prologue, "Next Slide, Please," Joshua makes clear to the reader that he will create his own "time machine," "a kind of wacky chaos," he calls it. When he was a child, he tells us, he "spent a good thirty minutes randomly rearranging slides [for the family slide projector], leaving gaps in the sequence and slotting several transparencies sideways or upsidedown." He tells himself, "My shuffling of images managed to convey nuances that linear sequence could not really communicate. Each click of the changer was a revision and a gloss."[39] The juxtapositions, cross-references, counter-references, repetitions, effects before causes, dramatic ironies, reflexivities, anticipations, and so on define the aesthetic structure of the novel and provide the reader with a superb instance of what I have elsewhere called barrier time and what Ian Watt has called delayed decoding.[40] Thus, we time travel with Joshua long before he becomes the key chrononaut with the White Sphinx Project itself; the discussion of the possibilities of visiting the past come long after the reader has actually experienced the visit; the mundane sandblasting in Blackwater Springs, Florida comes after his adventures with the chalicotheres. On the other hand, the accidental death of Hugo Monegal is paired with the accidental death of the hominid Genly, and Joshua's induction into his foster family in Santa Clara brackets his first meeting with the hominids.[41] And Bishop toys with the time dilation effect by spinning the clock of the present thirty-three days while allowing the clock of the Pleistocene past to tick away two years, not attempting the exact temporal fit achieved in Wells's novel between the Time Traveller's Thursdays, but certainly echoing Wells's expansion of a few hours into a few days since the Time Traveller's journey into the year 802,701 occurs between four and eight o'clock one afternoon and evening.[42]

Between the two narratives and the two novels, then, clusters of any number of binary oppositions present themselves to the reader—American/English, postmodern/Victorian, past/future, then/now, optimism/pessimism, beginnings/

closures, dream/reality, protohuman/posthuman—as Bishop and Wells inscribe a history of hominids. *No Enemy but Time* stands in a very convoluted relationship with Wells's novel. It is simultaneously a reply, a parody, a supplement, an interrogation, an affirmation, a rebuttal, an homage—paradoxically both an ancestor and a descendant. Most of all, though, it is a problematizing of one of the defining myths of science fiction. In *A Poetics of Postmodernism*, Linda Hutcheon argued that "[p]arody is a perfect postmodern form, in some senses, for it paradoxically both incorporates and challenges that which it parodies."[43] "The collective weight of parodic practice," she continues, "suggests a redefinition of parody as repetition with critical distance that allows ironic signalling of differences at the very heart of similarity."[44] Parody, however, is an inadequate term for glossing Bishop's novel.

Can we time travel? At the very end of the novel, Joshua Kampa closes his eyes and thinks: "Time ceased to have any conventional meaning. History had been repealed, the future indefinitely postponed."[45] Bishop has indeed repealed history in a sense. He has looked long and lovingly at Wells's *The Time Machine*, a work that he could not literally inhabit, but to it he has added an extension, a remodeled wing, a lean-to if you wish, and through it he has firmly, clearly, joyfully restated the permanent appeal of the work that we are celebrating with this book. Bishop once said that "another of my hopes is to bring a certain degree of seriousness and consequentiality to science-fiction without gutting it of its imaginative vigor or rendering it pretentious."[46] He has more than realized this agenda with his homage to H. G. Wells and discovered for us, in the words of Borges, that "work that endures is always capable of an infinite and plastic ambiguity."[47]

Notes

1. Jorge Luis Borges, "Tlön, Uqbar, Orbis Tertius," trans. Alastair Reid, in *Fictions*, ed. Anthony Kerrigan (New York: Grove Press, 1962), p. 29.

2. Jorge Luis Borges, "The Approach to Al-Mu'tasim," trans. Anthony Kerrigan, in *Fictions*, p. 42. The story, which Borges called "both a hoax and a pseudo-essay," was written in 1935; see "An Autobiographical Essay," *The Aleph and Other Stories 1933–1969*, ed. and trans. Norman Thomas di Giovanni (New York: Dutton, 1970), p. 239.

3. I discuss this phenomenon in my *Shadows of the Past in Contemporary British Fiction* (Athens: University of Georgia Press, 1984), pp. 79–130.

4. George Macdonald Fraser, *Royal Flash* (New York: New American Library, 1971), pp. 242, 247.

5. Higdon, pp. 116, 117.

6. Northrop Frye, *Anatomy of Criticism* (Princeton: Princeton University Press, 1957), pp. 15–18.

7. Julia Kristeva, "Word, Dialogue and Novel," in *The Kristeva Reader*, ed. Toril Moi (New York: Columbia University Press, 1986), p. 37. Almost simultaneously, Roland Barthes was enunciating the same idea. In "Death of the Author," he wrote: "A text is made of multiple writings, drawn from many cultures and entering into mutual relations of dialogue, parody, contestation, but there is one place where this multiplicity is focused and that place is the reader, not, as was hitherto said, the author." (Roland Barthes, *Image Music Text*, trans. Stephen Heath [New York: Noonday Press, 1977], p. 148.) Barthes's essay was first published in 1968.

8. Julia Kristeva, *La Révolution du Langage Poètique* (Paris: Éditions du Seuil, 1974), pp. 338–39. The passage reads: "Quel que soit le contenu sémantique d'un texte, son statut en tant que pratique signifiante présuppose l'existence des autres discours, au sens fort du terme de 'présupposition', celui qu'il a dans l'analyse de la locution. C'est dire que tout texte est d'emblée sous la juridiction des autres discours qui lui imposent un univers: il s'agira de le transformer. Par rapport au texte comme pratique signifiante, tout énoncé est un acte de présupposition qui agit comme une incitation à la transformation."

9. *The New Encyclopedia of Science Fiction*, ed. James Gunn (New York: Viking, 1986), p. 53. Also see the entry in *The Encyclopedia of Science Fiction*, ed. John Clute and Peter Nicholls (New York: St. Martin's, 1993), p. 126.

10. *Anatomy of Wonder 4: A Critical Guide to Science Fiction*, ed. Neil Barron (New York: Bowker, 1981), p. 250.

11. Michael Bishop, *No Enemy but Time* (New York: Pocket Books, 1982), quoted on back cover.

12. Bishop, inside cover.

13. Fredric Jameson, *Postmodernism: Or, The Cultural Logic of Late Capitalism* (Durham, N.C.: Duke University Press, 1991), p. 103.

14. Quoted in Jameson, p. 109.

15. See *Contemporary Authors*, ed. Cynthia R. Fadool, vols. 61–64 (Detroit: Gale Research, 1976), p. 68, and *Contemporary Authors, New Revision Series*, ed. Ann Evory and Linda Metzger, vol. 9 (Detroit: Gale Research, 1983), p. 57.

16. For Poe see Bishop, pp. 15–16, 61; for Swift, p. 61; for Tolkien, p. 94; for Lamb, p. 135; for Browne, p. 143; for Collier, p. 152; for Yeats, pp. 236–37; for King, p. 282.

17. Ibid., p. 255.

18. Ibid., p. 276.

19. Ibid., p. 322. In his novella, "The White Otters of Childhood" (1973), Bishop further signals his interest in Wells by naming a leading character after the protagonist of *The Island of Doctor Moreau*.

20. H. G. Wells, *The War of the Worlds*, Atlantic Edition (London: Unwin, 1924), p. 397.

21. Bishop, p. 7.

22. Ibid., p. 7. Bishop had obviously read such works as Louis Leakey, *Adam's Ancestor* (New York: Harper and Row, 1960), Mary Leakey, *Olduvai Gorge* (London: Collins, 1979), and Donald Johanson and Maitland Edey, *Lucy: the Beginnings of Humankind* (New York: Simon & Schuster, 1981).

23. By "self-authenticating evidence," I refer to those items appearing in the present time during the Richmond Thursday evening, which are explained by the events in the future: for example, the Time Traveller's physical appearance, his limp, the damage to the machine, his cut, the distance the machine has moved, and the white flowers.

24. Bishop, pp. 28–29.

25. Ibid., p. 135.

26. Philip Rightmire, "Homo Habilis," *Encyclopedia of Human Evolution and Prehistory*, ed. Ian Tattersall, Eric Delson, and John Van Couvering (New York: Garland, 1988), p. 267.

27. Bishop, p. 295.

28. V. S. Pritchett, *The Living Novel* (London: Chatto & Windus, 1946), p. 164.

29. Bishop, p. 60.

30. Ibid., p. 344.

31. Joseph Campbell, *The Hero with a Thousand Faces* (New York: Pantheon, 1949), p. 246.

32. Bishop, p. 341.

33. In *The Definitive Time Machine: A Critical Edition of H. G. Wells's Scientific Romance with Introduction and Notes*, ed. Harry M. Geduld (Bloomington: Indiana University Press, 1987), Geduld lists three sequels to the novel: Egon Friedell, *The Return of the Time Machine* (New York: Daw, 1972); George Pal and Joe Morhaim, *Time Machine II* (New York: Dell, 1981); and Christopher Priest, *The Space Machine* (New York: Popular Library, 1978).

34. Bishop, p. 71.

35. See Note 19 and Phil Garner, "The Prophetic World of Michael Bishop," *Atlanta Journal and Constitution* (4 April 1946), reprinted in *Authors in the News* (Detroit: Gale Research, 1976), II, pp. 31–32.

36. Doris Lessing, *The Fifth Child* (New York: Vintage, 1989). Looking at Ben, her "goblin child" (96), his mother identifies her son with "all those different people who lived on the earth once—they must be in us somewhere" (114) and later feels "she was looking, through him, at a race that reached its apex thousands and thousands of years before humanity, whatever that meant, took this stage." (130) During the 1995 *Time Machine* conference, I spoke briefly with Lessing, telling her that I had once bracketed a fiction course with *The Time Machine* and *The Fifth Child*. She was most intrigued by my students' seeing kinship between Ben and the Morlocks.

37. Bishop, pp. 88, 182, 226.

38. Ibid., pp. 9, 222.

39. Ibid., pp. 11, 12, 13.

40. See my *Time and English Fiction* (London: Macmillan, 1975), pp. 9–11, 74–76, and Ian Watt, "*Almayer's Folly*: Memories and Models," *Mosaic* 8 (1974), 165–82.

41. For Hugo Monegal see Bishop, chapter 15; for hominid Genly, chapter 14; for Joshua's foster family, chapters 5 and 7.

42. Ibid., p. 15.

43. Linda Hutcheon, *A Poetics of Postmodernism: History, Theory, Fiction* (New York: Routledge, 1988), p. 11.

44. Ibid., p. 26.

45. Bishop, p. 394.

46. *Contemporary Authors*, vols. 61–64, p. 68.

47. "The First Wells," in *Other Inquisitions* 1937–1952, trans. Ruth L. C. Simms (Austin: University of Texas Press, 1964), p. 87. The passage reads: "Work that endures is always capable of an infinite and plastic ambiguity; it is all things for all men, like the Apostle; it is a mirror that reflects the reader's own traits and it is also a map of the world. And it must be ambiguous in an evanescent and modest way, almost in spite of the author; he must appear to be ignorant of all symbolism."

Doomed Formicary versus
the Technological Sublime

BRIAN W. ALDISS

What Wonders 'gin to be our lot
When Evolution spins the plot!
—Shakespeare, *Vortigern*

 The zebra problem has been solved. It is a black animal with white stripes, rather than a white animal with black stripes. This is known because occasionally a freak animal is born, and it is black without white stripes. Aware of this, the animal—as if in shame—tends to remain on the outside of the herd, and is thus more vulnerable to danger.

Those who write about the future are the black zebras of the literary world, forced to the outer fringes of the group. That greatest of all futurists, H. G. Wells, remains on the outer fringes of literature, and it is a puzzle as to why that should be.

The Time Machine represents a revolution in storytelling. It may stand in a tradition of marvelous travel tales, but it presents us with something new: a story whose mainspring is a dramatization of the grand, grim process of evolution. Unprecedented as this was in 1895, one might think that by the time a century had passed, the bemusement of literary critics might have given place to a general acknowledgment of H. G. Wells's stature and the new gifts and vistas he brought to a traditional form of literature.

Such is not the case. One reason may be the deep-seated one: that there has always been a doubt about the notion of exploring the future. Such explorations have been left to Nostradamus, false prophets, and the author of the Book of Revelation. Scholars have only reluctantly accepted these explorations as literature. The question of writers of works set in the future is, in these days, whether to cast them in a predominantly literary or a predominantly scientific mold; since

Formicary vs. the Technological Sublime 189

the dilemma can never be solved one way or the other, we call the dilemma *science fiction*, an uneasy compound of two conflicting modes, the one intended to instruct, the other to entertain.

It's no new dilemma, and it was faced by Thomas Burnet when he came to write *The Sacred Theory of the Earth* in the late seventeenth century and sought to explain the Bible in scientific terms. Prophecy or futuristic fiction? The two seem inextricably mixed. Burnet also saw that even when you have found a suitable style of writer, you have to find a suitable audience, one receptive to visions of the future. (There was no fandom in the 1680s.) Many people, including intellectuals, are lost when it comes to contemplating the future or anything not strictly of the terrestrial here and now. I have quoted previously the learned and famous Oxford name who asked me, after proclaiming how much he had enjoyed my *Helliconia* novels, "But you couldn't really have two suns in the sky at once, could you?"[1]

The question reveals not merely a pre-Copernican viewpoint, but a reluctance to face the modern sublime—that modern sublime which embraces anything imposing in scale, whether human-made or natural. This new sublimity, leaping ahead from Burke's description of "objects of great dimension" being sublime and introducing feelings of terror and awe into the human breast, springs from the ability of modern consciousness to confront so much more knowledge than was accessible to its earlier avatar—knowledge, I mean, about the universe and about ourselves.

There are words that express sublimity. One such word is the word *future*. It has a compelling power of its own, at times alluring, at times lowering. Wells it was who, in *Anticipations*, formulated a way of thinking constructively about the future. Most people, of course, shrink from the idea.

Given this general reluctance to face the future, as a traveller on foot may be reluctant to enter a great forest, not knowing where it might end, how is it that Wells became, with his science fiction, the most generally read author on the planet?

Well, we can see in *The Time Machine* Wells's amiable method of procedure, a pattern often pursued in his later books. We are coaxed into the future, the unknown, from the here and now, often from the domestic with which most readers are familiar. In that opening paragraph, we meet with chaps round a table, glasses in hand; the fire's burning, there's an "after-dinner atmosphere" (1, 3). And in no time we are captive to a miracle: the model time machine vanishes from the table-top and embarks on its interminable journey toward the second law of thermodynamics.

Thus, Mr. Wells too escapes from the "every-dayness" he hated—escapes as a lay person not a theologian, as a black zebra, into the sublime of the far future, the end of the world, the dying sun, the silence like no other silence but death. This eschatological journey was not an unfamiliar one; but Wells casts it in scientific terms. His eponymous machine is a McGuffin, and what powers the story are the unseen mechanisms of evolution: *le Morlock, c'est moi.*

There had been attempts before Wells to use the greatest discoveries of the nineteenth century in fiction. Richard Jefferies's *After London* (1885), for example, dramatically illustrates the death of a great city. Yet Jefferies produces no reasoning for his calamity; we make no intellectual leap as we do when we come to Wells's Richmond.

A much more spirited attempt to come to terms with the dawning scientific climate was made by a novelist who attended Charles Darwin's funeral service in Westminster Abbey, Thomas Hardy. Hardy had been among the earliest of those who acclaimed *The Origin of Species.*

In 1873, only two years after the publication of Darwin's *The Descent of Man*, Hardy published *A Pair of Blue Eyes.* Particularly in chapter 22 of this novel, there are passages that one feels cannot have escaped Wells's eye. These magnificent instances of Burke's sublime are too long to quote in full. A paragraph must suffice. Knight has slipped over a mighty chalk cliff, and is about to fall to his death. He is staring at the cliff face:

> By one of those familiar conjunctions of things wherewith the inanimate world baits the mind of man when he pauses in moments of suspense, opposite Knight's eyes was an embedded fossil, standing forth in low relief from the rock. It was a creature with eyes. The eyes, dead and turned to stone, were even now regarding him. It was one of the early crustaceans called Trilobites. Separated by millions of years in their lives, Knight and this underling seemed to have met in their death. It was the single instance within reach of his vision of anything that had ever been alive and had had a body to save, as he himself had now. [. . .] He was to be with the small at his death.

When the sea is described—"that narrow white border was foam [. . .] but its boisterous tosses were so distant as to appear a pulsation only, and its plashing was barely audible. A white border to a black sea—his funeral pall and its edging"—and when the sun is described—"it appeared, low down upon the sea. Not with its natural golden fringe [. . .] not with the strange glare of whiteness which it sometimes puts on as an alternative to colour, but as a splotch of vermilion red upon a leaden ground"—when we read these Hardyesque descriptions, we are inevitably reminded of that remote and awful twilight, thirty million years hence, which confronts the Time Traveller. Yet Hardy is unable to make his vision central; it is but an adornment in a tale of thwarted romance. So formidable is the essence of Wells's fable that he wisely ensconces it within the cozy setting of a company of men, sitting about, smoking their pipes, and chatting together. The sublimity is domesticated. This comfort-discomfort equation—this domestic-alien equation, if you like—is very Wellsian. It was a steadier for readers' nerves in 1905 and 1906 to find that *Kipps: The Story of a Simple Soul*, a comfortable book, was published between two uncomfortable books, *A Modern Utopia* and *In the Days of the Comet*.

Wells was to a large extent unaware of the workings of his own mind. It was not an easy mind, filled as it was with conflicts and disappointments; for which reason he kept himself constantly active, plotting and disputing and writing journalism to keep the demons at bay. His weariness with this way of life is embodied in that beautiful short story, "The Door in the Wall." Patrick Parrinder has noted Wells's split personality.[2] We might go further and suspect him of Multiple Personality Disorder.

Amid much evidence of that condition, I'd mention two novels of the 1920s that are strangely mirror images of each other: *The Dream* and *Christina Alberta's Father*. In the former, one Sarnac, two thousand years from now, dreams of Edwardian England and believes he is humble little Henry Mortimer Smith. In the latter, humble little Mr Preemby of Edwardian England imagines himself to be the great King Sargon of ancient Sumeria (one of the heroes of *The Outline of History*). This is at a time when Wells suffered from mental illness and felt his divided life to be falling apart. Sargon, Mr Preemby, and Sarnac, men of different ages and cultures, fight with each other as, within Wells's psyche, draper's assistant fights with Lord Beaverbrook's friend, past with future, Eloi with Morlock.

He turned this variousness in his disposition to good effect in his writing, as writers so often make paper amends for their own shockingly disruptive characters. Short though it is, *The Time Machine* is extremely various. It's a page of history, a love affair, a mystery, an adventure, a horror story, social criticism, and, over all, a detour—dazzlingly conducted—in evolution and cosmology. Thus it becomes a secularization of old religious fears, often using quasi-biblical language to gain its most splendid effects: revelation transposed in terms of thermodynamics.

The brief epilogue cleverly sums up the whole matter. On the one hand, "the future is still black and blank." There the Time Traveller may be wandering. On the other hand, he may have travelled back in time to wander "some plesiosaurus-haunted [...] coral reef" (E, 91). We as readers are free to speculate on this point.

All of which goes some way toward explaining the popularity of the early scientific romances at the time of first publication and ever since. But Wells had another active sense, attuned to his times. Like many other men, in sway to the technological sublime, in love with the future, he was for the enslaving and *grooming* (his word) of Nature—of cats, dogs, horses, mountains, even seas.

When Wells visited Niagara Falls, he was less interested in the falls themselves than in the power station that harnessed the torrent of water. For him this was the "will made visible, thought translated into easy and commanding things."[3] In his book *Imagining America* (1980), Peter Conrad remarks that Wells has passed from the natural Sublime of the nineteenth century to "the mechanical sublime, which regulates the mind and technologically supersedes nature. [. . .] The turbid ghost of the falls now inhabits the sleek machines."[4]

Wells the atheist responded to what is called in Scott Fitzgerald's story, "Absolution," "something ineffably gorgeous [. . .] that had nothing to do with God."[5]

The ineffable—something that can hardly be put into words. That is the concern of much science fiction. The whole business of the New World was to tame the wilderness, to supplant it by man's works, much as the End of the World is tamed, made domestic, by the Time Traveller's visit. Electricity illuminated the new sublimity. The Hoover Dam as symbol of America reinventing itself, the city as shimmering hieroglyph. Isn't much of today's flood of SF America's attempt to reinvent itself?

David E. Nye's book *American Technological Sublime* (1994) emphasizes that modernization was not simply a machine process; thought and attitudes changed as well. Electricity, of which Victor Frankenstein speaks as infusing "a spark of being into the lifeless thing"[6]—and *future* is a word derived from the future participle of the Latin verb *esse*, "to be"—electricity proves to be a new form of lifeblood. During the building of the Hoover Dam, the tallest dam in the world, many people preferred to visit it at night, when the gigantic emergent structure was bathed in artificial light. Immensity was all.

When the Empire State Building was completed in May 1931, the *New York Times* reported, "From the height of more than a thousand feet pedestrians were little more than ants and their movements hardly could be detected."[7] The earlier Flatiron Building—that beautiful creature of 1905—provoked a similar comment, although changing the metaphor round: not humans as ants but ants as humans—"primitive but human, hurrying grotesquely over the most expensive spot on earth."[8]

Possibly that striking phrase, "doomed formicary," which Wells employs in his final book, *Mind at the End of Its Tether* (1945), to describe the human race, derives from some such skyscraper altitude.[9] Such were the attitudes Wells espoused, attitudes of paradox: the more gigantic the works of mankind became, the more he was dwarfed; the more he was dwarfed, the greater his power was seen to be.

While *The Time Machine* depicts the extinction of the human race from, as it were, the heights of a literary Empire State Building, it delights too in one man's conquest of Time itself. Even toward the end of his life, Wells praises tall buildings, for in tall buildings especially his art finds physical expression. Tall buildings provide the perfect view of "our doomed formicary." In *The Happy Turning*, the last but one of his many books to be published in Wells's lifetime, he says, "I dream of a purely architectural world. But that architecture goes far beyond the mere putting-up of buildings and groups of buildings here and there. The architects of Dreamland lay out a whole new world. Their gigantic schemes tower to the stratosphere, plumb the depths of the earth, groom mountains, divert ocean currents and dry up seas. My identity merges inextricably with every dreamland architect."[10]

Note that in Wells's list of desirables there's almost nothing to which we would not violently object today. Drying up seas? Fine, try the Aral Sea, one of the world's greatest ecological disasters. . . . We're listening to the voice of a black zebra, now separated from its herd.

Yet although the heyday of the technological sublime that was Wells' forte has passed with the rise of thermonuclear power, the paradoxical attractions of works like *The Time Machine* remain and will be likely to outlast the Empire State Building. To quote again from *The Happy Turning*: "Truth has a way of heaving up through the cracks of history."[11]

Notes

1. The two suns seen from Helliconia are Batalix and the predominant Freyr. Helliconia, in other words, is a planet in a binary system.

2. Patrick Parrinder, introduction to *The Discovery of the Future with the Common-Sense of World Peace and the Human Adventure* (London: PNL Press, 1989), p. 8.

3. H. G. Wells, *The Future in America: A Search After Realities* (London: Chapman and Hall, 1906), p. 74.

4. Peter Conrad, *Imagining America* (Oxford: Oxford University Press, 1980), pp. 25–26.

5. F. Scott Fitzgerald, "Absolution," in *The Bodley Head Scott Fitzgerald*, vol. 5, ed. Malcolm Cowley (London: Bodley Head, 1963), p. 279.

6. Mary W. Shelley, *Frankenstein, or The Modern Prometheus*, ed. M. K. Joseph (London: Oxford University Press, 1971), p. 57.

7. Quoted in David E. Nye, *American Technological Sublime* (Cambridge, Mass.: MIT Press, 1994), p. 135.

8. Quoted in ibid., p. 135.

9. H. G. Wells, *Mind at the End of Its Tether*, in *The Last Books of H. G. Wells*, ed. G. P. Wells (London: The H. G. Wells Society, 1968), p. 77.

10. H. G. Wells, *The Happy Turning*, in *The Last Books of H. G. Wells*, ed. G. P. Wells (London: The H. G. Wells Society, 1968), p. 36.

11. Ibid., p. 40.

Afterword

In the Company of the Immortals

PATRICK PARRINDER

> It was at ten o'clock to-day that the first of all
> Time Machines began its career.
> —Wells, *The Time Machine*

The Time Machine, subtitled "An Invention," was first published in book form at the end of May 1895. The date on which the Time Traveller set out on his first voyage is more mysterious; all we know is that he left on a Thursday at 10 A.M. and returned later the same day. His second voyage began at around noon the next day and is presumably still going on. Since 1895, not only have millions of readers and viewers encountered Wells's *Time Machine*, but time machines themselves, of one kind or another, have continued to multiply. What Wells set in motion a hundred years ago was both a brief, visionary story and an unstoppable idea.

Time Machines and *Time Machines*

If I want to own something called a Time Machine today, I can choose between a Lotus computer, an ATM card issued by a Midwestern bank, and a handmade model based on Wells's description and suitable for display on the mantelpiece. Leaving aside the Wellsian brand name, huge numbers of people in the twentieth century have cooked their dinners with automatic timers, used time-delay mechanisms to take their own picture, and perhaps been buried alongside time capsules. The experience of time travelling has been simulated by cinematic techniques, museum displays, and multimedia, and soon it may be available in virtual reality. The construction of a real Wellsian time machine still eludes us, but it may not be a mere fantasy. Time travel as a scientific theory is now taken more seriously than at any time since Wells began publishing his fictional speculations about the fourth dimension.[1]

Twentieth-century science fiction, as this book has shown, is full both of time machines and of rewritings of *The Time Machine*. Some of the modern time-travel stories and films are explicit adaptations and sequels, or at least acknowledge Wells's influence—but most do not, for the reason Olaf Stapledon rather magnificently gave when he wrote to Wells that "A man does not record his debt to the air he breathes."[2] Darko Suvin has argued on structuralist grounds that "all subsequent significant SF can be said to have sprung from Wells's *Time Machine*."[3] Many of the literary and filmic rewritings of *The Time Machine*, including those by Wells himself, are analyzed or referred to in the foregoing essays. Among the papers delivered at the 1995 *Time Machine* centenary conference that could not be included here were a rewriting of Wells's story for the virtual reality age by computer expert Alan Mayne and a survey of sequels to *The Time Machine* by SF novelist Stephen Baxter (who is himself the author of one of those sequels).[4]

Although Wells never planned to write a sequel to *The Time Machine* and would have discouraged anyone else from doing so, he left the perfect opening for one. The Time Traveller's disappearance on his second voyage meant that the career of the "first of all Time Machines" must remain perpetually unfinished. It was Wells, too, who began the reduplication of imaginary time machines. Starting with "The Chronic Argonauts" in 1887, there were, on W. M. S. Russell's reckoning, as many as eight different versions of Wells's time-travel story. In the final version (as Paul Alkon reminds us), there is not one time machine but two.[5] What the Time Traveller calls the "first of all Time Machines" is not the first, since he has evidently forgotten the scale model that the Psychologist sent on its "interminable voyage" (1, 9) after the previous week's dinner. Not only is the model time machine itself a time machine, but in normal engineering practice the model would be built and tested in advance of the full-sized vehicle. And this is what has in fact happened. The model was demonstrated at the first of the Time Traveller's two Thursday dinner parties. As he begins his story on the second Thursday, Wells's protagonist says of the full-sized time machine:

> I expected to finish it on Friday; but on Friday, when the putting together was nearly done, I found that one of the nickel bars was exactly one inch too short, and this I had to get remade; so that the thing was not complete until this morning. It was at ten o'clock to-day that the first of all Time Machines began its career. (3, 18)

Logically, of course, there must have been other prototype time machines, though the dress rehearsal with the model might have been the first occasion that one of them had actually travelled in time. "I don't want to waste this model, and then be told I'm a quack" (1, 9), the Time Traveller cautions his friends. What is certain is that there is more than one such machine at large in the time dimension when the story ends.

Revision and Remaking in *The Time Machine* and Its Criticism

Brian W. Aldiss rightly observes that "Short though it is, *The Time Machine* is extremely various."[6] Wells's narrative is an almost classic example of the basic artistic technique of repetition with variation, since revision and remaking characterize not only the Time Traveller's invention but almost every other aspect of the story. We learn from the opening paragraph that another of our hero's inventions has already been patented and put into production—the chairs in the smoking room, "being his patents, embraced and caressed us rather than submitted to be sat upon" (1, 3). The Time Traveller's excessively comfortable chairs do not necessarily provide the ideal support for listening to him lecture on a "recondite matter" (1, 3), but that is only one of the ambiguities in a first paragraph that still awaits its explicator.

Wells's constant resort to mirroring and remodeling effects is one of the most remarkable features of *The Time Machine*. Many of these instances act as nodal points in the criticism and interpretation of the story and, as such, are frequently highlighted in the present book. They help to account for the multiplicity of ways of reading the text. For example, the Eloi and Morlocks represent two alternative outcomes of human degeneration; the Time Traveller frequently revises his understanding of the process of future degeneration; his hunger for meat anticipates the Morlocks' grisly appetites; and his dialogue with his listeners anticipates and models the reader's responses. The Palace of Green Porcelain is a kind of time machine, and the two shriveled flowers that the Time Traveller brings back in his pocket are like stolen exhibits from some future museum. In the "Further Vision," the solar eclipse witnessed by the Time Traveller in A.D. 30,000,000 is a temporary image, or simulacrum, of the heat-death of the solar system, which the Traveller cannot experience directly. If the solar system were to die, the Traveller and his machine must surely die with it.

As soon as he has safely returned to his own time, the Traveller offers his guests the choice of considering his story as a "lie—or a prophecy" (12, 87)—in effect, two different kinds of story mirroring and distorting one another. His second journey is apparently conceived as a repeat performance of his first journey, only something goes wrong and the mirror is shattered. The last that the narrator sees as he bursts into the laboratory after his friend has promised to return and "prove you this time travelling up to the hilt, specimens and all" (12, 89) is the ghostly transparent figure "sitting in a whirling mass of black and brass" (12, 90)—not the human being who, a few minutes earlier, had looked him in the eyes, but a momentary image presented, as the Time Traveller tells the Psychologist, "below the threshold" (1, 11). Earlier, teasing his listeners with the logic of the fourth dimension, the Time Traveller had asked whether an instantaneous cube could exist. We are left asking the same about an instantaneous human being.

The theme of reduplication continues in the epilogue, where the narrator imagines that the Time Traveller might have gone back into the remote past—a mirror image of his journey forward along the time dimension. Then the narrator's sense of blindness toward the future is contrasted with the Time Traveller's doom-ridden insights. "If that is so, it remains for us to live as though it were not so," the narrator comments (E, 91). The contrast and reduplication of ideas has now given way to a kind of Orwellian doublethink. We pass on to the narrator's final comment that even in the world of the Eloi and Morlocks "gratitude and a mutual tenderness still lived on in the heart of man" (E, 91). By now, we recognize that remodeling and repetition with variation must necessarily structure the criticism and interpretation of the Time Traveller's story, as well as the story itself. By introducing commentary and interpretation into his narrative, Wells was able to prompt both his ordinary readers' responses and the body of critical commentary that would eventually grow up around *The Time Machine*.

Given the choice whether to consider Wells's romance as a lie or a prophecy, many of its original reviewers agreed on its prophetic qualities. Before its serialization was even finished, its author had been hailed by the *Review of Reviews* as a "man of genius."[7] Within the next few months, the *Daily Chronicle* had declared Wells's story a "new thing under the sun," while the novelist Israel Zangwill found the portrayal of the Morlocks worthy of Swift and the "Further Vision" more somber and impressive than the Book of Revelation.[8] This vein of admiration continued throughout Wells's lifetime, though it soon became an excuse for critical disparagement of his later work. He neither had done nor could be expected to do (it was often implied) anything else half as good as *The Time Machine* and its immediate successors. The academic scholars and critics who turned to Wells from the 1960s onward have continued to focus on *The Time Machine* and to stress its sublime and visionary aspects. Bernard Bergonzi saw it as an "ironic myth," Robert M. Philmus unraveled its "logic of prophecy," and Darko Suvin located it at the "turning-point of the SF tradition."[9]

Since the 1960s, the process of revision and reinterpretation inherent in the reading of Wells (and of every other established author) has been enlivened by the impact, sometimes direct, though more often diffused, of new waves of literary theory. Bergonzi, Philmus, and Suvin brought myth criticism and genre theory to bear on *The Time Machine*. Another essay by Suvin offered a structuralist analysis, illustrated by numerous diagrams, of Wells's narrative.[10] Deconstruction was represented by Veronica Hollinger's 1987 essay "Deconstructing the Time Machine."[11] (Surprisingly, there is as yet no full-dress account of *The Time Machine* from the perspectives of feminism or gender studies).[12] In the present book, not only the above-mentioned theoretical currents, but the influences of formalism, Marxism, cultural history, postmodernism, and postcolonialism are clearly discernible.

One aspect of *Time Machine* studies not directly represented here (though it forms an indispensable background and has been the subject of lively debate and controversy) is that of textual editing and textual genetics. The reconstruction of Wells's compositional processes and of his early intellectual and literary development by scholars such as Bergonzi, Philmus, David Hughes, Bernard Loing, and Gordon N. Ray provides the *sine qua non* of contemporary understanding of the text. Such labors with respect to *The Time Machine*, though not to Wells's other works, may now be virtually complete, at least for our generation. But the publishing history of *The Time Machine* has still to be written, and critics have still to come to terms with David C. Smith's discovery—announced in the course of his closing remarks at the 1995 conference—that Wells on one occasion credited his wife Jane as the story's virtual coauthor.

The production of edited and annotated critical texts began in 1987 with Harry M. Geduld's *The Definitive Time Machine*, a reprint of the 1924 Atlantic Edition text with extensive notes and numerous valuable appendices.[13] Unfortunately, the text was not truly definitive, since it ignored Wells's post-1924 revisions (not that there were many of these) and thus fell short of its professed aim of presenting the writer's final intentions. Moreover, the claims Geduld made for his edition were at variance with the recent revolution in textual scholarship, which has undermined the very idea of a definitive text. In the 1990s at least four new scholarly versions of *The Time Machine* appeared, each of them constructed on slightly different editorial principles.[14] The main issue of debate was whether Wells's original (1895) or revised (1924 and after) text should be followed. These recent editions should be consulted by anyone concerned with textual bibliography, though unfortunately, due to continuing copyright restrictions and to the licensing policy of the Wells Estate, most of them are difficult to obtain outside the country of first publication.

One outcome of this editorial ferment is that *The Time Machine* has now become (what, for the vast majority of readers, it was not until very recently) a classic text loaded with the apparatus of scholarship. This was necessary and inevitable, since hardly anyone without notes is likely to register instant comprehension of Wells's references to "Nebuchadnezzar phases" (2, 15), "plough[ing] you for the Little-go" (1, 7), and the like. At the same time, it is encouraging that *The Time Machine* continues to be reprinted in cheap and popular versions without any apparatus, such as the recent United States "Penguin 60s" edition, which offered a complete and uncut text for $.95.[15] There have, in fact, been cheap paperback reprints of *The Time Machine* ever since Heinemann printed a "popular edition" of the novel from the original plates of 1895 (my own very battered copy dates from 1905). The future vitality of the text will depend on the availability of popular editions as well as the currency of adaptations, spin-offs, and critical and scholarly reinterpretations of Wells's original.

Futures for *The Time Machine*:
Political, Physical, and Metaphysical

What sort of future, then, can we predict for *The Time Machine*? There are likely to be two overlapping, but nevertheless divergent, patterns of response, the first approaching the story as a prelude to the rest of Wells's prolific and controversial output and the second concentrating on the theme of time travel and its place in physical, metaphysical, and science-fictional speculation. As it happens, these two orientations were reflected in the two organizing bodies responsible for the 1995 *Time Machine* conference: the London-based H. G. Wells Society and the Eaton Program for Science Fiction and Fantasy Studies.

Founded in 1960, the Wells Society has as its aims the "promotion and encouragement of an active interest in, and appreciation of the life, work and thought of Herbert George Wells." It is in many ways the successor of an earlier H. G. Wells Society, which flourished briefly in Wells's lifetime before changing its name to Cosmopolis. The present-day Wells Society brings together at least three different kinds of Wellsians, those (including the biographers Michael Foot and David C. Smith, both of whom attended the 1995 conference) with an all-embracing enthusiasm for every aspect of Wells's activities and those whose interests are either predominantly literary or predominantly political. Political Wellsians believe he is best honored by advocating the causes of world government, world education, and human rights, which he championed in books like *The Open Conspiracy* and *The Rights of Man*. Although *The Time Machine* is not obviously relevant to Wells's later political campaigns, it does contain more than an element of prophetic social satire, as Israel Zangwill, for one, pointed out at the time of its first publication. The more closely we examine Wells's early scientific romance, the more unmistakably can it be seen to contain some of the seeds of his later political ideas.

Wells's advocacy of a World State stands in the twentieth century for an unrepentant universalism—an intellectual grand narrative comprehending the whole of space and the whole of time from the point of view of scientific rationalism and the encyclopedism of the Enlightenment (a movement to which he paid frequent tribute). *The Time Machine*, in which the human race is shown dividing into two and becoming extinct, records the tragic failure of Wellsian universalism and progressive thinking in general. At the same time, the story itself clearly rests on universalist assumptions. The Time Traveller can only study that portion of the future of terrestrial life that is visible, at various far distant times, from within a twenty-mile radius around what is now Richmond in southwest London. Yet neither he nor the narrator find it necessary to consider other parts of the globe before writing their joint epitaph on the "growing pile of civilisation" and the "Advancement of Mankind" (E, 91). The Time Traveller is saved from having to extend his geographical range by his discovery of the Palace of Green Porcelain, the future universal museum in which, just as in the Victorian age, our remote civilized descendants have put together a Great Exhibition of the whole natural and cultural world and brought it to London. In the light of the Palace of Green Porcelain, we must inevitably read the universalism of *The Time Machine*— on one of its many levels—as a sublimation of the late-nineteenth-century triumph and impending fall of British global dominance.

Wells's advocacy of world citizenship and a New World Order (a phrase he invented long before it became a buzzword used by U.S. presidents) can still excite political passions today. Opponents of the movement toward global uniformity, or at least conformity, which is such a palpable feature of present-day life, often feel there is something to be gained by discrediting the World State's most outspoken champion. Nevertheless, most critiques of Wellsian universalism seem to be carried out in the name (whether acknowledged or unacknowledged) of a rival form of universalism. Beginning in 1938 with Christopher Caudwell, Marxist ideologists have attacked Wells as a "petit-bourgeois" writer whose works, including the portrayal of the Morlocks in *The Time Machine*, were inspired by hatred and fear of the proletariat.[16] Neo-Christian apologists such as Hilaire Belloc and C. S. Lewis pilloried him as a godless Darwinian.[17] More recently, the conservative populist John Carey has combed *The Time Machine* and Wells's other romances for evidence of what he believes is Wells's near-pathological desire to "get rid of people."[18] Wells today is frequently scrutinized from the point of view of ideologies such as anticolonialism, antifascism, antiracism, and feminism. There is much to admire, and a good deal to criticize, in his record on all these issues; but, Wells being the sort of writer he is, *The Time Machine* as well as his later books is likely to go on being interrogated for indications of his covert values and prejudices.

According to one recent writer, "What makes *The Time Machine* so enduring, even a century after its conception, is its sharp political and social critique." The author, perhaps surprisingly, is not a literary or political commentator, but the theoretical physicist Michio Kaku, and the quotation is taken from *Hyperspace*, his popular account of superstring theory. Kaku outlines two possible ways of constructing a time machine along the lines recently suggested by Kip Thorne and his collaborators.[19] In 1988, Thorne argued in an article in *Physical Review Letters* that time travel was theoretically possible by means of so-called wormholes.[20] The existence of black holes and wormholes is somewhat controversial, but once a wormhole of the type theorized by Thorne had been created, a time traveller could supposedly pass through it. Kaku comments that "Anyone who has read *The Time Machine* [. . .] may be disappointed with Thorne's blueprint for a time machine."[21] Only time will show whether or not serious scientific concern with time-travel possibilities is still in its infancy.

Among the many "commonsense" objections to the theory of time travel, the most fundamental was surely that voiced by Israel Zangwill in 1895—that to reach the future the traveller would have to journey beyond his natural term of life and so would be dead on arrival. Roslynn D. Haynes has argued that this entails a misunderstanding of the concept of the fourth dimension put forward by Wells. Appealing to Einsteinian special relativity, she maintains that the Time Traveller, while his machine is in motion, exists in a separate frame of reference outside terrestrial time.[22] Be that as it may, the fact that the Time Traveller is somehow cheating his own death alerts us to the link between stories of the future and the age-old fascination with immortality. Although I can only pursue this link very briefly here, it may once again suggest why *The Time Machine* holds such a central place in modern science fiction and fantasy.

Jorge Luis Borges said of Wells's scientific romances that "They are the first books I read; perhaps they will be the last."[23] *The Time Machine* is both a world-ending narrative and the story of a man who lives to see how the world ends. One of its most remarkable rewritings is to be found in Borges's story "The Immortal," in which an ancient traveller (who may be a Roman centurion, or maybe

Homer) treks across the desert until he comes to the City of the Immortals on the opposite bank of a muddy stream. The traveller drinks from the stream, thus becoming an immortal himself, and spends some time among the mindless troglodytes who inhabit the side from which he has come. He then crosses over and enters the abandoned city, which resembles the world of the Eloi and Morlocks in several respects. He first traverses a wilderness of underground chambers and then climbs up to ground level on a ladder of metal rungs sunk into an enormous wall. Towering above him is a huge antiquated palace, which he regards as a fabrication of the gods; but the palace is a labyrinthine nightmare, and the gods, whoever they were, have died out. When he escapes from the city and returns to the opposite bank, he finds one of the troglodytes waiting for him like a faithful dog or, we might say, like Weena at the mouth of the Morlocks' well. Finally Borges's traveller realizes that the troglodytes are themselves the immortals. They have evacuated the city, lost their humanity, and forgotten almost everything they once knew.[24]

Applying Borges's logic to Wells's story, we might speculate that on his second journey, the Time Traveller must have become indistinguishable from the Eloi or Morlocks, or that he may have recognized them as former time travellers. The name of the Eloi echoes the Hebrew for "gods," and the Traveller certainly thought of them initially as gods. In the banqueting hall soon after his arrival, he refers to their "inextinguishable laughter" (4, 27), a phrase echoing the laughter of the immortal gods in the *Iliad* (I, 599). The gods, we might say, have a choice between two kinds of life—the endless contemplation of human mortality, or ("If that is so, it remains for us to live as though it were not so") mindless oblivion like that of Borges's troglodytes. A time machine is in the end a transitory vehicle and a mere invention, but he who travels on it into the future becomes one of the immortals. Returning to tell their stories, time travellers bring us as readers into the company of the immortals.

Notes

1. See for example Paul J. Nahin, *Time Machines: Time Travel in Physics, Metaphysics, and Science Fiction* (New York: American Institute of Physics, 1993).

2. Robert Crossley, ed., "The Letters of Olaf Stapledon and H. G. Wells, 1931–1942," in *Science Fiction Dialogues*, ed. Gary Wolfe (Chicago: Academy, 1982), p. 35.

3. Darko Suvin, *Metamorphoses of Science Fiction* (New Haven and London: Yale University Press, 1979), p. 221.

4. See Stephen Baxter, "Further Visions: Sequels to *The Time Machine*," *Foundation*

65 (Autumn 1995), 41–50. Baxter's *The Time Ships* (London: HarperCollins, 1995) is in fact both a sequel and a prequel to *The Time Machine*.

5. Paul K. Alkon, "Was the Time Machine Necessary?", in this volume.

6. Brian W. Aldiss, "Doomed Formicary versus the Technological Sublime," in this volume.

7. Patrick Parrinder, ed., *H. G. Wells: The Critical Heritage* (London and Boston: Routledge, 1972), p. 33.

8. Ibid., pp. 38, 40.

9. Bernard Bergonzi, *The Early H. G. Wells* (Manchester: Manchester University Press, 1961), and "*The Time Machine*: An Ironic Myth," in *H. G. Wells: A Collection of Critical Essays*, ed. Bernard Bergonzi (Englewood Cliffs, N.J.: Prentice-Hall, 1976), pp. 39–55; Robert M. Philmus, "The Logic of Prophecy in *The Time Machine*," in *H. G. Wells: A Collection of Critical Essays*, pp. 56–68; Suvin, *Metamorphoses of Science Fiction*, pp. 208–21.

10. Suvin, *Metamorphoses of Science Fiction*, pp. 222–42.

11. Veronica Hollinger, "Deconstructing the Time Machine," *Science-Fiction Studies* 42 (July 1987), 201–21.

12. See, however, Nancy Steffen-Fluhr, "Paper Tiger: Women and H. G. Wells," *Science-Fiction Studies* 37 (November 1985), 311–29.

13. Harry M. Geduld, ed., *The Definitive Time Machine: A Critical Edition of H. G. Wells's Scientific Romance* (Bloomington and Indianapolis: Indiana University Press, 1987).

14. The editions are as follows: *The Time Machine*, ed. Jonathan Benison (Genoa: Cideb, 1994); *The Time Machine: The Centennial Edition*, ed. John Lawton (London: Dent; Vermont: Tuttle, 1995); *The Time Machine and The Island of Doctor Moreau*, ed. Patrick Parrinder (New York: Oxford University Press, 1996); and *The Time Machine: An Invention*, ed. Leon Stover (Jefferson, N.C.: McFarland, 1996). The Benison and Stover editions reproduce the 1895 Heinemann text.

15. H. G. Wells, *The Time Machine* (New York: Penguin, 1995). In Britain, a superficially similar edition brought out by Phoenix (a J. M. Dent imprint) and paying royalties to the Wells Estate turned out to contain chapters 3 to 6 only: H. G. Wells, *The Time Machine* (London: Phoenix, 1996).

16. Christopher Caudwell, *Studies and Further Studies in a Dying Culture* (New York and London: Monthly Review, 1971), pp. 82–83, 94.

17. Wells's supposed "human racism" is voiced by the scientist Weston in Lewis's novel *Out of the Silent Planet* (1938). Wells is also caricatured as the popular novelist Horace Jules in Lewis's trilogy. However, Lewis added the following disclaimer on the reverse title page of *Out of the Silent Planet* (London: Pan, 1952): "The author would be sorry if any reader supposed he was too stupid to have enjoyed Mr H. G. Wells's fantasies or too ungrateful to acknowledge his debt to them."

18. John Carey, *The Intellectuals and the Masses: Pride and Prejudice among the Literary Intelligentsia, 1880–1939* (London: Faber, 1992), esp. pp. 128–29.

19. Michio Kaku, *Hyperspace: A Scientific Odyssey Through Parallel Universes, Time Warps, and the Tenth Dimension* (New York and Oxford: Oxford University Press, 1994), pp. 60, 249.

20. Michael S. Morris, Kip S. Thorne and Ulvi Yurtsever, "Wormholes, Time Machines, and the Weak Energy Condition," *Physical Review Letters* 61 (1988), 1446–49.

21. Kaku, *Hyperspace*, p. 249.

22. Roslynn D. Haynes, *H. G. Wells: Discoverer of the Future: The Influence of Science on his Thought* (London and Basingstoke: Macmillan, 1980), pp. 56–59.

23. Parrinder, ed., *H. G. Wells: The Critical Heritage*, p. 332.

24. Jorge Luis Borges, "The Immortal," in *Labyrinths* (Harmondsworth: Penguin, 1970), pp. 135–49. For further connections between Borges and Wells see Robert M. Philmus, "Borges and Wells and the Labyrinths of Time," in Suvin and Philmus, eds., *H. G. Wells and Modern Science Fiction*, pp. 159–78.

Contributors

BRIAN W. ALDISS is a writer of science fiction and contemporary novels, a poet, and an actor. His autobiography, *The Twinkling of an Eye*, was published in 1998. His critical history of science fiction, *Billion Year Spree* (1973), changed the way we think about the field. Since then, he has produced four volumes of literary criticism.

PAUL ALKON, Leo S. Bing Professor of English at the University of Southern California in Los Angeles, is the author of *Samuel Johnson and Moral Discipline, Defoe and Fictional Time, Origins of Futuristic Fiction,* and *Science Fiction Before* 1900.

LARRY W. CALDWELL is Professor of English and Comparative Literature at Evansville University in Evansville, Indiana. He has written on modern narrative and H. G. Wells.

DANIÈLE CHATELAIN is Professor of French at the University of Redlands. She is author of *Perceiving and Telling: A Study of Iterative Discourse* (1998) and is working on a book on Flaubert and science.

ROBERT CROSSLEY, Professor of English at the University of Massachusetts, Boston, has written often about Wells and is currently working on literature of the world's end and on the history of fiction about Mars. His most recent books are *Olaf Stapledon: Speaking for the Future* (1994) and *An Olaf Stapledon Reader* (1997).

KIRBY FARRELL's latest book is *Post-Traumatic Culture: Injury and Interpretation in the '90s* (Johns Hopkins, (1998). He is Professor of English at the University of Massachusetts at Amherst, and the author of *Play, Death, and Heroism in Shakespeare* and other books on Renaissance literature, as well as several novels.

J. R. HAMMOND is the founder and current President of the H. G. Wells Society. His books include *H. G. Wells and the Modern Novel* (1988), *H. G. Wells and Rebecca West*

(1991), and *H. G. Wells and the Short Story* (1992). He is a Research Fellow at Nottingham Trent University, England.

SYLVIA HARDY is a former lecturer, now a Research Fellow, at the University College of Northampton, England. She has been Chairman of the H. G. Wells Society and Editor of the *Wellsian*. She is writing a book on H. G. Wells and cinema.

DAVID LEON HIGDON is Paul Whitfield Horn Professor of English at Texas Tech University. He is the author of *Time and English Fiction* (1977), *Shadows of the Past in Contemporary British Fiction* (19841), and numerous essays on twentieth-century British novelists. Currently, he is editing Joseph Conrad's *Under Western Eyes* for Cambridge University Press and completing a study of various types of intertextuality in postmodern fiction.

JOHN HUNTINGTON is Professor of English at the University of Illinois at Chicago. He is the author of *The Logic of Fantasy: H. G. Wells and Science Fiction* (1982), *Rationalizing Genius: Ideological Strategies in the Classic American Science Fiction Short Story* (1989), and *Ambition, Rank, and Poetry in 1590s England* (forthcoming).

CARLO PAGETTI is Professor of Modern and Contemporary English Literature, Faculty of Letters and Philosophy, University of Milan, Italy. He has published on English and American fiction, utopian literature, and science fiction. His critical works include a study of H. G. Wells, *I Marziani alla corte della Regina Victoria* (1986), and a book on SF and the scientific imagination, *I sogni della scienza* (1993). He has recently translated Shakespeare's *Henry VI* trilogy into Italian.

PATRICK PARRINDER's books on Wells include *H. G. Wells* (1970) and *Shadows of the Future* (1995). He has edited *H. G. Wells: The Critical Heritage* (1972) and, more recently, the Oxford World's Classics edition of *The Time Machine and The Island of Doctor Moreau*. He has also written *Science Fiction: Its Criticism and Teaching* (1980), *James Joyce* (1984), and a study of English and American literary criticism, *Authors and Authority* (2nd ed., 1991). He is Professor of English at the University of Reading, England.

W. M. S. RUSSELL is Emeritus Professor of Sociology at the University of Reading, England. He was President of the Folklore Society from 1979 to 1982. He is a member of the H. G. Wells Society and has published several papers about Wells and many articles on science fiction.

FRANK SCAFELLA is Professor of English at the University of West Virginia. His specialties are Hemingway and twentieth-century American Literature, as well as H. G. Wells.

GEORGE SLUSSER is Professor of Comparative Literature at the University of California, Riverside, and curator of the Eaton Collection. He has written or edited twenty-nine books on science fiction and fantasy. His forthcoming publication is *Stalkers of the Infinite: The Science Fiction of Arkady and Boris Strugatsky*.

JOSHUA STEIN holds master's degrees from the University of California, Riverside, and the University of Liverpool. He is an adjunct faculty member in the English Department of the University of California, Riverside, and is currently finishing his doctoral dissertation, "Interpretations of/for 'SF': (Ab)Using (De)Constructions of a Genre."

Index

Ingram Content Group UK Ltd.
Milton Keynes UK
UKHW042058100323
418405UK00004B/100